THE AFRICAN ENTREPRENEUR

THE AFRICAN ENTREPRENEUR

A STUDY OF ENTREPRENEURSHIP AND
DEVELOPMENT IN KENYA

PETER MARRIS
and
ANTHONY SOMERSET

AFRICANA PUBLISHING CORPORATION

NEW YORK

Published in the United States of America 1972
by Africana Publishing Corporation
101 *Fifth Avenue,*
New York, N.Y. 10003

© *Institute of Community Studies* 1971

Library of Congress catalog card no. 70 180668
ISBN 0-8419-0098-1

Printed in Great Britain

In Memory of
BETTY SOMERSET

CONTENTS

LIST OF TABLES   *page* ix

ACKNOWLEDGMENTS   x

1   THE IMPORTANCE OF ENTREPRENEURSHIP   1

PART I   THE SOCIAL SETTING

2   AN HISTORICAL PERSPECTIVE   23

3   THE ORIGINS OF ENTREPRENEURS   55

4   THE AFRICAN BUSINESS CREED   77

PART II   THE ORGANIZATION OF BUSINESS

5   MANAGEMENT   105

6   THE FAMILY IN BUSINESS   132

7   CUSTOMERS AND COMPETITORS   151

PART III   AIDING THE DEVELOPMENT OF
BUSINESSES

8   ACCESS TO CAPITAL   179

9   EDUCATION AND TRAINING   206

10 CONCLUSIONS   225

APPENDIX I   SUPPLEMENTARY TABLES   244

APPENDIX 2   INTERVIEW SCHEDULES   266

REFERENCES   280

INDEX   283

vii

LIST OF TABLES

1   Occupations of Businessmen's Fathers   *page* 59

2   Previous Occupations of Businessmen   62

3   Tribal Distribution of ICDC Loan Recipients   71

4   Landholding of Businessmen   119

5   Diversity of Interests amongst Industrial and
    Commercial Businessmen   123

6   Attitudes to Relatives in Business   139

7   Attitudes to Family of African and Asian Businessmen   143

8   Success of Different Kinds of Business   169

9   The ICDC's Contribution to Capital Invested   187

10 Sources of Original Capital excluding ICDC Loans   189

11 Availability of Bank Overdrafts   192

12 Education of Businessmen and the General Population   211

13 Education and Size of Business   212

14 Education and Size of Profit   213

15 Education and Progress of ICDC-supported Business-
    men   215

    Appendix 1   Supplementary Tables   244

ix

ACKNOWLEDGMENTS

This study depended on the information, advice, criticism and practical help of Kenya businessmen and officials, social scientists with a special interest in African entrepreneurs, research assistants and colleagues. We can only acknowledge a few of these here by name. But we would like to thank the Ford Foundation for financing the study, the Institute for Development Studies at University College, Nairobi, for providing us with a base, and the Industrial and Commercial Development Corporation in Kenya for their co-operation. Apart from ourselves the research reported here was done by Caroline Hutton, Andrew Hayanga, Gibson Kamaru, Joseph Kariuki, James Karuga, John Danson Kibinda, Isaiah Mutonyi, Shem Migot, Samuel Ngugi and teams of interviewers from Alliance High School and University College, Nairobi. Donald Rothchild collaborated on the survey of Asian businesses. The research was administered by our secretary, Diana Rodricks, who also typed the first draft of this book. The final draft was typed by Renee Allinson. A list of the critics whose comments on the draft forestalled at least some of our errors of interpretation would be distinguished, but far too long.

Peter Marris
Anthony Somerset

THE IMPORTANCE
OF ENTREPRENEURSHIP

'Economic development requires financial resources. Indeed,
it requires far more than have yet been made available. But
the resource it requires most is creative innovation.'

Robert S. McNamara[1]

In 1967 there were scarcely 200 African businesses in Kenya larger
than a country store or a craftsman's workshop, and even these
few were mostly still small affairs. Yet few and small as they were,
the progress of these enterprises raises questions which go to the
heart of problems of economic and social change. African businessmen are engaged in the same endeavour as planners, governments,
agencies of international aid—to gather resources and adapt them
productively to new situations: and since they are struggling daily
with the practical difficulties of a particular firm, their experience
illustrates fundamental anxieties of development with a unique
clarity of detail. In the chapters which follow, therefore, we have
tried to unravel the complex social and economic factors which
determined the careers of African businessmen in Kenya, in the
hope that an analysis in a small compass may reach to a better
understanding of more general questions.

Our inquiry is concerned above all with a quality in economic
life whose influence is easy to recognize but hard to define, and
harder still to place systematically in economic theory. Wherever
development has most vitality, there seems to be an element of
original adaptation, a restless adventurousness in the search for
opportunity which cannot be simply explained by the presence of
exploitable resources. Let us call this quality entrepreneurship: a
practical creativeness, which combines resources and opportunities

---

[1] In his presidential address to the Board of Governors of the World Bank, 29 Sep-
tember 1969.

in new ways. It is not necessarily inventive: entrepreneurship turns invention into profit, but need not originate it. Nor is it a quality of economic analysis, since an entrepreneur handles a specific enterprise, not, like the development planner, economic possibilities at large. It is essentially a very practical talent for combining assets in a form which has not been attempted before. The originality may lie in the techniques of production, the market served, the labour used, the organization of the firm, the raw material: and it may exploit what was previously neglected or wrest its resources from established, less productive uses.[1] But in one way or another it improvises a new arrangement of economic relationships. This entrepreneurial talent is the theme of our study —what helps or hinders it, where it comes from, how it may stultify itself in the struggle to survive. But first we should explain why it seems so essential a part of development and why, in particular, it may be important to foster it amongst African businessmen whose economic contribution is, for the time being, only marginal.

The resources which rich nations possess that poorer nations lack are obvious enough—factories, technical schools, university places, power generators—and the proportions in which they need to be combined can be roughly estimated. So the development plan for an African nation can be seen as a purchasing requisition —so many head of high level manpower, so many food-processing factories, so many cement factories, two dozen economic advisers, five Japanese ceramic technicians, two Israeli co-operative managers, a trunk road, a dam. The economy grows by assembling, piece by piece, the elements of more powerful systems. But even assuming that the skills and institutions of an advanced economy are indeed transferable, their timing is still crucial. If the market cannot yet sustain an industry, if skills are trained which cannot be employed, or jobs created which no one has been prepared to fill,

---

[1] 'Seen in this light, the entrepreneur and his function are not difficult to conceptualize: the defining characteristic is simply the doing of new things or the doing of things that are already being done in a new way (innovation). It is but natural, and in fact it is an advantage, that such a definition does not draw any sharp line between what is and what is not "enterprise". For actual life itself knows no such sharp division, though it shows up the type well enough. It should be observed at once that the "new thing" need not be spectacular or of historic importance. . . . To see the phenomenon even in the humblest levels of the business world is quite essential though it may be difficult to find the humble entrepreneurs historically' (Schumpeter).

the investment will be wasted. Development is therefore as much a problem of co-ordinating resources as acquiring them.

Economic planning tries to guide investments in a sequence so that none is frustrated. But since the planners have to work from incomplete information and can scarcely control or predict the movement of capital and markets, a plan is at best an uncertain protection—even if its logic can be rescued from the intrusion of political interests. The plan has still to be implemented, and skill in large-scale economic management is rarest where it is most needed. From inexperience, the urgency of growth, the disruptive pressures of political insecurity, dependence on overseas markets and foreign investors, the imbalance of resources is likely to be less manageable in a poor country, and the complementary parts of a viable project harder to bring together. Unemployment is high, but jobs go begging for lack of qualified applicants; skills go to waste for lack of a market, or capital to make them productive; loans are not issued for lack of promising proposals; imaginative policies cannot be undertaken because able administrators are preoccupied elsewhere. The unevenness of development frustrates integration: everything depends on something else not yet ready. So although the resources are less than in a rich country, they can be less intensively exploited and less easily planned. Assets lie idle, waiting. The talent which can find ways of bringing them into use is therefore very valuable.

Anyone who uses this talent can be called an entrepreneur— owner or manager, co-operative society official or agricultural officer, an administrator deeply involved in a favourite project or the representative of a development fund. There are entrepreneurs in politics, social services, universities, too, who reorganize resources to new ends. But professional innovators are rare. For the most part, those who create an enterprise remain to manage it, and entrepreneurship is only an episode in their careers, an intermittent quality of their occupation. The study of entrepreneurship cannot begin by equating it with a class of occupations. Some assumptions have to be accepted about the economic activities where entrepreneurship will be most needed, and where it will come from.

The relevance of studying African business depends, therefore, on three beliefs which underlie much of our argument: that the encouragement of small firms, especially in industries, is vitally

3

important; that these firms cannot succeed without much entrepreneurial skill; and that this skill must in future come from Africans, of whom the present generation of progressive businessmen are the likely pioneers. The assumptions are speculative, but the situation in Kenya seems to support them.

The largest concerns in Kenya are mostly European-owned, or branches of international companies. They recruit and train African managers, and may co-opt distinguished Africans onto their boards, but they do not depend on African entrepreneurship. This perhaps is their weakness. They tend to pre-empt only the most obvious opportunities, in conditions contrived to favour their chances by a government anxious for their investment. The element of entrepreneurship is diffused amongst prospective investor, government and supportive agencies, who may manipulate the economy to accommodate a preconceived pattern of organization. Such companies can remain an enclave of sophisticated management, poorly integrated with the rest of society, and stultifying as much as encouraging its potential economic vitality.

Overseas capital can provide large factories; loans from other nations can provide roads, railways, dams. But these investments will stimultate growth throughout the economy only if the openings to which they might lead are imaginatively exploited. The opportunities, individually, will be too small to appeal to overseas investors, and too particular for any general economic plan to foresee. Without an entrepreneurial bustle of activity on a smaller scale, the set pieces of development will stand apart like parlour furniture, too grand to be of use. The ability of the Kenya economy to generate wealth from its own resources will depend most of all on this intermediate level of business. Such relatively small firms are characteristic of all advanced industrial societies. In the United States over 90 per cent of all manufacturing concerns employ less than 100 people—most of them less than 50. In West Germany the proportion is 85 per cent, in Britain 95 per cent, in Japan 99 per cent. These firms employ between 40 and 60 per cent of the industrial labour force in most rich countries and produce between 30 and 50 per cent of industrial output. They supply a large part of the components of the steel and motor car industries (which buy from thousands of them) and use much of the output of the great chemical industries.[1] Small-scale manufacture is

[1] In 1956, the Ford Motor Company purchased from an estimated 20,000 different

4

not merely a transitional stage in industrial development, but acts everywhere and all the time to integrate and adapt the parts of the economy. In Kenya, too, such businesses will surely be crucial.

The importance of entrepreneurship, as we have conceived it, depends then on the following argument. Like planning and management, it is concerned with the co-ordination of resources —and co-ordination is as fundamental a problem of development as accumulation. But it is more concrete than planning and more creative than management, which handles more or less predictable and familiar sequences of action, not the origination of economic structures.[1] In principle, planning and management might partly substitute for entrepreneurship, in the sense that a perfect plan would create a system needing only competent managers to set in motion. In practice, very large undertakings which dominate their circumstances can sometimes wrench the economy into line about them and exact assurances against unforeseen risks. Even so, predictability is bought at a price in waste and frustration elsewhere. If the same principle is applied to the economy as a whole, detailed control becomes very clumsy—and is probably impossible without ruthless and sweeping powers of command. Entrepreneurship is therefore essential above all to intermediate businesses in a developing country, since here the co-ordination of opportunities and resources cannot be prescribed by any humane and realistic plan.

At the same time, the future of these businesses in Kenya raises political issues as urgent as any economic concern. Until very recently, this level of enterprise has been dominated by Asians, whose loyalty to Kenya is now widely, if unfairly, mistrusted. Apart from some European importers, wholesaling was still in 1967 mostly in Asian hands; Asian bakeries and garages served the needs of the countryside; Asian sawmills exploited the timber of the forests; Asian contractors put up every substantial building where the largest European firms did not want to compete.

[1] 'One necessary distinction is that between enterprise and management: evidently it is one thing to set up a concern embodying a new idea and another thing to head the administration of a going concern, however much the two may shade off into each other' (Schumpeter).

suppliers, U.S. steel from 50,000 and U.S. rubber from 14,000—many of them small firms. See Staley, and I.L.O., *Services for Small-Scale Industry*, pp. 7, 9.

Historically, these immigrants from India introduced African society to a money economy, and linked subsistence farming with the commerce of the world. Out of their profits they built factories and transport companies. As much as the European settlers, they have been the early entrepreneurs of Kenya's economy. But the commercial structure they created depended on caste and kinship. Though they pioneered shopkeeping far into the African country-side, they remained apart, jealously guarding for their family and friends the opportunities they had sought out. In time they have come to be deeply resented. They are now politically too insecure and socially too self-enclosed to exploit the opportunities of an African state. As intermediaries between the small-scale, rural economy and the international economy which contains it, they can only give way to Africans.

Entrepreneurship is therefore also an aspect of the transfer of power for which Independence stands. But in economic life, the redistribution of opportunities has to disentangle a structure of relationships deeply embedded in the colonial past.

The aftermath of colonialism

Colonization imposed upon Kenya a deliberately segregated European commercial agriculture, with its own mills, dairies, bakeries, food-processing factories, and its own urban centres, banks and commercial agencies. Africans worked in the farms, and made their homes there as squatter-labourers. But by law they could neither own land in the European settlements, nor grow the valuable export crops on their own farms. This policy was grounded in the principle that European agriculture would sustain the economy, and develop the resources for a gradual civilization of African society, while in return the African population was to contribute its labour. As Africans were drawn into a money economy, as their standard of living rose and industries established themselves in an expanding market, so the groundwork of a progressive modern state would be laid. From the outset, the policy required a firm distinction between European and African farmlands: on the former, the economy depended. But the African reserves were essentially a source of labour—and even if African husbandry could be improved, it would not be desirable to develop it commercially to the point where it might become a counter-attraction

6

to employment on the European farms. The future for Africans lay in their gradual absorption into a modern European economy, where the two races would eventually participate as equals. But even in 1950, the colonial administration still assumed that African inexperience would preclude any serious claim to equality for at least another generation. The evolution of a viable multi-racial civilization had to be protected against premature demands, by Europeans and Africans alike, for political autonomy.

These two racially and administratively segregated economies were mediated by a third, equally distinct. From the final decade of the nineteenth century, Indian traders from Gujerat began to penetrate inland from the coast, at first along the old slaving routes, then along the Uganda railway, establishing a commercial network that stretched from the wholesaler in Mombasa to the remotest country store. By 1910, isolated Indian shops were selling cloth and groceries amongst the African farmers of Western Kenya, supplying district officers and missionaries with the amenities of their civilization, buying hides and skins and local produce. At the same time, the colonial administration looked to India for clerks and artisans to keep its books, file its documents, and service its railways, cars and machinery. Denied the right to buy land either in the European settlements or the African farmlands, these Asians bought and built the townships. An urban population of skilled manual workers, minor officials, technicians, shopkeepers and factory owners, they integrated the economic structure, and reinforced its social rigidity. Parochial and community-minded, they pre-empted the commercial and industrial opportunities most within reach of African skill, enclosing them within a culture more impenetrable and inward-looking than colonial civilization itself. But the presence of this Indian middle class, sophisticated enough to put its political interests effectively before the British parliament, also helped to forestall the settlers' demands for home rule under local European control. Colonial government remained the arbiter of racial interests, protecting each within its established economic function, and resisting its encroachment on the rest.

This structure began to break down as a viable distribution of economic opportunities long before it became politically untenable. As time went by, and the demarcation between European and African lands became only more rigid, the conception of the

7

African reserves as reserves of employable labour became less and less realistic. Traditional subsistence farming could not provide for the growing population, but the European farms were no longer eager for labour. By the 1930s they could hardly contain the natural increase in the families who had originally settled there. European farmers began expelling their workers' cattle, and drastically reducing the plots around the workers' homesteads. In the African farmlands over-cultivation and over-grazing threatened to exhaust the eroding soil. But the colonial government did not revise its basic economic assumptions. African farmers were still forbidden to grow valuable commercial crops such as tea or coffee, on the grounds that they were plantation crops unsuitable for scattered small-holdings, where inferior cultivation and lack of supervision would spread disease. Nor would European farmers willingly admit competition for overseas markets restricted by the depression. Colonial agricultural policy tried therefore to improve animal husbandry and cultivation only within the social and physical boundaries of traditional peasant farming, in the face of growing political alienation. In these circumstances, the opportunities for rural trade grew slowly. And borrowing the prejudices of the English gentry, the district administration treated commerce with indifference, disdainful of the shrewd, hard-working Indian shopkeeper, and reluctant to encourage its African wards into anything so morally corrupting.

This whole political and economic structure collapsed in the eleven years between the declaration of a state of emergency in 1952 and Kenya's independence. In 1953, African farmers were first permitted to grow coffee, Kenya's most valuable export crop. Ten years later, a quarter of a million small-holders owned half the total coffee acreage in the country. Tea—the second largest export crop—was introduced to African small-holders later, but by 1964 their share of the acreage was already nearly a quarter. In 1960 land ownership in the European-settled area was opened to all races. On the eve of independence in 1962 thousands of African families began to stake out their homesteads on the Kinangop plateau, and farming schools and settlement-scheme officials set up their quarters in the country homes of the former owners, amongst the lawns and beds of cannas. In the next three years, over 1,000,000 acres—about a third of all the acres of mixed farming once European-owned—was transferred to African farmers under the government settlement schemes. Another half million acres had been bought independently by Africans as individuals or co-operatives, and about 300,000 acres acquired by local or national government.

This agricultural revolution swept aside the segregation of commercial and subsistence farming which for half a century had dominated economic policy. Settlement schemes and the Land Bank opened the European farms to both large- and small-scale African ownership. The consolidation of holdings and their registration, the promotion of tea, coffee, pyrethrum and dairy co-operatives opened the most fertile African farmlands to the opportunities of commercial agriculture. But the revolution had no counterpart in commerce and industry.

Between the two world wars, African shopkeepers had begun to set up business around the rural markets. Butcheries and tea rooms served the crowds who gathered on market days. As time went by, grass shelters were rebuilt in brick or stone, provision stores appeared, and business extended from market days throughout the week. The first local bus services began to link country districts, defining the centres of trade. But shopkeeping remained an intermittent occupation, subsidiary to farming. Shops were often closed, as the owner ran out of stock or was busy elsewhere, and often failed. And since their stock was bought from the local Indian shopkeepers, at retail prices, they could not compete with them, and depended on whatever opportunities there were too out of the way or too petty to be worth the Indians' trouble. Most African shopkeepers, therefore, carried a poor stock at high prices, which still left them with the barest margin of profit. They probably survived at all only because Indians were confined by colonial policy to certain designated trading centres: when the trouble or expense of visiting the trading centre outweighed the difference in price, customers might turn to an African shop. On this slender support, most seem to have balanced on the edge of bankruptcy for a year or two, and slid at last into destitution—the shelves bare, and the shopkeeper back in his fields.

After the second world war, the distribution of market centres was brought under the control of district councils. An attempt was made to rationalize the size and density of market centres. Plots in each were allotted in limited numbers, standards of building set, and shops outside the markets forbidden. But these measures did not prevent the proliferation of short-lived and impoverished general stores, all selling much the same narrow range of groceries at equally unattractive prices. A Colonial Office economic survey in 1951 concluded:

> The entry of Africans into trade and commerce is slow and one of the chief difficulties is the lack of sufficient capital with which to finance a business. Other limiting factors are lack of knowledge and training in business practices and also the difficulty in obtaining supplies at genuine wholesale prices, for frequently the prices charged by Asian wholesalers approximate very closely to the retail selling costs.

Measures to meet the first two difficulties were introduced in 1956. A fund of £230,000[1] was created to finance loans to likely African shopkeepers, selected by local boards; provincial trade officers were appointed, and courses for traders organized. But the third difficulty, which arose from the racial segregation built into the whole structure of the colonial economy, survived the achievement of Independence.

If Africans were ever to establish themselves in commerce on equal terms with their Asian rivals, they needed, firstly, enough capital or credit to purchase the same range of stock at the same wholesale prices, and, secondly, they needed to break the Asian monopoly of wholesaling. In 1964, the Industrial Development Corporation added commerce to its concerns, and began to offer loans and credit guarantees to African shopkeepers. While the earlier loan scheme generally gave £100 or £200, and never more than £500, the Industrial and Commercial Development Corporation (as it now became) took £500 as its lower limit. By 1966, the ICDC had issued nearly £90,000 in loans and £10,000 in credit guarantees to about 170 traders, including several wholesalers. At the same time, the Kenya National Trading Corporation was set up as a subsidiary of the ICDC 'to promote the interests of Africans in the wholesale trade and, by reducing the number of middlemen, to lower the cost of living'. In its first year it redirected

---

[1] The official unit of currency in Kenya is the shilling, divided into 100 cents. But, as is common in Kenya, we have sometimes written large sums as pounds, since they are easier to read. A pound always means twenty Kenya shillings. At the time of our study, a Kenya shilling was equivalent to a British shilling, but since the devaluation of sterling it has been worth more.

the bulk of wholesale sugar distribution to African concerns, and forced Asian retailers for the first time to buy an essential stock from African suppliers. Meanwhile—in response to political pressures—the breweries and cigarette manufacturers had begun to turn from Asian to African distributing agents. By 1966, Asian shopkeepers were beginning to withdraw from the rural market centres. But there was still scarcely a single African retail business to be found in any of the main shopping streets of Mombasa, Kisumu or Nairobi. In the commercial centre of the capital, we knew of three African retailers in 1967, outside the city market—a chemist, a typewriter agent and a greengrocer: in the same area, we counted over a thousand Asian shops, and several dozen European.

In both agriculture and commerce, racial inequality was obtrusive and frustrating. Industry was more remote from African experience, and the demand for a share in industrial ownership less widespread. The narrowness of Kenya's industrial base, rather than the race of its owners, at first preoccupied policy. The Industrial Development Corporation was set up in 1954, but a scheme of small industrial loans to encourage African businessmen was only initiated in 1960, with a fund of £50,000 from U.S.A.I.D. To this, the Corporation later added an equal amount from its own resources. By the middle of 1966 it had issued £83,944 and approved £108,942 in loans to African concerns. But as the ICDC became more involved with the promotion of African businesses, their difficulties began to emerge more distinctly from the problems of promoting industry in general. Participation with overseas capital in new industry was to be the responsibility of the Development Finance Company, while the ICDC would concentrate on investment where technical advice, protection, training and supportive facilities would be needed. Under the 1966/70 Development Plan, the ICDC was to build five industrial estates, where African firms could lease factory buildings, and share common services and equipment, at a cost of £4,000,000. It was to spend another million in investment in individual enterprises, while the Development Finance Company would invest £4,500,000 to attract overseas capital. About half the Government's planned expenditure on industry was therefore directed towards local African enterprise. Meanwhile, a Small Industry Research and Training Centre, provided by the Japanese government, opened in 1965 at Nakuru, and a Management Training and Advisory Centre a year later. But still Africans had far to go before they would control a substantial part of the industrial economy. In 1967, for instance, there were 62 companies quoted on the Nairobi Stock Exchange, with net assets just under £67,000,000. Only three had a majority of African directors, and over half had entirely European boards. In all, 14 per cent of the 376 directorships in these companies were held by Africans, and 5 per cent by Indians.[1] In the same year there were three African firms to be found in the whole of Nairobi's industrial area.

This legacy of racial segregation hands to both African entrepreneurs and their political leaders a socially entangled economic environment, where the urge to oust aliens from a controlling influence cuts across and confuses the needs of industrial and commercial growth. Asian businessmen work very long hours for a modest livelihood, backed by a sensitive commercial intelligence and a financial structure founded on communal trust. They cannot simply be replaced by Africans, as in a bureaucracy people of one race may substitute for another once they have been trained. The nature of their enterprises cannot be defined independently of the men who run them. The aims of the firm, the distribution of tasks, the handling of customers and creditors all depend on the social situation of those in charge—the opportunities they can exploit by their knowledge and relationships, the social conventions they understand and the language they speak. An African wholesaler cannot simply take over from his Indian predecessor. The Indian takes away with him his range of acquaintance and trust amongst his community; the social conventions which informed his relationships with employees, suppliers, customers; his particular flair. The African will have to reconstruct the business around different assets and a different social understanding. His market, his sources of capital and labour, his pattern of organization will change in ways which only experience can teach. The successful transfer of commercial and industrial opportunities therefore involves entrepreneurship as much as innovation does. It cannot be guaranteed by redirection of capital, training and licences, any

[1] A list of the 50 'top' company directors in 1968 included only nine Kenyans and two Ugandans, and six of these Kenyans were British by origin. Apart from one Irishman, the rest were all British. See *Who Controls Industry in Kenya?*, pp. 145–6. This report of a working party set up by the National Christian Council of Kenya analyses the management structure of the major Kenya industries.

more than sustained development can be guaranteed by investment.

Our study is therefore concerned with entrepreneurship as an
aspect both of economic progress and the redistribution of power.
In this context, we have tried to identify the African businessmen
whose activities seem most creative.

The design of the study

Most African businessmen are craftsmen or shopkeepers who work
with one or two assistants in a rural market and earn barely
enough to support their families. At the other extreme there are a
few company directors in European enterprises, often politically
influential, who share the prosperous suburban life of their
expatriate colleagues. In between are a few hundred independent
businessmen who own garages, dry-cleaners, sawmills, wholesalers,
bakeries and small factories employing perhaps a dozen men and
women and with potential profits of several hundred pounds a year.

Neither the rural shopkeeper nor the company director is
characteristically an innovator. The farmer or employee who
invests a few hundred shillings to start a local shop, risks his
savings in a familiar enterprise. He imitates the stock and prices of
his neighbours, and hopes for the best. Such shops have come and
gone for thirty years. They often fail; or if they succeed, the owner
may realize the accumulated capital, and reinvest it in the farm
which has always been his deepest economic attachment. Only a
few become the basis of an expanding, ambitious commercial
enterprise. The company director, too, is characteristically an
African representative or partner in an organization whose plan
and financing comes from others. He contributes the goodwill and
concern of African society and his personal experience: but he is
unlikely to be the initiator of the business or to bear the risk.

The innovators amongst African businessmen are those who
break out of the routine of petty shopkeeping and self-employed
craftsmanship, and risk their capital in more ambitious enterprises.
They, too, are imitators in the sense that wholesalers, garages,
bakeries, sawmills and dry-cleaners have been in Kenya for many
years. Some have indeed bought out European firms. But they are
the first Africans to run such businesses with their own resources,
and as they search for markets and struggle to establish working

13

relationships with their suppliers, their bank, their partners, employees and customers, they create a business whose form is new, even if its product is commonplace.

These men are already entrepreneurs on a small scale, and the pioneers of middle-sized African manufacturing firms should most naturally emerge from amongst them. Most of them, we assumed, would have received loans from the Industrial and Commercial Development Corporation, since these loans are the largest offered to African business by Government, and their most obvious source of capital. The Corporation has deliberately set out to stimulate expanding concerns and original ventures rather than just establish competent shopkeepers or craftsmen on a more secure footing. So for lack of any more comprehensive list, we took the recipients of ICDC loans as the principal subjects of our study. Even if they had proved not to be very creative, at least we would have shown that entrepreneurship was not to be found where the Government was seeking it. But in the event the men who gained the ICDC's support do seem to have included most of the enterprising African industrial entrepreneurs, and many in commerce.

In April 1966, we took from the ICDC's files the names of 51 businesses to which industrial loans had been issued since the scheme began. They were scattered all over Kenya, and of many kinds—a company of carvers, shaping vases and candlesticks from the delicately veined pink stone of the Kisii hills; a modern mining company with 100 employees by a railway siding in Nairobi's suburbs; sawmills, sometimes flourishing, sometimes lost in pastoral decay beside a country stream, the machinery tipped idly on its side amongst a few baulks of timber; dry-cleaners and tinsmiths; garages with up-to-date showrooms and garages cluttered with the hulks of stranded buses; furniture workshops in city streets, and at the end of minor country lanes. A few had already failed, and we traced their owners where we could. But we could gather no first-hand information of three unsuccessful enterprises, and one other turned out to be a minor, undeveloped activity of an agricultural co-operative, not yet a business in its own right. So we interviewed the owners of 47 businesses—seven sawmills, six garages, six bakeries, six dry-cleaners, four carpenters, two plough contractors, two metal workshops, a small garment factory, a canning factory, a mining company, a radio factory, a diesel injection pump repairer, printer, shoemaker, electrical contractor, photographer, sisal decorticator, typewriter repairer, a plastic factory, tour and safari agent, and the soapstone carving factory. Five of these had already closed down. The three other discontinued businesses, whom we could not contact, were a garage, a clothing and a glue factory.

At the same date in April 1966, the ICDC had issued 98 commercial loans to wholesalers, retailers and transport companies. We decided to interview only half of these, since they were not nearly so varied. We also excluded five in the Northern Province, where trouble with the Shifta rebels imposed restrictions on access, and five at the coast, to save a disproportionate amount of travelling. We selected at random 44 of the remaining 88 businesses, but two refused to co-operate, and we failed to reach two others.

For all these 87 businesses, commercial and industrial, we used the same form of interview. The first part was concerned with the business itself—its sources of capital and relationships with the ICDC; its management and structure; its customers, suppliers, competitors and employees; its costing and accounting; its progress and setbacks. The second part asked about the personal history of the initiator of the enterprise—his education and experience, his religion and family, the land and other businesses he owned, the committees and councils on which he sat. Lastly the interview discussed his views on African, Asian and European business in Kenya, what the greatest obstacles to African business were, and how Government might help to overcome them. Though many of the businesses were owned in partnership, or as private companies, the men most responsible for starting and managing the enterprise could usually be identified at once. Where the leadership was collective, we chose the present manager: but then the partners would meet us together, and the concluding discussion ranged between them. We spoke in English when everyone understood it, otherwise in Swahili or the businessmen's own language, using an interpreter. Most often, it took about four hours to gather all the information we asked—though the essential topics could be covered in two when the people were very pressed for time, and occasionally the interview extended over several long visits. The businessmen were unfailingly courteous and patient and on the whole persuaded that the inquiry was worth while, even though it brought them no personal benefit.

If these men stood out from the common run of African business activity, in what way were their thinking, their background or their careers distinctive? Some of them began as petty shopkeepers in a rural market, or as mechanics with no other capital than a spanner, working in the shade of a tree. How many other shopkeepers and craftsmen in country markets might make the same progress? There might be some, too, already as substantial as the businesses helped by the ICDC, though they had never borrowed from it. To provide a comparison by which to assess the 87 ICDC-supported businesses, therefore, we also surveyed market centres in ten regions of Kenya. These trade centres are usually laid out in a square of shops surrounding a market place where, once or twice a week, women bring vegetables for sale. There may be earthenware too, plastic combs and mirrors laid out on a blanket, bows and arrows, sacks of charcoal, a line of women weaving sisal ropes. A space apart, there is often a cattle market. The shops, perhaps 50 or 100, are mostly retail stores selling the same scanty stock of cigarettes, cloth and general groceries, ranged on rough wooden shelves behind a counter. But there may be, too, several bicycle repairers and blacksmiths, hotels and bars, tailors and butchers, a barber, a photographer, a hides and skins dealer, a posho mill, a furniture maker or watch repairer, and two petrol pumps in front of the most prosperous store. Some of the shops are always closed, or open sporadically when the owner has no work on his farm, and others seem more a way of passing the time congenially in the bustle of the market place than a serious enterprise. But though they depend much on market days, most are open all week, and the shops near towns or in the most intensive farming country may be busy enough any day.

We could not select the markets we surveyed systematically, since the interviews were to be carried out by senior students from Alliance High School in their holidays, working in their own locality, and markets had to be chosen conveniently within their reach. But we were able to select comparable markets corresponding to the main ethnic and regional divisions of the country—apart from the pastoral areas, whose nomadic peoples still mostly leave shopkeeping to others. We avoided markets with many Asian shops, since African businesses have concentrated more prosperously in centres apart from them.

In all 848 interviews were completed with the men and women

who run these shops—usually the proprietor or managing partner, or occasionally his wife where she took charge. Eighty-five of the businesses were in an untidy but busy market, once the home of coconut sellers, on the outskirts of Mombasa and nine in a municipal estate on Mombasa Island; 64 in two markets in the Taita hills, which rise steep and fertile from the plain 100 miles from the coast; 94 in a market in the dry Kamba country about 30 miles east of Nairobi; 114 in two Kikuyu markets, in Kiambu and Nyeri districts, both prosperous tea and coffee growing areas; 127 in two markets in the Rift Valley near Nakuru, until a few years ago a centre of European farming; 107 in two markets in the Kisii hills; 112 at an important road junction on the Kano plains, 15 miles from Kisumu; 80 in two Luhya markets of Western Kenya; and 56 in five small markets amongst the Kalenjin, an inaccessible but beautifully wooded range of rich green pasture, where the people have only in recent generations taken to settled agriculture. We tried to include all the businesses in each market, but altogether 40 refused, and about 60 were not available. Since, in every market, some premises are closed, permanently or temporarily, the exact number of functioning businesses is hard to determine, and the total may be nearer 1,000 than the 947 accounted for by our teams of interviewers. But between 85 and 90 per cent of the businesses were covered in every market.

We asked essentially the same questions as we had asked of the ICDC-supported businesses, but more briefly, so that each interview could be finished within an hour or so. Both these inquiries started with the business itself, as it stood at a point in time, rather than with the community of which it was part. And this abstraction of a particular, defined economic activity from its social environment and history seemed inevitably to introduce a selective bias. The businessmen in a neighbourhood, for instance, may not be the same as the businessmen of a neighbourhood: the most enterprising may have gone further afield, even outside Kenya. Over time, too, commercial and industrial activity may have passed through phases of growth and decay, recruiting in different periods other kinds of entrepreneur. Some of this can be discovered from the careers of businessmen, but we also undertook a study of a particular community, tracing the history of its trade and business over the past 100 years, and the present whereabouts of its substantial businessmen. We interviewed 55 of these men, all of whom had established their concerns outside their home area. By these three inquiries, we hoped to explore the range of African business.

In both the market surveys and the interviews with ICDC-supported businesses, we asked about Asian competition, and relationships with Asian wholesalers. We heard many complaints. While most African businessmen seem tolerant of European interests in Kenya—perhaps because Africans are not yet confident to compete in such large-scale enterprise—and believe that Europeans are generally helpful to African businesses, resentment against Asians is widespread. In 1966 and 1967, while the research was going on, the newspapers were full of anti-Asian letters, and pressure to limit Asian freedom of trade was growing. Legislation to restrict trading licences for non-citizens was introduced in the summer of 1967. We wondered whether Asian businessmen would respond to these pressures by looking for African partners, and doing more to help African business through credit, training and advice—and if not, what from their point of view were the difficulties? Were the organization and principles of Asian business essentially different from African? At the same time, Donald S. Rothchild, of the University of California, was interested in the future of the Asian minority from the point of view of a political scientist. So we decided to collaborate on a survey of Asian businesses in and around Nairobi, with the help of a team of Asian students from University College, Nairobi, who spoke between them the principal languages of India and Pakistan.

In Nairobi itself, we walked down every commercial street and shopping centre and through the industrial area, selecting every tenth Asian business we noted. It was, perhaps, a crude way of drawing a sample—biased against businesses which conduct their affairs from the upper floors of office blocks, and those which successfully disguise their Asian character. But such improvised procedures are often the only way of sampling a population where up-to-date, reliable records are not systematically compiled; and there is no point in imposing refined methodology on sketchy basic data. The sample seemed likely to represent the retailers and wholesalers against whom African complaints of discriminatory prices and unfair competition were strongest, and the small manufacturing and service trades where African employees might best hope to get experience. It amounted to 215 businesses in Nairobi streets and 41 in the industrial area. Thirty-nine in the industrial area were interviewed, as one owner refused and two were away; elsewhere two were not available, 14 refused, and 199 were interviewed. In all 93 per cent of the sample was successfully contacted. Finally, we interviewed all the Asian business owners in Kiambu and Limuru—two small townships about 20 miles from Nairobi more characteristic of rural Asian commerce. Here there were 45 businesses altogether, but two of the owners were sick and we could interview only 43 of them.

The chapters which follow are based on the information from these four sources—87 businesses supported by the ICDC, 848 African businesses in market centres up and down Kenya; a study of one location in Nyeri district, which included 55 interviews with businessmen from the area; and 281 Asian businesses in and around Nairobi. They are not exactly representative of all such businesses in Kenya—apart from the ICDC, they are not drawn from a national sample (and even here, so many more businesses have been granted loans since our study, they may no longer be altogether typical). But they do suggest the scale and nature of the problems of African enterprise.

Even if we can understand the importance of entrepreneurship and identify the activities where it will most likely appear, it is still a difficult concept to assimilate in any theory of development. A creative response is by nature hard to foresee. 'From the standpoint of the observer who is in full possession of all relevant facts, it can always be understood *ex post*; but it can practically never be understood *ex ante*; that is to say, it cannot be predicted by applying the ordinary rules of inference from the pre-existing facts.'[1] In retrospect we may be able to understand how a school of Impressionist painting arose, how religious nonconformity or political exile created a new class of entrepreneurs, but no one has yet predicted such outcomes. The study of entrepreneurship therefore tends to be historical and comparative, taking Europe's industrial revolution as its starting point. But these interpretations cannot then be translated into policy, since the unique circumstances of an historical evolution are not reproducible.

Social or psychological theories which generalize from historical instances have much the same drawback. However deeply religious beliefs, the deprivation of a social class, the childhood formation

[1] Schumpeter.

19

of personality may influence the creativeness of a response to economic circumstances, such factors seem beyond our power to manipulate in any predictable or coherent way. Only the government of a totalitarian society could legitimately attempt it, and the attempt itself seems then to pre-empt the choice of response and rob it of any originality.

For purposes of policy, therefore, it might seem more practical to take the existence of entrepreneurial talent for granted, and concentrate on the resources within government control which might foster it. But the simplification turns out to be misleading, even as a guide to policy, because the use of resources is conditioned by inhibitions, prejudices, social pressures and values which cannot be discounted. The analysis of entrepreneurship is caught between the need to understand all the complex influences— economic, political, historical, social and psychological—which combine to generate entrepreneurial behaviour, and the need to resolve these into general principles of action. It is drawn either to the comprehensive analysis of a unique instance, which cannot then be generalized, or to the analysis of the kind of supportive institutions whose success or failure cannot then be interpreted in isolation.

In presenting our findings, we have tried to resolve the dilemma by proceeding from one kind of analysis to the other—starting with an historical exploration of entrepreneurship in one community, and ending with the relevance of capital and trainable skills. In this way, we hope to show how different levels of analysis relate to each other, and how all may be combined to interpret the way an African enterprise works—for it is here, in the working relationships of a business, that any immediately practicable improvement has to be made. The same circumstances will never exactly reappear elsewhere. But we believe the form of the argument, if not its details, could be applied much more widely than to African business in Kenya alone.

Finally, two notes on the text: we have included only a few tables in the discussion, but another 46 tables are given in Appendix 1, pp. 244–65, arranged by the chapters to which they refer; quotations from interviews which have been translated from Swahili or a vernacular language are marked by a 'T'.

PART I
THE SOCIAL SETTING

2

AN HISTORICAL PERSPECTIVE

A modern African business tends to stand out incongruously from its surroundings. The up-to-date machinery, the office desk with its telephone and pen-holder, the orderly receipt books and ledgers seem to have little in common with the shabby stores which straggle about the market place, or the bicycle repairer stirring a tin of old nuts and bolts as he squats on a verandah. Where the business blends less obtrusively, it is because it has moved into a main street once dominated by Asian or European firms, and turned away from the traditional centre of African custom. This sense of discontinuity, even with the recent past, dramatizes the novelty of these African enterprises: and the impression is at least partly true. Scarcely any of the substantial businesses we studied were more than a few years old. Their owners were mostly the sons of peasant farmers who, as they struggled to master the techniques of modern industry and commerce, saw themselves as pioneers, 'children newly born' into a world where the traditions of their own society could teach them nothing.

Yet this sense of abrupt transformation is also in part misleading. The businessmen themselves emphasize it because they are trying to impose on their workers and customers new rules of relationship justified by their perception of modern European practice. And the European perception is distorted because we do not see the past of African society in historical perspective. Against our own ambiguous, changing, discordant beliefs and institutions we set an image of old Africa as classical anthropology preserved it—perfectly consistent, timeless, the ritual gesture fossilized in the amber of comparative scholarship.[1] So we over-play the twentieth-century development of Africa as a unique historical drama—as

---

[1] This is not meant to imply scorn for classical social anthropology. It sought to discover the fundamental principles of human organization, and from this point of view, it was at least as important to record the range of independently generated normative social structures as to trace the evolution of a particular society.

if our technology and systems of government had broken into an iron-age culture ignorant even of the possibility of change.

The more we discover about African history, the more this illusion of stability recedes. As far as memory and oral tradition reach, people were on the move, as famine, growing populations, or the pressure of more powerful tribes pushed them in search of food and safety. Tribes were overwhelmed, their remnants assimilated to their conquerors; the weaker borrowed the weapons and tactics of the stronger; migrants adapted their patterns of cultivation and social organization to new terrains. The African experience of change has, it begins to appear, as long and turbulent a history as anywhere else in the world. At least in those societies which survived, there must always have been a respect for innovation beside the respect for custom, an ability to recognize and reward pioneers. If this is so, the way in which a particular society accommodated change—the values and relationships which determined where, and by whom, innovation was possible—may influence its adjustment to the contemporary world more than any other aspect of its traditions. The continuities or discontinuities between the role of entrepreneurship in pre-colonial times, as a society conceived it, and the demands of modern business define the problems of adaptation.

In this section, therefore, we try to set entrepreneurship in an historical perspective. Does economic innovation always face the same fundamental problems? Is the talent for it passed on from one generation to another, within the same family or the same community? Where do the discontinuities fall? Since it was beyond our resources to trace the history of economic innovation over a wide area, our account covers only the last 100 years in one small part of Nyeri district in Kikuyu country. But within these narrow limits, we have tried to suggest how such questions might be answered. In the past as in the present, the impulses which generated entrepreneurship seem to have been compounded of a similar balance of exploitable resources and a sense of deprivation. And a network of social relationships was as crucial then to the success of business as it is now. The values which sustained individual enterprise have altered very little. But the nature of the economic opportunities themselves changed over time, and as they changed, so they fell to different kinds of people, in different situations.

An Historical Perspective

The account which follows traces the progress of commercial enterprise since pre-colonial times in one community—Mahiga location on the foothills of the Aberdare mountains—and especially of its trade with the Masai. A similar trade flourished in the neighbouring settlements, and in Kiambu further to the south. But since its history can only be discovered from old men, who still remember the events of the last century, we have concentrated on the one community where we made enough contacts to record and compare, in some detail, the memories of the few survivors from those days. In all, there were seven men still living in Mahiga who had grown into manhood before the turn of the century. From three of these, and about sixteen younger men, we gathered most of the information from which this account is reconstructed.[1]

Wealth and status in Mahiga society

Mahiga location lies along the ridges which run down the eastern slopes of the Aberdare range. Above lie the forests which once covered the whole countryside: for though Mahiga now has a population over 12,000, the area was uninhabited less than 200 years ago. On their western side, the Aberdares drop down into the Rift Valley, where the Masai used to graze their great herds of cattle, before the colonial treaty of 1904 dispossessed them. This geographical setting determined the nature of the trade which developed. The mountains and forests were a natural barrier, protecting each people from the raiding parties of the other. But there were tracks through the forest and across the moorland on which hardy traders could pass. The economies on either side of the range were complementary. The Masai possessed cattle, sheep and goats, which for Masai and Kikuyu alike were the measure of wealth, but they grew no crops: while the Kikuyu country was fertile and well watered, producing crops in abundance. Each had

[1] The three oldest informants were Kirere Kihara, Kirianjau Munyu and Kiburu Kinja. Kirianjau was then the oldest man in Mahiga: he was circumcised in about 1889 (through circumcision a young Kikuyu, round the age of eighteen, graduated into manhood). Kirere and Kiburu were circumcised about five years later: both were Masai traders themselves, and the sons of prominent traders, before 1900. For the later period, the most valuable information came from Mangore Waithaka and Kiiru Ngecu—both circumcised on the same day, probably in 1905—who were also traders. Their accounts, gathered through many sessions, agreed very closely with each other, once it became clear that apparent inconsistencies related to different periods in the evolution of the trade.

a surplus of what the other needed, and they were kept apart by obstacles which made exchange a more practicable means of securing it than warfare.

But geography does not explain why the Kikuyu were always the entrepreneurs of this trade, initiating its organization and bearing its risks. Looking back, the Masai seem to have stood in greater need of it. In the dry season, the arid pasturage of the valley floor could barely sustain them, and their livelihood was repeatedly threatened by cattle epidemics. But the people of Mahiga could sustain themselves even in a poor season, and their rivers never ran dry. Yet neither perceived their situation in this sense. The Kikuyu were the eager traders, the Masai their condescending customers, and this inequality of prestige was accepted by both as self-evident. To understand why, we need to understand how wealth and status were distributed in Mahiga society.

The first settlers seem to have reached Mahiga about 1800. They found the land dense with forest and, it is said, wholly uninhabited.[1] According to tradition, these pioneers were hunters, who established their land rights by setting traps. The holdings were as extensive as the range of a hunter's traps, and the main Mahiga ridge—an area of about eight square miles—was claimed by not more than ten men. Some of the claims amounted to only a few hundred acres, but Magana, the most hardworking and ambitious of the hunters, established his right to nearly as much land as all the rest together. At the present day, there are eighteen lineages (*Mbari* in Kikuyu) descended from Magana still living on the land he first settled.

Within a generation or two, the children and grandchildren of the settlers had cleared the fertile valley of the Gura river, and cultivated fields were extending up the hillsides. Land rights were granted according to lineage, each son as he grew up claiming a portion of his father's estate. But unlike some other parts of Kikuyu society, the head of the lineage had no power to adjust the boundaries of holdings within the family group. Once cultivated land had been allotted, its possessor held virtually unencumbered right to it: he could sell or lease it, and no other member of the

[1] A remnant of the Ndorobo people—forest-dwelling hunters—still survived in 1900 at Kiganjo, about twenty miles from Mahiga, and may originally have inhabited the Mahiga forests. In Kiambu, further south, land was originally acquired from Ndorobo. But our Mahiga informants say their area was wholly uninhabited when their ancestors arrived. The first settlers may have reached lower Mahiga before 1800.

family, apart from his sons, had any claim upon it. This individualistic pattern of land tenure fitted a society where unbroken land was still plentiful. A man could always be provided for, so long as he was prepared to work hard to clear the forest, while to have granted him rights where cultivation had already been established would have robbed another household of the reward of its labour. And because land was plentiful, outsiders as well as members of the family could often obtain cultivation rights in the forest. They were tenants at will, who could be required to return the land whenever its owners asked, but meanwhile they paid no rent. Many of them later bought land, and some of the descendants of these tenants became rich and influential men.

Land could, then, be acquired in one of three ways: by inheritance, as the son of a landholder; as a tenant, either freely through the friendship of its owner, or for the gift of a ram; or by purchase. In the last century, purchase was nearly always redeemable. The seller could claim his land back at any time, if he returned the equivalent in sheep and goats that he had been paid for it. But in practice, redemption was rare. A man would only sell when he was too poor to acquire otherwise the sheep he needed to fulfil his obligations, and the buyer could safely assume he would never be in a position to reclaim his land. A sale could be made final by the further payment of a goat and fat ram, but until this century— when land had become scarcer and unsecured purchases more vulnerable—no one bothered except as an act of generosity towards the original owner.

Under such a system, a poor or landless man could grow prosperous by hard work and good management. And equally, the children of a well established family might be disinherited through their father's incompetence, as the following story shows:

My grandfather was famous and respected, and from him my father inherited a large farm. But he was not a good farmer, and never became prosperous. He had only three or four sheep or goats, and whenever he needed one for slaughtering, he would sell a piece of his land. While I was still a child, I was ashamed to look after such a small flock. So I ran away to the Rift Valley, and worked as a shepherd boy for two shillings a month. . . . I saved nearly all my wages, and after a while I was able to buy three goats, which I drove over the

Aberdares and left with my father. So I went on working and buying livestock, until I was old enough to be circumcised. By then I had a big flock, and thought it was time to start reclaiming my father's land. I knew that if I spoke politely the men would refuse, because I was still young. So I decided to speak harshly. Arming myself with my sword, I went to see a man who had bought land from my father.

'Why are you cultivating this land?' I said.

'I bought it from your father.'

'What did you pay for this land?'

'I gave your father one sheep.'

'Very well. Come to my father's house tomorrow for your sheep. Do you understand? I don't want to see you cultivating this land in future.'

The man went to my father and asked him, 'What is the matter with your son? Is he mad? Haven't you warned him against insulting older men?' But my father answered, 'Do not ask me such questions. That is the way my son behaves. Take your sheep and give us our Land.' Later I reclaimed land from eleven other men in the same way—altogether twenty-three acres which my father had sold.[T]

This story dates from colonial times. But it seems clear that from the first the fortunes of a family fluctuated from generation to generation, and wealth or respect depended more on intelligence and enterprise than inheritance. Even an outstandingly successful man often did not leave his children with any advantage. He married many wives, and his land was dissipated amongst many sons. The younger ones, born in his old age, might be left as orphans to make their own way in poverty. Their father's wealth was an achievement to emulate by their own efforts, not a start in life.[1] The values of society did not, indeed, pay much respect to the man who was prosperous only by the accident of birth: he was said scornfully to have got his wealth from his parents' bed.[2]

[1] This theme appears in the lives of several present-day businessmen from Mahiga. Their father was rich, but died when they were young, and their childhood was spent in poverty. One of them recalled a song his mother used to sing to encourage him:

Giki kiriro murarira	Why do you weep?
Kia mwana uri ithe akiria thina	For the child with a Father has troubles,
Na uria wakuithirie ithe tene	While he who lost his father long ago
Ariagira maza	Eats at table.

[2] *Aria matongeire uriri.* The phrase referred to a man with many sisters and few

In these circumstances, livestock rather than land became the crucial asset. Land was the means of life, but it was cheap: in the last century one sheep or goat exchanged for between half and two acres, according to the fertility of the soil. And since the market in land seems to have been virtually unrestricted by claims of kinship or discrimination against outsiders, a man with a large flock could always acquire the land he needed. But livestock were scarce, and social prestige depended on them. All solemn occasions called for the slaughter of sheep and goats—the settlement of disputes, treatment of sickness, cleansing of ritual pollution, the councils and feasts of the senior men. Those who could not contribute their full share were unable to take an equally respected part in the society of their peers.[1] At every stage in life, from boyhood through circumcision and marriage to entry into the elders' council, gifts of sheep and goats had to be presented. So a poor man might be driven to continual attrition of his landholding to maintain his own or his son's place in society.

Sheep and goats were, then, the key to economic security and social status. Flocks could be increased by careful husbandry, or by bartering the farm surplus in the neighbourhood. But it must have been difficult to maintain large flocks over a long period in a settled agricultural community, where grazing land was restricted. The stock of animals had continually to be replenished. And the most abundant source of livestock, for those ambitious and able enough to take the risk, lay across the mountains amongst the Masai. A few bold men dared the military prowess of the Masai to raid for stock, but it was hazardous and provoked reprisals. The lasting profit came through trade, and a man who built up his flocks by successful trading became not only wealthy, but earned the highest respect. All the prominent traders became *athamaki*—wise men or judges, the acknowledged leaders of society. But such honour at home depended on a deferential attitude towards the land of its source.

[1] Routledge, for instance, describes a council meeting he attended early in this century, where elders who had not made the full payment sat apart from the rest, received inferior meat at the feast and 'formed something of a butt for good-natured jokes' (Routledge, p. 201).

---

brothers, whose family therefore received far more in bride price for its daughters than it had to pay out for its sons.

The Kikuyu perception of Masai society

Before about 1870, two distinct groups of Masai lived within reach of Mahiga—the Laikipiak to the north, and the Purko across the Aberdares in the Rift Valley. The Laikipia plateau was an easier journey, but the people had a fierce reputation: and since they sometimes cultivated as well as kept cattle, they perhaps depended less on trade with the Kikuyu. From the first, the Mahiga traders seem to have dealt mostly with the Purko Masai. In the 1870s, after a generation of warfare, the Purko and their allies finally overwhelmed the Laikipiak: it is said that in the decisive campaign, the Purko called upon their Kikuyu friends, who fought beside them. Thereafter, nearly all trade was with the Purko.

The Purko Masai practised a strictly pastoral economy. Their customs forbade the hunting of wild animals, or any form of cultivation. Even breaking the surface of the ground to dig a waterhole or bury a corpse was forbidden. They regarded other peoples who farmed or hunted for subsistence as inferior. Their young men and warriors tried to keep to a diet of milk, blood and meat even through the severest droughts, though women and children might eat grain and vegetables obtained from agricultural tribes in the long dry season. But the pride and independence of this purely pastoral life left them with a precarious economy. To get enough milk to carry them through the dry seasons, they had to maintain enormous herds of cattle. Even when grass was most plentiful, it took two milking cows to feed one adult Masai: as the pastures withered, it might take fifteen and in a drought even thirty cows barely provided one man's subsistence.[1] From time to time, too, cattle disease ravaged the herds, threatening survival. The size of the herds and flocks the Masai sought to maintain reflected, in truth, an underlying insecurity. But to their Kikuyu neighbours, it represented simply enormous wealth.

Neither Kikuyu nor Masai, therefore, saw themselves as equal partners in trade. The Purko regarded the Kikuyu as socially degraded because they farmed. While the people of Mahiga,

---

[1] These estimates are from Jacobs, Ch. III. Apart from his thesis, we owe most of our understanding of Masai society to discussions with Alan Jacobs, who generously gave us much help.

looking with envy and admiration on the vast Masai herds, compared their own conditions most unfavourably:

> Who can ask who had the better life? In Masailand there was meat and milk, but here there was only soil. So why would anyone want to live here? We lived on sweet potatoes and arrowroot then—and we live on sweet potatoes and arrowroot still.[T]

> In Mahiga only a few rich men owned any cattle at all, but in Masailand even a poor man owned many. Here we counted a man's wealth by his sheep and goats, but there they counted his cattle.[T]

This sense of inferiority lay deeper than a simple economic comparison. To an outsider, indeed, the Kikuyu seemed strikingly prosperous. Captain Lugard, who passed through the southern tip of Kikuyu country in 1890, remarked on its 'teeming abundance', and was able to buy 20,000 lbs. of grain and beans in a few days, 'in spite of the fact that a flight of locusts had recently devastated the country . . . and that this was not the best time of the year for food purchase.'[1] But in Kikuyu eyes, the Masai were not only richer, they possessed a superior culture: they were physically stronger, bred on milk and blood; warriors to be feared; the example of a prouder and more dignified way of life, of which cattle were the mainstay and the symbol.

The Kikuyu seem, in the remoter past, to have assimilated aspects of Masai culture to their own. The common word for God in Kikuyu is of Masai origin, though the two languages are of quite different roots; Kikuyu warriors adopted a Masai style; and even Kikuyu social organization may in part be influenced by the Masai. Their age-set system belongs, more commonly, to a pastoral than an agricultural people, and was practised with so many local variations in Kikuyu society that it appears as a cultural borrowing, never wholly integrated. Hence the Kikuyu may also have felt inferior because they saw their own culture as partly derivative, an attempt to emulate a pastoral tradition which they could never rival, because their own economy was essentially different.

At all events, the Kikuyu accepted as natural that they should be

---

[1] Lugard, p. 328.

the initiators of trade, and bear all its risks. To establish a trading relationship, a Kikuyu would make a gift worth two sheep or goats to his Masai customer: nothing of equivalent value was expected in return. No one can recall that a Masai trading party ever came to Mahiga: in need, the Masai would send a message.[1] The Kikuyu humped their packs over the mountains, and swallowed their dignity under the jeers of the waiting Masai escort—who used to cry 'Here come the donkey-men!' as the caravan plodded out of the forest with its bulky loads.

Most Mahiga men who took part in the trade regarded the wealth of the Masai as altogether beyond their reach. They were content to improve their status relative to other Kikuyu, and as they approached middle age they visited Masailand less often. But for a few, Masai wealth became the standard of reference, promoting a restless striving for profit which became the dominant theme of their lives. These men were Mahiga's first professional businessmen.

The organization of the Masai trade

The two main obstacles to trade were the Aberdare mountains and the hostility of Masai warriors. A man with goods to barter could not simply carry them to Masailand for exchange. Even if he succeeded in finding his way up through the forest, and across the cold, bleak moorland, unharmed by wild beasts, he would lose his goods and probably his life before he reached a friendly homestead. So traders always travelled in caravans, of any number from 30 to 200 people, under the direction of a leader. These leaders were professional traders, sometimes virtually full-time businessmen employing several assistants and their own file of porters.

The caravan leader traded on a larger scale than the other members of the party. But he owed his position less to capital than to his ability to arrange protection for the caravan. He did this, not by hiring an armed escort, but by developing friendships with influential Masai households. Every trade expedition was organized around a request for goods, received by the caravan leader from

---

[1] Occasionally, Masai warriors would return with a Kikuyu trading party to buy spears. But the livestock they brought for barter was driven for them by their Kikuyu companions, and they travelled as guests, not traders. They never carried home any bulky goods, such as flour or tobacco.

one of his Masai friends, and the success of the expedition depended on the effectiveness of their co-operation. The Kikuyu leader assembled the supplies, while his Masai customer provided protection for the caravan, and prepared the market. The caravan leader needed to be a good organizer and shrewd judge of articles of trade, but his crucial asset was his detailed knowledge of Masailand, and above all his personal contacts with a network of Masai households.

Throughout this period, the relationship between the two tribes was curiously blended of interdependence and hostility. Skirmishes might happen at any time, and a caravan could return to Mahiga to find that their livestock had been captured by Masai raiders in their absence. Yet trade was rarely disrupted.[1] Masai from other homesteads might be hostile, but the caravan leader could be sure that so long as his arrangements were made in advance, friendly Masai would meet him at the border, and escort his party safely. Each trading expedition therefore began with a meeting between the leader and his Masai customer, where they settled the goods to bring, and the time and place at the boundary of Masailand and the forest where caravan and escort would meet. If the rendezvous was for twenty days hence, each man tied twenty knots in a rope, untying one knot each evening thereafter, until the rope was clear. The rendezvous was then for the following day. Since it took about two days to cross the Aberdares, the caravan set out when there were two knots still in the rope. The initial meeting might take place in the course of a previous expedition. A major trader could have as many as ten Masai friends, and while on one trip he would contact another household to arrange the next. A trader of less consequence might have to wait until his only friend visited him or sent a message to say that he was again in need.

Once these plans had been settled, the trader set about assembling his goods. Millet flour would come from his own farm, and honey from his hives, but for other goods he might have to travel widely over Kikuyuland. Ochre, for instance, was cheaper in

---

[1] Sometimes, when tension was high, caravans consisting only of women were formed. The wives of a famous trader are said to have led his caravans on several occasions, when it was too dangerous for him to travel himself. Even when fighting had broken out between the tribes, women could still travel safely to and fro. The women were good bargainers. When tension eased, they reverted to carrying goods as casual traders or porters in caravans led by men.

Chinga, ten miles to the south; the best gourds grew in Muranga, twenty miles south; tobacco and snuff were available locally, but the Masai valued higher the tobacco from Ndia and Embu, thirty or forty miles to the east; a Mahiga blacksmith would forge spearheads and knives, but the ingots had to be obtained from Muranga, where iron ore was mined and smelted. To acquire all these goods, the trader had to drive livestock for exchange. He travelled with porters, but unless he had an experienced assistant, he supervised his own purchasing, since quality was important. Gourds, for instance, had to be of the right shape and colour: young Masai women much preferred the straight, unblemished gourds, and curved or blotched gourds would only sell to older women at a discount.

While the trader was gathering his stock, news of the impending expedition spread throughout Mahiga, and even the neighbouring districts. Every young man wanted to grasp the opportunity to barter his grain for a sheep, or even a share in a sheep. 'When you were young, and a caravan was going to Masailand, who would want to be left behind?' When the caravan assembled, there were often 'very many people—as many as you see today at a market'. These casual traders outnumbered the caravan leader with his porters and assistants: most carried only the surplus millet from their farms, but some, like the leader, had prepared more valuable articles of trade—ochre, spears or gourds. Each man carried his spear, but left his shield behind, because it was awkward to manage on the steep forest paths, and no one was detailed to guard the caravan. Everyone except the leader carried a load: 'We were going to trade, not to fight.'

The caravan usually camped for one night on the mountain, at a height of about 10,000 feet. The nights were often very cold, and casual traders, eager to make as much profit as they could, sometimes carried such heavy loads that they were too exhausted to eat. Casual traders carried their own food and made their own cooking arrangements, though the caravan leader sometimes provided food for his assistants and porters. The expedition had to carry enough rations for the entire round trip, which seldom lasted less than ten days and more often two or three weeks. Trade goods might sometimes be exchanged for milk and meat from the Masai, but especially in the dry season, when most trade took place, this could not be relied on. A cache of food for the return journey was usually buried near the margin of the forest on the edge of Masailand, though there was a risk that it would be unearthed and eaten by animals before the caravan came back.

Besides those hazards, hostile Masai might still harass the party in spite of all the arrangements. A Mahiga man remembers an expedition in about 1892, where he nearly lost his life. The caravan was large and unwieldy, made up of parties from several locations under their own leaders, and it may have been the lack of overall leadership which failed to avert trouble. A few weeks earlier, a group of Purko had raided Mahiga for sheep, but Kikuyu warriors had caught up with them at the forest edge and killed several of them. While the caravan was pausing to trade with a party of Masai women, a few miles short of its destination, a group of Masai warriors came up, demanding to know who were the people from Mahiga, intent on revenging their comrades. 'One Masai lifted his spear, but he was cautioned by another, and they moved to the main group of traders at the front of the caravan. Suddenly I saw several traders fall to the ground, struck by spears. Everyone panicked. What could I do? I thought of running away, but then reflected "How shall I answer people at home, when they ask me where I have left the women?" I started to run towards the fighting, but a young Masai girl seized me and held me so tight I couldn't move—she had been fed on Masai milk, and was very strong. By now we were surrounded by Masai warriors. I saw an elder from the homestead we were visiting, and appealed to him for help. He took me by the hand, and led me to a safe place. Here I met a Kikuyu friend of mine, and we started running: suddenly I saw him rolling down the hill three feet behind me with a spear through him. Two warriors were chasing me. I doubled back up the hill and hid with two other traders until they went away. Later, when we reached the homestead of our Masai friend, we found that our caravan leader was safe, but many traders had been killed. . . . Another caravan had been attacked at its camp in the Aberdares a while before. But if members of one caravan were killed, we still joined the next. If we had stayed at home, where would we have got wealth?'[T] Such incidents seem to have arisen partly from the tension within Masai society between the elders and the young warriors, who had their own, largely separate organization. It was the elders who arranged and supported trade with the Kikuyu.

When all went well, the caravan was met at the forest edge by its Masai contact, and escorted with his party to their homestead. The journey might take several days more, and when food was short they might be approached by other families along the way. But the Masai host did not usually allow any trading until they had reached his home, and the needs of his own household had first been satisfied.

When the journey was over, before trade started, the caravan leader collected dues from all the casual traders who accompanied him. For those carrying food, the payment was four or five pounds of flour: others contributed according to their goods—a small gourd, or a little honey. This fee was a recognition of the protection and economic benefits they shared through their leader's relationship with the Masai. The articles collected were then added to the trading stock of the leader, or his assistants, to whom he might distribute them as payment for their work.

For those who brought valuable goods, the rates of exchange were evidently very profitable. Gourds, knives and spears seem to have been worth double their buying price in Kikuyuland. Two spears, for instance, which a Mahiga blacksmith would sell for a single sheep or goat could be bartered for two in Masailand—three or four if the animals were skinny. Honey, which both tribes used to brew beer for ceremonial occasions, was especially valuable. Since the hives were slung from branches deep in the forest, its collection was difficult and dangerous. Several Mahiga men specialized in the honey trade, and one in particular, who spent most of his time in the forest tending his hives, is remembered to have become very rich.

But only a few traders carried such valuable stock. For the majority who sold only their farm surplus, the trade was much less profitable, and the return less certain. Even a casual trader who travelled speculatively with spears or gourds, though he might have to wait a few days, could be sure of his price when buyers arrived from outlying homesteads. But the value of food fluctuated with its scarcity. When there was dearth in Masailand, two loads of flour would buy a sheep, at other times five or six loads.[1]

[1] As many traders brought only a single load, several men might have to share one animal. And since the customer selected the loads he wanted, the partners were not necessarily friends, or even known to each other. A council made up of the caravan leader's assistants, or of representatives of groups of traders, usually determined how the benefits of the animal were to be shared. If it was a female, each trader would

Occasionally, the Masai would refuse to barter livestock for food at all, and a trader would have to accept skins. So while the professional trader returned from his expedition driving a flock of twenty or thirty sheep and goats, a casual trader might have nothing more to show than a fifth share of one animal, or a mere goatskin.

Entrepreneurship in the Masai trade

Although most people took part in the Masai trade at one time or another in their lives, there was clearly a much smaller group who devoted most of their energies to the trade, and made profits of an altogether higher order. What distinguished these entrepreneurs? Where did their crucial advantage lie?

In the first place, no one could become a caravan leader without Masai contacts, and his success depended on the skill with which he cultivated them. He needed to travel widely in Masailand, and speak the language fluently. Masai rarely knew more than a few words of Kikuyu, and trading relationships were always conducted in Masai. The casual traders relied upon the caravan leader to translate for them. A Mahiga man who had lived as a herd-boy in a Masai homestead recalled that when Kikuyu trading caravans came there, the casual traders and porters did not speak to the Masai at all. The Masai referred to them as 'the Kikuyu who belong to this leader'. But besides his familiarity with Masai custom, a major trader could also reinforce his relationships by personal ties. He might marry one of his daughters into the homestead of a Masai friend, where she would serve as a reliable messenger between them. Or he might send one of his young sons to help a Masai customer who was short of labour to herd his cattle, where the boy could learn the language and grow up strong on the Masai diet. When he returned after a few years, his son would already have begun to acquire the knowledge and contacts he needed to succeed in his turn as a trader.

In this way, leadership in trade tended to pass from father to son within particular families. The two biggest traders of the 1880s—

receive its progeny in turn, according to the value of his load: a male would be exchanged for a female, or fattened and exchanged for two other animals. Even when the partners were strangers, and lived in different communities, the arrangements seem to have been scrupulously honoured.

one of them himself the son of a prominent trader—both had sons who became caravan leaders. The families of both men spent much of their time in Masailand, and were regarded by other Kikuyu as part Masai. One of them is said to have established a home there, where he sent two of his Kikuyu wives to live—they assimilated Masai values so well that they refused to work in the fields when they visited Mahiga.[1]

A young man from a family prominent in the Masai trade had an obvious advantage. He may have spent part of his childhood in Masailand, he knew the language, and he had probably accompanied his father's caravans from the time of his circumcision, or even before. But energetic and able men from other families could still compete. The outstanding trader who sent his wives to live in Masailand is said to have come from a poor home: and two out of five other substantial traders of the same period were not from trading families. The opportunities for entrepreneurship did not ultimately depend on any inherited asset. A young man who took the trouble to learn Masai, studied the articles of trade, and cultivated his customers, could build up a stock. For instance, a man who started as a trader in foodstuffs but soon became a caravan leader's assistant, recalled his first successful bargain:

> On my second trip to Masailand I was lucky. I'd already learned a little Masai, and I talked politely to a woman called Nguruma. She agreed to buy my flour for a young sheep—I did not have to share with other traders. I cooked four sweet potatoes, gave one to Nguruma, one each to her two sons, and ate the last myself. Then Ngurumu's husband arrived, complaining that she had sold the sheep too cheaply. But she said I was a kind man who had given them sweet potatoes, and I was allowed to keep the sheep. . . . I fattened it and exchanged it for a young sheep and a ram. I gave the ram in dowry for my wife, but kept the sheep. Soon I was the owner of ten,

[1] Characteristically, these relationships were not reciprocated. Masai would not let their daughters marry Kikuyu, since wives of Kikuyu were required to cultivate, nor would they ever send their sons to a Kikuyu homestead—though in times of famine (as after the rinderpest epidemic of 1889–90 and the drought of the following year) many Masai women and children took refuge amongst the Kikuyu. The services of a Kikuyu herd-boy were paid for by a gift of two sheep a year. The marriage payment for a Kikuyu girl was high by Kikuyu standards, but did not include the cattle a Masai would give for a girl of his own tribe.

and they all came from that one sheep I had from Nguruma in Masailand.^T

In this manner a man could work his way to become a substantial trader, perhaps a caravan leader's assistant, and eventually through the contacts he made undertake his own expeditions.

Why, then, did only a few men exploit these opportunities fully? Nearly everyone possessed at least a few sheep or goats, which were readily exchangeable in local markets for the valuable articles of the Masai trade. Why did most still toil over the mountain with surplus flour, from which they could expect little profit? Perhaps, as one man who had been a prominent trader suggested, it was simply lack of business acumen. 'Many people's heads are filled with darkness. They cannot work out for themselves the profitability of different trade articles. Was I there to educate them?' But intelligence beside, success was also seen as a matter of risk taking and hard work. Indeed, the economy of Mahiga turned on these qualities, which were honoured as the acknowledged qualifications for respect and leadership. At every level of participation in the Masai trade, there were obstacles to overcome. Each level called for more intelligence, more effort than the one below, and the risks were higher. At the same time, the profitability of the trade was closely related to the complexity of the difficulties which the trader surmounted.

At its simplest, the trade was open to any man who worked hard enough to grow a surplus of crops. On most landholdings there was uncleared bush, and the size of the cultivated farm depended on the energy of the owner. A man would clear land for each of his wives, and the family lived on the harvest of the women's labour. But if he was ambitious, he also cleared a plot for himself, which he cultivated by his own labour. The yield of this plot was reserved for trade. So, ironically, the more a man demeaned himself by the values of the Masai, and worked in the fields alongside his womenfolk instead of only tending his flock, the better his chance of approaching their standard of wealth. It seems that there was much variation in the part a man took in cultivation. But so long as he worked hard enough to grow a surplus, trade was neither very risky nor skilled. The surplus was not vital to his family's welfare, since the harvest never failed altogether, and no reserve against famine was needed. If he failed to exchange it at much profit, no serious harm was done. And once he had joined a caravan, he could take part in trade without any experience of the Masai or their language: the leader or his assistants would act for him.

At an intermediate level, where a trader dealt in more valuable articles like honey, spears or gourds, both risks and skills were higher. He now needed a working capital of livestock to buy his stock-in-trade from the local markets. 'Goods for trade, as people used to say, come entirely from the home': the trader was gambling the resources of his household. If he possessed only a few sheep and goats, he was venturing all his little wealth in an adventure where any accident could leave him destitute of the means to meet his social obligations and maintain his status. At the same time, he had to know what articles to acquire, of what quality, and at what price. For most people, these risks were too great: they preferred to build up their flocks more slowly and more safely by natural increase. But for those who could handle the risk, the profits were substantial.

Finally, at the most sophisticated level, were the leaders of the trading expeditions. Besides venture capital, and a knowledge of trade goods, they needed to be skilled organizers: they had to assemble their goods over a wide area, recruit assistants and porters, distribute rations and pay, and look after the interests of all the casual traders who joined the caravan. Above all, each needed a network of social relationships amongst the Masai, on whom he could rely for protection and a market. This was the scarcest and most valuable asset. Only a few men ever attained to this, but the rewards were great. All the richest men in Mahiga were leaders of trade.

We do not know enough about the personal history of prominent men of those times to determine exactly why they excelled. Some inherited their father's experience and contacts in Masailand, but others succeeded without a tradition behind them. They must all have been exceptionally able, ambitious and hardworking men. Probably none of them inherited any very substantial capital. The wealth of one generation tended to be dispersed in the next, since a rich man married several wives and distributed his land amongst many sons—the four richest men of the 1880s all had more than five sons, two of them more than ten. It may be that the most determinedly ambitious were the younger sons of rich fathers.

These late born children had to succeed by their own efforts: their fathers often died in their early childhood, leaving them little claim on his divided estate. But their fathers' achievements remained a standard by which to set their own aspirations. This pattern of motive certainly appears amongst some prominent traders early in the twentieth century.

But whatever the individual circumstances which characterized the origins of these men, the most important factor was the entrepreneurial values of society as a whole, which gave scope to ability and enterprise. These values derived from the nature of Mahiga economy. Throughout the nineteenth century, it was still a frontier economy where an ambitious young man could hack his way into the forest and—as Mahiga people used to say—look back over his shoulder with pride at the land he had cleared. Inherited land rights mattered less than the industry with which it was cultivated, and as we have seen, even the sons of rich men seldom inherited much fortune. Prosperity was therefore an individual achievement, won by hard work and good husbandry, and this was reflected in the distribution of status. No one could become an acknowledged leader of society by birth or wealth alone: but if he had grown rich by his own efforts, he was likely to be honoured as a man of wisdom (*muthamaki*)—as much in recognition of his ability as his wealth. A successful trader was almost certain to become a *muthamaki*, and the most influential of these leaders was also the biggest trader, not simply because he was rich, but because of the hard work and organizing skill which had earned him his fortune. Nor were these qualities seen as a natural endowment. If a man achieved little, he was scorned for his idleness without considering what his abilities fitted him to do. Wealth, ability and hard work emerged in a single conception of worth. Children were encouraged to compete for status while they were still young. The uncircumcised youngsters from ten to seventeen years organized their own 'council of boys' (*Njama Ya Ihii*), to which only about one in eight of the age group were at any one time admitted, and their leaders were the élite of their generation—the 'little *athamaki*', whose parents were very proud of them.[1] Even before he was circumcised, a boy could begin to cultivate, to trade, to accumulate his own property: talent was

[1] Five out of six of our informants, who had been trade leaders or assistants to caravan leaders, had been members of the boys' council in their youth.

41

watched for and encouraged from the earliest years, in a spirit of open competition. And once he reached manhood, the young man who strove hardest to make his fortune was most admired.

To this the Masai trade added a further dimension. It provided an opportunity for commercial entrepreneurship which became a major activity of the economy: in the dry season between December and February as many as three Kikuyu caravans a month would visit a single Masai neighbourhood. At the same time, the Masai acted as a frame of reference by which Mahiga judged itself, setting its most ambitious men on a restless drive to emulate a standard of wealth which remained unattainable within their own culture.

Our analysis of the Masai trade shows how closely the values of Mahiga society corresponded with the values of Victorian Britain. The qualities of industriousness, intelligence and aggressive competition which Mahiga admired, its conception of legitimate wealth and honour, appear with much the same emphasis in the Protestant beliefs of the commercial nation which colonized it. In both societies, the values reflected the realities of economic opportunity. If anything, the entrepreneurial spirit of the Kikuyu was more single-minded, for there it did not have to contend with an older feudal tradition of inherited class status. At the same time, the Kikuyu on the frontiers of their territory were used to looking outside their own society to a culture of seemingly superior wealth and self-respect, on which to model their aspirations. It seems, then, that the people of Mahiga should have been particularly ready to assimilate the opportunities created by colonial rule. They were used to exploiting the circumstance of a dominant alien culture, and the values of that culture conformed to their own.

But the transition was neither so simple nor so direct. The old trade dwindled away without any comparable commercial enterprise taking its place. Though the same restless search for opportunity still drove people, the structure of opportunities in the new order was more unstable, more constrained by arbitrary limits, and they explored it at first uncertainly. When, after a generation, they came to see this new opportunity structure more clearly, education supplanted trade as the ruling passion. The true heirs to the Masai traders of the nineteenth century were not Mahiga's businessmen, but the leaders of its drive for schools. Yet even in business, there is a thread of continuity. In the next sections, we shall try to show

how commercial entrepreneurship struggled to adjust to an opportunity structure which remained, throughout the era, less favourable to its chances.

The decline of the Masai trade

In 1904, a year before the incorporation of Kenya as a British colony, the Protectorate government persuaded the Masai to accept a treaty, by which they were to vacate their land in the Rift Valley to make way for European settlement along the line of the new railway. They were compensated by the grant of two Masai reserves—one to the south, and the other on the Laikipia Plateau to the north. Most of the Purko Masai, with whom the Mahiga people had been accustomed to trade, were moved to Laikipia, which they had been gradually colonizing since their victory over the Laikipiaks in the 1870s. This made trade much easier. A secondary trade route to the area had already been established after the Laikipiak war, and it was physically much less hard work, since the plateau could be reached without crossing the Aberdares. As the colonial administration extended its control and the risk of attack from hostile Masai receded, trade also became less dangerous.

In these circumstances, the personal friendships with Masai households mattered less. Though individual traders might still run a risk, caravans could pass safely without protection. Expeditions were no longer arranged in advance in response to a specific request. Men would assemble trade goods they thought they could sell, and travel with them from one household to another.[1] Traders still spoke of visiting Masai friends, but these friends might be no more than acquaintances, and the success of the expedition no longer hinged on the relationship. And as the importance of Masai friendship declined, so did the position of the caravan

[1] According to our informants, trade goods were carried to the Masai homesteads. But there was also, evidently, a considerable trade at Rumuruti market. The Rumuruti District Report for 1909–10 notes 'Kikuyu in larger numbers come from Nyeri District to the market at Rumuruti. They bring in foodstuffs, tobacco and calabashes which they sell to the Masai and the station staff'; and again for 1910–11, 'it is seldom that a week goes by without several caravans of Kikuyu coming to this station'. The earlier report adds 'It has been found expedient not to allow the Kikuyus to wander about among the Masai with their produce, as it leads to numerous complaints and squabbles. . . . The Masai say that the Kikuyu steal their stock, and the Kikuyu say the Masai steal their foodstuffs, and sometimes murder them' (Kenya Archives, DC/LKA/1/1).

leader. 'Any fool could trade then—it required no talent. There were so many traders that none of us could make much profit, and there was nothing a good trader could do to stand out from the rest. In the old days it had been different.'

But with this ease of access came powerful competition. Asian shopkeepers established themselves first in Nyeri, and then at Rumuruti, the administrative centre of the Masai district. The Kikuyu traders were dependent on them for the new kinds of goods which their customers began to demand—umbrellas (a fashion copied from the herd-boys on European farms), sugar, calico sheets and blankets. Once an Asian shop reached Rumuruti in 1905, profit margins in these articles dwindled, for the traders had to buy their stock in Nyeri at prices little less than the shop in Rumuruti would sell them to the same customers. Where, before colonial rule, the Kikuyu had unique access to the supplies on which the Masai depended, their opportunities were increasingly restricted to the sale of their agricultural surplus. For the rest, they now acted more and more as marginal middlemen, whose only chance of worthwhile profit lay beyond the reach of the spreading Asian commercial network. As roads improved, and shops could be supplied more regularly and cheaply, the itinerant trader was at a growing disadvantage. They were also handicapped by their dependence on a rapid sale of all the goods they brought: traditionally, the caravans had always bargained away their stock in a few days, returning before their rations were exhausted. Lacking any base in Masailand, they could not compete with the Asian shopkeeper, who could afford to store slow-moving articles until he got his price.

This period of easy but declining profit lasted scarcely ten years. By 1913, the situation had once again radically changed. The terms of the original treaty with the Masai were to last 'as long as the Masai as a race shall exist'—a promise lightly given when the scrub-covered and isolated Laikipia Plateau seemed unattractive to European settlement. In 1911, the colonial government had second thoughts. The land acquired by the 1904 treaty had been parcelled out, and pressure was growing for the alienation of more Masai territory. A second treaty was forced upon the Masai, by which they lost the plateau in exchange for an extension of the Southern Reserve—a larger but arid tsetse-fly-infested region. By 1913, the last of the Masai had been evicted.

The 1911 treaty reversed the effect of its predecessor. Communication between Mahiga and Masailand was now more difficult than ever before. To reach the Southern Reserve, a trader had to cross the Aberdares on the old route, and continue past Naivasha for another three or four days. The journey took at least a week, and it might be a month before the expedition returned. The casual organization of the years between the treaties would no longer do. Trade became increasingly concentrated in the hands of a few full-time professionals with capital and experience, who could once again make substantial profits. But they were the rearguard of a system of exchange which had lost its geographical logic.

Transport presented a formidable problem, not only because of the distance, but because a much larger stock had to be carried if the expedition was to be profitable. At first, the organizers hired porters, who received a wage of ten shillings or one sheep for the trip. But porters had to be fed, and food was expensive and scarce in the Rift Valley. More porters were needed to carry the rations for the party—maize meal bought from Asian shops in Nyeri. The overhead costs of the trade were therefore much higher than before. After a while, donkeys replaced porters, until the railway reached Nyeri in the late 1920s, and the traders began to move their goods by rail—especially the perishable or fragile tobacco and gourds.[1]

One trader of this period described his routine of organization as follows. Starting from Mahiga, he would travel thirty or forty miles to Embu to buy tobacco, accompanied by his clerk, four donkeys, and perhaps some porters. Then they returned to Nyeri district, where the tobacco was put on the train to Kijabe in the Rift Valley. Next he visited the District Commissioner in Nyeri, to get permission for the expedition, and perhaps renew his trading licence. At the same time, he bought maize meal from the largest Asian store in the township. He then returned to Mahiga, where he hired more porters: four or five men marched with him regularly, and he hired others as he needed them. The caravan now

[1] Traders readily accepted the reliability of rail shipment, transferring to Europeans the trust they held for the Masai. 'Europeans, like the Masai, could be trusted because they were rich. Sometimes when we were trading in Masailand the Masai could not give us our sheep, but we knew they would be kept for us and that we would get them on the next trip. In the same way we knew that when the railway clerk had given us a receipt for our goods, we would receive them safely at Kijabe.'

set off southward, buying ochre and spears along the way. In Fort Hall he bought gourds, and collected those he had already bought and stored there on his way back from the previous expedition. These too were sent by rail to Kijabe from Fort Hall station, so the caravan crossed the Aberdares only lightly loaded. The party dropped down the escarpment, picked up their trade goods from Kijabe station, and loaded the porters and donkeys for the four-day march across the Rift Valley to the Masai reserve.

Personal friendships with Masai households, whose importance had declined in the preceding period, were now even a disadvantage. The trader could sell his goods more quickly, at a better price, if he conducted his business in a public place where customers from a wide area would be attracted. He no longer needed protection, and he only stood to lose custom through jealousy if he appeared to favour particular families. The traders began establishing depots, where they were not dependent upon Masai hospitality. At first these were flimsy structures of leaves and branches, built near friendly Masai homes, and designed only to last the length of the expedition. But in time they were set up at gathering points like salt licks, became more durable and more permanent. By the 1920s there were at least eighteen Kikuyu businessmen—five of them from Mahiga—with depots scattered throughout the Narok district of Masailand, each permanently staffed by assistants and continuously open. So the trader gradually became a shopkeeper, with a fixed place of business and a stock which derived more and more from Asian shopkeepers, less and less from his homeland. Eventually he was absorbed into Masai society. There are today market centres in Masailand where, as far as we could tell, the shopkeepers are all of Kikuyu origin, though they now bear Masai names.[1]

Thus the Masai trade began as a vital exchange between two complementary economies, one rich in cattle, the other in crops, and ended as petty shopkeeping amongst a backward people,

[1] As early as 1913, the Nyeri District Commissioner was worrying about this migration. His report for 1913–14 complains: 'I am very much averse to allowing the Natives to leave the District for the purpose of trading in the Masai Reserve (Southern) for sheep. It is in this way that a very large number of Kikuyu become de-tribalized, and so as to avoid their taxes and other responsibilities remain in Masailand' (Kenya Archives, DC/NYI/1/2). About 1930, however, the most successful Kikuyu traders in Masailand withdrew, and sought more profitable opportunities elsewhere.

picking up the profits of markets too remote to attract Asian commerce. The Kikuyu entrepreneurs of the nineteenth century had grown rich from the delicate balance of hostility and co-operation whose risks and opportunities they mastered. Their successors in the Masai trade never commanded a crucial asset comparable with the network of Masai friends. They were still skilful organizers, but their organization could not compete with the more sophisticated Asian retailing on which it soon became dependent. Under the colonial economy, the opportunities they could still exploit in Masailand became increasingly marginal. Meanwhile, better opportunity was arising elsewhere.

The European succession

As the Masai were dispossessed of the Rift Valley and the Laikipia Plateau, European settlers took their place. But not only physically: they also became a standard of reference and source of opportunity to the people of Mahiga, as the Masai had been before them. Like the Masai, they were powerful and rich and, like the Masai, they were at first mostly cattle keepers. The wealth of these strangers so far outdistanced even the proud Masai that the Kikuyu promptly transferred to them their envy and admiration. 'When the Europeans came, the prestige of the Masai fell like the price of wattle-bark.' Where before rich men in Mahiga had been called 'Masai-like', now they were 'European-like'. The settled areas of the White Highlands became the focus of Mahiga ambitions. Young men went to work there, hoarding their meagre wages to buy their flocks; older men went to trade. And they perceived the qualities of Europeans as they had perceived the Masai: they were trustworthy, because they were rich, and a rich man did not need to cheat; but they were also potential enemies, because their superior power threatened the integrity of Kikuyu society. The ambivalence of the old relationship was handed on too. Thus at least in the first generation, there was a striking continuity in Kikuyu perceptions of Masai and European, and even in the way the economies on either side of the Aberdares complemented each other. The Europeans, like the Masai, were short of agricultural products, especially maize, to feed their stock and their farm labour; while the Kikuyu were as eager as ever for livestock, and grew maize and vegetables in surplus.

47

Small-scale maize trading between Mahiga and the settled areas seems to have started almost as soon as the first European farmers arrived. But at first traders lacked confidence and familiarity to deal with the settlers on a regular basis. Much as the outstanding Masai trade leaders owed their success to their Masai contacts, so the first Mahiga maize trader to establish a substantial business with Europeans had already had many years experience of their society. He had worked for several years in an Asian shop in Nairobi, where he learned to read, write and count money, and he had served as a soldier in the first world war. He had saved enough from his wages to buy donkeys, without which transport costs would have been prohibitive; he had learned simple book-keeping; and he knew enough Swahili to communicate with his European customers. Most important of all, perhaps, he was familiar enough with European ways to gain their confidence, With these assets, he became a model for other men in Mahiga: by 1930 three other traders, with between five and ten donkeys each, travelled with him regularly—and many more joined the caravan occasionally for a fee.

The organization of this trade had, then, much in common with the old Masai trade. The journey was easier and shorter, but it was still undertaken in large parties, under a leader, with a principal, secondary traders and casual followers. And it depended still on stable personal relationships with customers. European farmers would place orders on one trip which were fulfilled on the next; and as they learned to trust the reliability of Kikuyu traders, genuine friendships grew up between them. The trading party would be put up on the farm, provided with pasturage for their donkeys, and even given milk and meat. As one Mahiga trader remarked of a settler from whom he used to buy sheep, 'rich men of all races get on well together'.

The trade flourished in the early 1930s. It was profitable because food could be bought for very little from Kikuyu women in Mahiga, and donkey transport was cheap. So long as prices were lower than a settler would pay to the Asian shops in Nyeri—and he sometimes telephoned to check—the market was assured. But by 1940, Asian traders had begun visiting Mahiga themselves with lorries to buy maize, and Kikuyu left the business for other more promising opportunities.

In the same period, while the larger entrepreneurs were trading with Europeans or Masai, other Mahiga men began to supply the communities of African wage earners growing up in the towns and farms. One partnership bought sheep and goats from the Tugen near Lake Baringo, and sold them to Kikuyu farm labourers in the Rift Valley.[1] Others traded snuff and bananas, or took the eggs and vegetables grown by the labourers on the settlers' farms to hotels in Nairobi and Nakuru. The earliest entrepreneurs could reap substantial profits from such trade, so long as communications were poor, and only the most imaginative perceived where the opportunities lay. As a surviving partner in the Tugen sheep trade remarked to us, 'what matters in any kind of business is shrewdness in seeing chances that other people have not seen'.

But as road and rail transport developed, customers became more sophisticated, and the network of Asian commerce spread, profit margins dropped and the capital needed to compete increased. As with the Masai trade, a permanent place of business began to hold advantages which itinerant trading could not match. 'We became tired of travelling. Our object was to make a profit, not to go on journeys.' As shopkeepers, however, the Mahiga traders were handicapped by illiteracy and lack of capital. The first school in Mahiga was not opened until 1922. Most businessmen could not read and write enough to handle the stock-taking of a shop on an Asian scale, even if they had had the money to start one. The techniques of retailing in the modern manner were all new to them. 'The trouble with business in those days was that we did not know how to do things properly, and made many mistakes. If we had known how to build stone shops like the businessmen of today we would have become very prosperous.' Instead, they tended to seek out opportunities where Asians could not so easily better them. For a while, until mechanical grinders were widely imported, water mills were popular. The heavy grinding stones can still be seen here and there beside a stream, though all but one of the mills themselves have gone. Then, between 1936 and 1942, men began to move out of trade into restaurants serving Kikuyu labourers in the Rift Valley farms and towns. Here there was little Asian competition, and capital costs were low. Once the site and

[1] As early as 1912, there was a flourishing trade route from Nyeri District through Rumuruti to Lake Baringo, by which 'an enormous quantity of tobacco and grain is sold now by the Kikuyu to the Suk and Turkana in return for goats, sheep and money'.

building had been acquired, only enough tea, sugar, milk and vegetables were needed to satisfy the first customers, and book-keeping could be very simple.

The present structure of Mahiga businesses is still influenced by this evolution. Nearly all the economic enterprise of the community, apart from farming, takes place outside its own borders. There are scarcely any substantial businesses in Mahiga itself, but we interviewed 55 businessmen from the area elsewhere in Kenya. Restaurants and bars, together with general retail stores, are still the commonest business interest, followed by butcheries and bus or taxi companies, which—like restaurants—do not depend on supplies where Asians have better contacts.[1] And these businesses have spread out from the areas most familiar to Mahiga people in the days of the Masai trade. The older businesses concentrated in or bordering the Laikipia Plateau—Nyeri, Kiganjo, Nanyuki and Thompson's Falls—or in Naivasha, across the Aberdares in the Rift Valley.[2] Younger men have moved on to Embu, or further into the White Highlands, gradually exploring beyond the traditional limits of Mahiga enterprise.

But as trade gave way to settled businesses, with substantial buildings and a staff of employees, problems of management arose which the men of Mahiga were unprepared to handle by their previous experience. In the pre-colonial economy, every man had worked on his own account, for himself and his family. Regular employment was unknown. The caravan leaders in the Masai trade sometimes had paid assistants, but these were also traders in their own right, and they were compensated out of the profits of the expedition more in the manner of stock holders than employees. Joint ownership was equally rare. Where it appeared of necessity —as in the purchase of a Masai sheep by several small traders together—it was dissolved again as soon as possible by sharing out the progeny of the animal. But modern business involved partnership. Few men had the capital to build a restaurant or stock a shop without assistance, and, especially to begin with, when cash was

[1] The 55 businessmen were owners or partners in 21 restaurants and bars, 21 general stores, 14 taxi or bus companies, and 13 butcheries. Five had an interest in whole-saling, 5 in charcoal dealing: no more than 2 or 3 were involved in any other kind of business. In all, these 55 men had interests in 130 businesses. We traced 10 other businessmen whom we were not able to interview.

[2] There were 24 Mahiga businessmen in these places, 16 of them over forty. Of the 31 men whose activities were centred on more distant places, only 6 were forty or older.

scarce in African communities, the partnerships had to be quite large. Amongst the 22 men over forty whom we interviewed, 6 owned their principal business in partnerships of ten or more, and 3 others in partnerships of five. Only 2 of the 33 younger men were involved in a group as large as ten, 3 in a group of five. The size of partnership seems always to have been related to the capital requirement of the business: butcheries and charcoal dealing, for instance—where there was a quick return on a small investment— were characteristically owned by a single proprietor, while partnerships predominated in all other kinds of business.[1]

At first, the people of Mahiga tried to resolve the notion of partnership into serial single ownership, much as in the past they had divided up the value of a sheep. A water mill, for instance, would have cost between 12,000 and 15,000 shillings around 1928 —more than one businessman could raise. So he formed a partnership with perhaps a dozen others. Each partner would then, in turn, take sole charge of the mill for a month. He could operate it himself, or through an employee, and took all the profit. In this way, the problems of joint management and mutual trust were sidestepped, and since there were scarcely any maintenance costs to the mill, the principle seems to have worked. Nearly all the first hotels were financed and run in the same manner, usually with two partners undertaking the business together at one time. Later, the partners were sometimes divided into two teams, each with its own leader, representing different neighbourhoods or groups of friends, which replaced each other every six months or every year. So long as the business was small and simple the system could be made to work. But it could be applied only clumsily to a business where continuity in the employment of staff was an advantage. It broke down altogether once depreciation and maintenance costs had to be taken account of, and stock transferred. No partner would want to undertake expensive repairs and replacements for the benefit of his successor. In a shopkeeping partnership, there could be endless argument over the value and amount of goods to be passed on whenever control changed hands. In the end, Mahiga society had to come to grips with the unfamiliar practice of shared ownership, and assimilate the new kinds of economic

[1] Ten of the 14 butcheries and charcoal businesses were singly owned, 18 of the 41 other businesses—taking only the principal interest of the 55 businessmen we interviewed.

relationship it implied.[1] So, as trade gave way to settled business, entrepreneurs encountered increasingly the problems of management which we analyse in the second part of this book. They were hemmed in by an alien economy whose principles of operation they could not easily grasp, but on which their chances depended; and they had to work out relationships within their own businesses for which they had no precedent in their traditions.

In the hundred years we have reviewed, an iron-age society without any written language, where the known world scarcely extended beyond its neighbouring tribes, was confronted by a culture which conducted its economy and government across thousands of miles by ship and rail, by car and plane, and managed it through a vastly complex system of signs, tokens and records. Thousands of years of technological evolution were compressed in the experience of a single generation. Yet the continuity is as striking as the changes. From the first arrival of the European farmers, the people of Mahiga set about adapting their traditions of economic enterprise to the new circumstances with extraordinary resilience; and if they were not always successful, yet they were never disconcerted. They carried into the colonial era a habit of looking for economic opportunity outside their own borders, in a society of greater wealth and power. And this sense of being, as a people, poorer than their neighbours reinforced the individualism of their own social structure to sustain a restless acquisitiveness. They did not withdraw from European power nor challenge it, any more than they had challenged the Masai. They searched out the commercial opportunities inherent in the new pattern of relationships, as they had done before.

But the inherent readiness to make contact with a superior culture, to emulate its achievements and assimilate them to the Kikuyu ideal of the self-made man did not lead only towards new forms of commercial enterprise. As pioneers in Mahiga tried to imitate European techniques, they began to realize how crucial was the knowledge which informed European practices. They had bought the superior European sheep and cattle, but had not

[1] 'Partnerships usually end in violence or lawsuits', according to the Nyeri District Report of 1926.

known how to protect them from disease; they had tried to adapt their patterns of trade, but had been continually overtaken by the immigrant commercial network. European and Asian enterprise had eroded the traditional ways of acquiring wealth, while it pre-empted the new opportunities for profit. In their frustration, ambitious Mahiga men began to see that if they were ever to approach European standards of wealth, they had first to master European knowledge. The search for economic opportunity became increasingly preoccupied with education.

They approached the problem with an ambivalence not unlike the mixture of co-operation and self-defence blended in their former relationship to the Masai. They wanted to learn what Europeans learned, since here the key to European power must lie—but on their own terms, so that they, rather than the missionaries or the colonial government, controlled it. They mistrusted the sincerity with which schools under European management would serve their ambitions, and they resented the missionaries' attempt to use education as a weapon to attack their customs. Leadership in Mahiga therefore came to centre on the struggle to establish and control schools. From 1930 onwards, prominent businessmen became deeply involved in the Independent school movement: three of the principal organizers of the Independent school in Upper Mahiga, for instance, were substantial traders and restaurant keepers. Education became the dominant passion, and the end to which all other activities were referred.

Mahiga was successful, out of all proportion to its population, in securing educational opportunities for its children. By 1938, a third of the places at the only government-aided secondary school in the district were filled by pupils from the Independent primary schools, few as they were, and amongst these the Upper Mahiga school was outstanding. But the entrepreneurial vitality which channelled the resources of the community towards these opportunities was, in a sense, working for its own destruction. Personal ambition turned to educational qualifications, and the prestige of business dropped. At best, it was a means to earn school fees for oneself or one's children, and a source of profits to invest in community schools. Entrepreneurial talents became handmaids to the academic talents which won secondary school places, university degrees, and positions of power and wealth in a modern bureaucracy.

The values of society had not fundamentally changed. But as the opportunity structure changed, the attitudes imposed by the educational means came to be at odds with the underlying drive for education itself. The narrowly academic schooling preoccupied with examinations, which passed for the European model, was essentially passive and conservative. It served to place young people favourably in an employment structure where educational qualifications were scarce, but taught them to trust in certificates and routine knowledge. Only the talent frustrated in the struggle for education still turned to entrepreneurship, and society no longer respected it. Thus as the opportunities changed, so did the kind of achievement to which people aspired, and this imposed on a tradition of individual initiative a superficially uncreative, status-conscious attitude of mind. The confusion of values prevented any straightforward handing down of an entrepreneurial outlook.

3
THE ORIGINS
OF ENTREPRENEURS

In Mahiga, as the colonial régime progressively undermined the traditional basis of trade, entrepreneurs struggled to reorganize their activities around the new opportunities which the disintegration of old structures was creating. But they were largely frustrated. Society as a whole turned its attention from trade to employment—especially the relatively well paid occupations to which educational qualifications were the passport. The same evolution was taking place all over Kenya. For thirty years African economic enterprise was confined to the trading centres which began to grow up around the barter markets and in the African parts of the townships: the profits were small, the enterprises themselves obviously inferior to their Asian counterparts, the prestige of the trader much below that of an educated man. Entrepreneurship was no longer—as it had once been in Mahiga —a highly respected and prosperous activity.

As Independence approached, the opportunity structure of society began to change again. But the gradual relaxation of constraints on African commercial life were not nearly as spectacular as the promotion of Africans throughout the occupational hierachy. The value of education redoubled, as young men with university degrees, higher school certificates, or even first school certificates succeeded their European predecessors as district officers and senior civil servants, and began to find their way into the management of European companies. In 1966 and 1967 when we undertook our study, the conventional aspirations of society still looked above all to education and salaried careers. These were the years when hundreds of local communities were pouring scarce resources into 'Harambee' secondary schools, financed and run on their own initiative, with an almost reckless disregard for the practical possibilities of sustaining them: and farmers were selling their land to find fees to place their children in them. The entrepreneurs we met were therefore different from most of their generation. They recognized a different order of opportunities, at least for themselves, if not their children, attaching their ambitions to achievements whose prestige and importance had still to be conventionally established. Where did they come from? What had driven them to pioneer a new kind of career? Is there some more or less universal pattern of circumstance, whose influence can be traced here too, from which entrepreneurs characteristically arise?

The vitality of entrepreneurship as a response to change seems to vary greatly from one society to another, or within the same society at different phases of its evolution. It may appear now in one class or group, now another—a minority religion, excluded by its unorthodoxy from conventional positions of prestige; an immigrant community; a class of society deprived of its traditional status. The characteristic circumstances cover a wide range of conditions, but they all have something in common. In a study of Indonesian businessmen, for instance, Clifford Geertz has described two typical yet contrasting patterns of entrepreneurial initiative. In a Javanese town, small but enterprising businesses were run by families of a reformist Muslim sect, self-contained and self-respecting, while in Bali the traditional aristocracy, bereft of political power, exploited old feudal loyalties to re-establish themselves as masters of large-scale organizations.[1] These patterns recur elsewhere. Like the Balinese aristocrats, the Samurai of Japan found in business a way of recovering a purpose and esteem they had lost in the disintegration of feudal society. Like the Javanese Muslims, nonconformist sects such as the Quakers—debarred from political life by their refusal to take any oath—turned to business during the industrial revolution. Some entrepreneurial minorities—the Chinese in South East Asia, the Indians in East Africa, the Jews—are both religious minorities and immigrants.

All these groups seem to stand in a fundamentally similar relationship to the opportunity structure of society. On the one hand, they feel themselves excluded from the generally recognized means to success. The Javanese and Balinese businessmen, for instance, though they differed greatly in their conception of business organization and their social origins, had in common

[1] Geertz.

their need to search out a new way to power and prestige—in Java because they were a nonconformist religious minority, in Bali because Dutch rule and the populist régime which succeeded it had deprived them of their political authority. Conversely, the religion, race, or past status which isolates such groups also gives them an internal cohesion which may help them to assemble a business organization—through the mutually protective loyalties of a vulnerable minority, for instance, or the social network of a self-conscious class.

At the same time, this sense of isolation is characteristically created or reinforced by beliefs which assert the superiority of the group to the rest of society. Religion, cultural or class traditions give them a reassurance of their worth which prevents them from being easily reconciled to their apparent expectations. These systems of belief can be seen as an expression of the social pressures which push them towards innovation; as themselves a cause of alienation from orthodox society; or as both, in a mutually reinforcing cycle. In this chapter we examine the origins of entrepreneurship as an outcome of social position, while the influence of beliefs and attitudes in themselves is the theme of the next. But each is a different aspect of the other.

The businessmen we studied in Kenya were not all entrepreneurs. Rural shopkeeping has been a commonplace activity for a generation—though, in their fathers' day, the first man to establish a permanent trading post or a permanent building was indeed an entrepreneur. A few of the men we met were the sons of these pioneers. But whenever businessmen undertook manufacture or services which before only Asians and Europeans had provided, or organized their concerns on a larger scale than an earlier generation, there was at least an element of creative originality in their venture. The businessmen supported by the ICDC stand out from the ruck of African shopkeepers as bolder, more ambitious men. If entrepreneurship characteristically arises from an interaction between social exclusion and access to resources which others ignore or cannot grasp, can a similar pattern be traced in the origins of these Kenya business pioneers?

Firstly, African entrepreneurs do not seem to arise from a minority religious group. All but 6 per cent of the ICDC-supported businessmen belonged to a Christian church, and identified with a variety of denominations—Roman Catholic, Anglican,

Quaker, Methodist, Baptist, the Salvation Army, Seventh Day Adventist. Most of them, however, had simply accepted the religion of the mission which ran their childhood school, and since in Kenya a single mission usually predominates in each area, this was also the accepted religion of their community. 'We didn't bother much about denominations, we just went to the only church there was and I went with the other boys.' Only 7 per cent claimed to belong to a minority religion where they grew up. Correspondingly, ties of religion did not facilitate business relationships, as happens amongst the members of an unorthodox sect. Eighty-nine per cent said their religion had been of no material help to them in business, even incidentally, and no one seemed concerned about the religious affiliation of his partners or workers. Even in the ten businesses where all the principal partners and workers were of the same faith, it seemed more accident than design. Many had not bothered to inquire about it. In 61 per cent of the businesses, the religions were so mixed, or of such little concern, that their directors had no sense that any one was dominant. As a whole, church membership neither segregated them from the majority of their community, nor bound them by any special ties to their fellow worshippers.[1]

Nor were they characteristically an ethnic minority in the areas where they established their enterprises. Twenty-five had been born in the same location, 24 elsewhere in the same district, another 25 in the same province,[2] so in all 86 per cent were working amongst their own tribesmen, and the majority close to their birthplace. Even the 14 per cent who came from another province included mostly Kikuyu from Central Province who worked in the Rift Valley, or the other way about, and in the Rift Valley too Kikuyu predominate amongst the African population, The businessmen had, however, often travelled widely in their careers —in the army, in prisons during the Emergency, trading and shopkeeping as far as Rhodesia or the Congo, studying in India, working in the cities. Over half of them had been living in their present neighbourhood for less than ten years. If they settled at last near their original homes, it was because here they found their

[1] Strictly, Christianity itself could be called a minority religion, since amongst the African population as a whole only about a third are Christian, according to the census. But Christianity is certainly not regarded as an unconventional faith to hold.
[2] These figures include Nairobi with Central Province, which it adjoins, though it is an extra-provincial district.

opportunity, rather than from attachment to their roots. But there is nothing to suggest either that businessmen come from minorities excluded from other opportunities or that they are more successful, if they establish their enterprises amongst strangers. And here again, as with religion, because they have no sense of isolation as a tribal minority, they do not organize their businesses by appealing to tribal loyalty. Most, as we shall see, repudiate it as irrelevant to business, preferring workers only for their competence and willingness to work.

If African entrepreneurship did not arise from a distinct tribal or religious minority within the community, was it then the outcome of frustration within a particular class? At first sight, the origins of the businessmen supported by the ICDC seem to reflect, simply, the variety of experience common to African society. They included some whose families had been expelled from the land by consolidation, and others from traditionally dominant lineages: sons of poor widows, who had struggled through an impoverished childhood, and sons of prosperous, respected men; illiterates and university graduates. Sixty per cent were the children of peasant farmers, rich or poor, and the rest of labourers, shopkeepers, craftsmen, schoolteachers or junior government officers, clergy, soldiers and policemen (Table 1).

Apart from the number of businessmen's sons in commerce,

TABLE I   *Occupations of businessmen's fathers*

Father's principal occupation during their childhood	Businessmen in Industry	Commerce	All
Peasant farmer: prosperous	21%	28%	25%
average	24%	21%	22%
poor	13%	15%	14%
Unskilled or semi-skilled	24%	5%	15%
Craftsmen, employed or self-employed	6%	5%	6%
Schoolteacher, clergyman, junior government officer	6%	—	3%
Police, army	2%	5%	3%
Businessman	4%	21%	12%
Total	100%	100%	100%
Father held position of leadership	23%	7%	16%
Total no.	47	40	87

and of leaders' sons in industry, this family background does not seem unusual.

The previous careers of the businessmen themselves, however, do distinguish them more sharply. Here, in the characteristics which identify them as a particular occupational group, we can begin to trace that interaction of frustration and opportunity which seems so often to generate entrepreneurship. For though they had been relatively successful in employment, acquiring experience and self-confidence, they were dissatisfied with their jobs and—as we shall see—felt their aspirations blocked by the conventional structure of opportunities.

Entrepreneurship and vocational frustration

Most of the businessmen were between thirty and fifty years old when we met them, and had already followed a variety of occupations before they turned to business. At one time or another, about a quarter had been hawkers and petty traders, and a similar proportion had run other kinds of business, worked as labourers, as skilled employees, or as clerks. Seventeen per cent had been schoolteachers or junior government officers, another 17 per cent soldiers or policemen and 13 per cent self-employed craftsmen. Only 8 per cent had even been full-time farmers. If their final occupation before they began their present business careers is compared with the occupations of all African men in Kenya, some striking differences appear.

Firstly, only 7 per cent were then farming, and 2 per cent were unemployed, while amongst the adult male population at large, 64 per cent are estimated to be either engaged in farming their small-holdings, herdsmen, or—perhaps 5 per cent—unemployed. Even if those who took up business as soon as they were released from detention (8 per cent) and the former hawkers and petty traders (12 per cent) are added to this group, they still represent a much smaller proportion outside recognized paid employment. There are about 2,000,000 men of working age in Kenya, of whom 36 per cent were reckoned to be employed or self-employed in 1964. But in roughly the same period, 71 per cent of the businessmen held paid jobs, and their work was more than averagely skilled. Fourteen per cent were teachers, or in positions of similar status, like medical dispensers or assistant agricultural officers; 18 per cent held clerical posts; 29 per cent were skilled manual workers or self-employed craftsmen; 7 per cent were in the army or police. Most of these categories absorb only about 1 per cent of the labour force as a whole, and skilled manual work 5 per cent. The commonest employment is unskilled, and accounts for at least a quarter of all occupations. But only 3 per cent of the businessmen had been in such humble jobs. On the other hand, very few had given up highly paid or prestigious posts for business.[1]

The pattern of careers was similar in both commerce and industry, except that a fifth of the shopkeepers and wholesalers had grown out of petty trading, and only 4 per cent of the industrialists. As a group, the businessmen supported by the ICDC stand out as men who had been relatively successful in employment, though they had seldom achieved positions of importance. They came into business characteristically from a middling occupational status, between the peasant farmer, labourer, or domestic servant and the small African élite of senior civil servants, doctors, lawyers, academics and company officials.

The career pattern of the businessmen in the market centres shows a similar bias towards relatively skilled employment. Their previous occupations differed less markedly from the population at large, but even so 62 per cent had been employed before they took up business, and 46 per cent had held skilled manual or non-manual jobs: in the African population as a whole only 36 per cent are employed at all and about 8 per cent have skilled jobs. The more prosperous of the market businessmen conformed even more closely to the businessmen with ICDC support in the distribution of their preceding occupation (Table 2).

[1] It is not possible to make an exact comparison with the population at large. There are no official figures for unemployment, and an estimated 10 per cent of employment is unreported and so cannot be classified. It is presumably mostly unskilled. The size of the labour force itself is not accurately known. Even in the reported categories of employment, the classifications are hard to follow. Sales and workers in transport and communications are each separate categories, as are 'unskilled workers and labourers', 'crafts, production and skilled workers', and 'service, sport and recreation workers'. These groups are obviously not naturally exclusive, and rest partly on distinguishing the field of activity, partly on its status. Employment, too, varies with age and origin. But for all these difficulties, the differences between the businessmen and the adult male population at large are so great, it seems very unlikely that any adjustment would alter the sense of the comparison. The figures for the general population are derived chiefly from Ray. A sample survey of occupations was attempted in the 1962 census, but it was unsuccessful. Too many of the returns from rural areas failed to state occupation usably.

TABLE 2 *Previous occupations of businessmen*

Last occupation before business*	All	Market businessmen[1] Profit under 300/–	Profit over 300/–	ICDC-supported businessmen
Unemployed, no occupation†	13%	15%	12%	10%
Farming	17%	17%	15%	7%
Hawker, petty trader	8%	8%	9%	12%
Employed or self-employed:				
unskilled manual	16%	18%	10%	3%
skilled manual	25%	23%	27%	29%
non-manual (clerks, teachers, etc.)	17%	15%	21%	32%
Army or police	4%	4%	6%	7%
Total %	100%	100%	100%	100%
Total no.‡	765	438	175	87

* Or present occupation for the 3% of the market businessmen who were still employed.

† Including those in detention or at school.

‡ Excludes one market where the question about previous occupation was not asked, and businessmen who did not give the relevant information. Businessmen whose profit could not be assessed are included in the first column.

It seems then that entrepreneurial initiative came typically from men who were already in comparatively well paid and secure jobs. Why did they give them up for business? The immediate inducement was not money. They knew that at first they would make very little, and sometimes accepted a sharp drop in income to set the business on its way. A locomotive driver, for instance, resigned to manage a company he had promoted, though it could pay him only a tenth of his previous salary. Train driving, besides, had been a secure and easy life—'there are no great responsibilities, if the engine breaks down you just telephone for the repairers and sit down to wait'—while the worry and responsibility of the company had almost been too much for him. He saw it as a challenge to his courage and integrity: 'I thought if I ran away I would be a coward: you must have that spiritual dedication to start a business and make it stand.' A baker, in the same spirit,

[1] This breakdown by monthly profit is explained more fully on p. 213.

explained why he was giving up a £1,000-a-year job with a European firm to return full time to his own struggling enterprise: 'I feel I'll be creating something, helping people. Your mind is all the time occupied. When I was baking myself I was working night and day—all I wanted was to get some people and start working, even all through the night if there was a demand. I was just interested in creating something. But in this job (with the European firm) I'm wasting my time, not contributing anything to the development of the country. If I felt I was really using my knowledge I'd be satisfied—but that's where you have difficulty in this country.'

To these men, business seemed their one chance of being independent, creative and of using their minds. As a whole, money did not seem the deepest concern of the ICDC-supported businessmen. Although they hoped to make more one day than they could ever earn from employment, the immediate rewards were often less. When we asked them about the satisfactions of business, only a fifth mentioned money. But half of them spoke of independence—the freedom to take your own decisions, to be master of your time; and a third of the contribution to development—creating employment, adding new resources. A fifth, too, mentioned the broadening of their experience. Employment was less worrying, less demanding, more irresponsible—but for these same reasons ultimately unsatisfying. Again and again, the business men stressed the value of autonomy:

The most important thing is being independent, because you work and rely on yourself. You use your brains and sweat and energy instead of relying on an employer who tells you what to do without you thinking.[T]

You enjoy the work more, you are your own master, and you know more people. When you are employed you don't use your mind fully. But on your own you have more scope to think for yourself. You come to learn, and enjoy that it is your own work. With your own business you have a sense of independence and responsibility. You are responsible for your own mistakes, and you are more alert. If you are employed, you just wait to be told.

Ha! Employment—no. If I was to be employed, I would be ordered about—and I have been free too long.

They felt not only free, but useful.

> Even if I could get 5,000 shillings a month in employment, so long as there are people lounging about looking for work whom I could help, the money wouldn't mean anything to me. I want to be able to help others, and relieve the misery of unemployment.[T]

> When you are running your own business, you are helping more people—the people you employ, and your shareholders. If you are employed, you are helping your own family only. Ten people employed help maybe forty people, but ten people with their own businesses help 400.

> Working for yourself gives you experience which you could never get if you were employed. Later you can use that experience to advise others. You don't learn for yourself, but for others. And you are creating employment for everybody. I could make more money employed elsewhere, but I am not willing to put up my hands. If I give up, others will follow, and the business which we are all very proud of will collapse.

Thus business gave them a sense of fulfilment which they could not find in employment: the jobs open to them were neither responsible nor interesting enough. Four-fifths of them said they would still prefer business, even if employment paid them better. What mattered was not so much money for itself, but to be master of their own achievement.

If they had been more educated, their prospects of employment would not have seemed so unsatisfying: in more senior jobs, they might have found a sense of importance in their work. But the career structure of Kenya is closely related to educational attainment, and they lacked the formal qualifications which would have entitled them to promotion above subordinate posts in the occupational hierarchy. This was the underlying cause of their frustration. The businessmen had more schooling than most— enough, perhaps, to give them a sense of their abilities—but not enough to open the way to influential positions. Three-quarters had never gone further than primary school, and half the rest had not continued their education long enough to achieve school certificate standard. Poverty, the disruptions of the Emergency years, ill health or their parents' indifference had thwarted their educational chances. Apart from four who had been trained as teachers after primary school, the few who did manage to acquire qualifications had not climbed the conventional ladder of examination successes but studied at night school, or paid their own way at colleges in India of doubtful academic standing. Thus the businessmen were excluded from careers which might have satisfied their desire to do something important and influential in their own eyes. And correspondingly, the élite who had attained these qualifications no longer had any incentive to turn to business.

The way in which formal qualifications block career opportunities helps to explain why—as we discuss more fully in chapter 9—education seems associated with success in simple small businesses, but not at the level the ICDC-supported businessmen had reached. Up to a point, the ablest and most ambitious children are likely to find opportunities of acquiring knowledge and skills, irrespective of their circumstances. Even if they are poor, their talent may attract support—as, for instance, some of the businessmen were helped through school by the European farmer who employed their parents. Or they may study at night school and correspondence colleges, or teach themselves a craft. So they will acquire confidence in their abilities and rather better jobs. But at the level of secondary school, this correspondence between education and ability becomes more and more tenuous. Since school places are much scarcer and more expensive, the chances that an able child will drop out are much higher. Indeed, the places are so few that even if every pupil were selected only for merit, and not partly by his parents' capacity to pay the fees, there would still be far more talented children outside secondary schools than in them. At this stage, education and entrepreneurship begin to diverge. The higher the qualifications a boy attains in school, the better his employment opportunities: money, responsibility and prestige are more and more surely open to him through a conventional career. But the boy who missed the chance must seek out an alternative path to justify the same intelligence. 'It's true that educated people don't want to go into business', a garage proprietor remarked. 'In government you can get a big car at once. In business you may have nothing to start with, not even a bicycle. But one day you may have an aeroplane.' Thus the entrepreneurs are recruited from the frustrated and talented who, because they have been excluded from the occupations of highest prestige, are determined to show that in business they can go one better.[1]

They were therefore seeking from business not merely money, but achievements which would earn them a status equivalent to the educated élite. And money, in itself, does not necessarily confer prestige. We asked a group of 92 secondary schoolboys, for instance, to rate 38 occupations according to several criteria— would they like the jobs? had it high prestige? did it require an educated man? a clever man? would it make them rich or happy? On all counts, they preferred senior jobs in government— district officer, health inspector, agricultural officer—as prestigious, well paid, educated occupations. But for other careers, their ratings were less consistent. They perceived a shopkeeper in a township as wealthier than a secondary school teacher, but less educated and of lower status, and they found the job less attractive. Similarly, they would rather have been clerks or junior government officers than rural retailers, butchers, teashop or bar keepers, which they saw as uneducated occupations of lower status; yet they believed these local businessmen made at least as much money. Thus the prestige of a job was, in their eyes, consistently related to the education it required, not to its financial reward. Businessmen were amongst the most prosperous, yet of less status than an office clerk, a veterinary assistant or a soldier: and the schoolboys' own preferences were invariably related to prestige, not wealth.[2]

[1] There are signs that some quite high-status civil servants are now being attracted towards business. This probably does not represent a different pattern of motivation, but rather the same pattern at a higher level of sophistication. Now that the Africanization of the civil service is largely completed, the prospects of pay and promotion are becoming less satisfying. Correspondingly, opportunities for sophisticated businesses are growing. Highly educated men now have the confidence to challenge the predominance of expatriate firms in these markets, and a greater frustration in their civil service prospects. As the African secretary of the Chamber of Commerce remarked to us: 'We want to show that Africans can compete on an equal footing with foreigners. It is a matter of respect.'

[2] The boys, in forms I to III of a Kikuyu high school, were asked to rate 38 occupations according to eight criteria on a five point scale. Two of the criteria not discussed above—happiness and the easiness of the life—were closely associated with wealth, while all occupations were seen as hard-working. Cleverness was associated with wealth, too, but here the schoolboys' judgment of occupations differing greatly in status or income tended to converge. Farming with 15 acres was rated much like business, while small farmers and manual workers were judged lowest on all counts. The findings are given in more detail in the supplementary tables, pp. 246–7.

If these views reflect prevailing attitudes, the businessmen's disparagement of money as a motive becomes more clearly understandable. A large income would not itself compensate for their occupational frustration, since it could not buy them a sense of social importance. They needed to associate business with the qualities of senior government service, whose prestige was universally acknowledged. Hence they emphasized their contribution to national development, to modernization and the growth of knowledge—purposes which business could claim to share with political leaders, administrators, the professional élite, and in which it could play an autonomous part. If they could prove themselves in business, in time their achievements would be acknowledged as equally significant, and their status would be vindicated.

Entrepreneurship and political frustration

This association of business with national ideals is confirmed by the businessmen's political careers. They had characteristically been active in the struggle for Independence. But as an African government came to power, and their own part in political life began to seem less meaningful, they transferred their patriotism to entrepreneurship. Business became a substitute for both administrative influence and political leadership, where lack of educational sophistication was less of a drawback.

The Kikuyu businessmen had nearly all committed themselves to the fight for Independence, and some of the older men had taken part in earlier campaigns, as leaders of the independent churches and schools, radical journalists, party agents. Half the ICDC-supported businessmen who came from the tribes subject to the Emergency regulations had been detained as Mau Mau sympathizers—two for less than a year, three for one or two years, seven for two to four years, and thirteen for longer. These thirteen, who had spent up to eight years in jail, would have been regarded by the colonial régime as 'hard core'—political organizers, and occasionally forest fighters, who adamantly refused to repudiate their allegiance in captivity.

Some of the businessmen were still active in politics—one a minister, another chairman of his town council, a third in the inner circle of the ruling party. In all, 9 per cent still took part in local party committees, and 10 per cent were town or county council-lors. But as time went by and their business affairs claimed more and more of their attention, they tended to limit their involvement. Fourteen per cent had withdrawn from politics, refusing further invitations to stand. The Chamber of Commerce and local school committees—in each of which about a quarter were active—remained as their principal interests. 'I'm a KANU[1] man, but I'm not interested to be elected as a politician', said a wholesaler. 'I stay with them because I've dealt with it for such a long time, I was one of the very early group. I helped to form KANU in Kiambu in 1960. Now I'm only interested in the business, but I'm paying them money. I'm a member of the Chamber of Commerce —that's my root. I don't belong to anything else, I'm not interested in any of these nonsense things. The Chamber and KANU and business is all I want.'

This withdrawal from politics was a redirection of their patriotic ideals, rather than growing indifference. Under the colonial régime, the frustration of African aspirations was undifferentiated. Land hunger, the poverty of education, econo-mic and political subordination, all alike seemed to arise from imperial oppression. The progress of business and the political struggle were interdependent. Business itself was sometimes as much an expression of nationalism as an economic venture in its own right.[2] But with the granting of Independence, they began to diverge. The nature of party politics inevitably changed, as it turned from mass movement to the manipulation of government, and became more competitive, more self-seeking, and more con-troversial. It began to demand more specifically political skills, and at the same time, was no longer so obviously relevant to the

[1] KANU—Kenya African National Union, the ruling party.
[2] The Luo Thrift Society, started by Oginga Odinga, for instance, attempted ambi-tious projects—such as a modern hotel in Kisumu—which were attractive as symbols of African progress, rather than profitable. Under colonial government, when politi-cal initiatives are restricted, the nationalist leadership may turn to business as a means of asserting their aspirations. But since the enterprises need to be impressive if they are to make their political point, they are characteristically over-ambitious. One of the businesses we interviewed seems to have been started for political rather than economic reasons, by local political leaders. 'The Forest Department took land from us and planted these trees, which were helping other tribes who came and took our wood. So we thought that by starting this business we would be able to use our own timber. And there was no African sawmiller here, so it would be a prestige for our own people to own their own mill. And we hope to force the Asians out.' But it had not so far proved economically viable.

national purpose. The political struggle had given place to an economic struggle. Europeans and Asians still dominated commerce and industry. African society was still backward, and desperately needed to create more employment, widen its industrial base, and generate the income to provide more education. As economic and political development evolved into distinct tasks, so they claimed different leadership, and different talents. The businessmen began to recognize that their particular contribution lay in their own enterprise, and subordinated all their other activities to it, as they often said: 'They wanted me to become a councillor, but I told them I have no time', 'We haven't a minute to spare for politics', 'I don't have time, and I refuse when people want to elect me', 'A businessman is like a local leader and you cannot lead in two ways. If you join local committees you may find the claims of business make you neglect your committee duties, and if you devote your time to committees your business will suffer.' So they transmuted African nationalism into African capitalism. To build up a business until its headquarters stood proudly in a main street of Nairobi beside the European companies; to provide employment and encourage its workers to build their own enterprises; to develop the township with shops, hotels, industries—these were national as well as personal ambitions.

An entrepreneur in Kenya is, then, likely to have identified himself with the struggle for Independence, and to be looked upon as a leader of his community. His political past may still help him —a quarter of the businessmen, for instance, had facilitated the negotiation of their ICDC loan by political contacts; and though they did not get more money or on better terms thereby, they got it on the whole more quickly. But lacking the education for an important position in government, or a taste for the factional conflicts of local politics, business now attracts him more as a means of furthering his patriotic ideals. Economic pioneering increasingly demands all his attention. It is the justification of his self-respect, as an African, and as an intelligent and creative man, whose abilities would be cramped in employment.

Thus the vocational dissatisfaction which drives men into business derives its idealism from a prevailing sense of frustrated national aspirations. Entrepreneurship is a reaction to the economic backwardness which excludes African society as a whole from international respect. This may partly explain the predominance of

Kikuyu amongst African businessmen. For just as vocational frustration touches most those who come closest to the opportunities they miss, so the humiliations of colonial rule were felt most bitterly by the people most involved with their institutions. At the same time, this familiarity with European society instilled an awareness which made entrepreneurial ventures more possible to conceive.

The predominance of Kikuyu entrepreneurs

Although the Kikuyu are the largest tribe in Kenya, their part of the ICDC's small business loans was two or three times greater than their numbers alone would justify, especially in industry— the most ambitious enterprises where Africans have least experience to guide them (Table 3).[1]

Apart from the Somali, the traditionally pastoral people have taken little part in business, as they have ignored most other opportunities in the modern economy. But for the rest, only the Kikuyu stand out as altogether disproportionately represented.

This could be the result of favouritism rather than entrepreneurial initiative, as businessmen of other tribes sometimes complained. The senior staff of the ICDC was Kikuyu, so predominantly was the Government. What else was to be expected? The charge is plausible, but we found no other evidence for it. The ICDC began granting loans before Independence, when its most active promoter of applications was an Englishman, who seems to have been guided only by his sense of economic possibilities. The ICDC had since sent its officers into non-Kikuyu areas to stimulate a wider distribution of applicants. And if discrimination had been deliberate, why should the bias be stronger in industry—where applicants were fewer and viable projects hard to find—than in commerce, where there was more choice? Apart from the ICDC's experience, there is evidence that Kikuyu seek out economic opportunities more widely than other tribes. Kikuyu businessmen had established themselves in most of the

[1] We have used here the figures for loan recipients rather than the figures from our interviews, since the sample of commercial businesses excluded the Northern Province and the Coast, as explained in chapter 2, and so is not geographically fully representative. But apart from excluding the two Taita businessmen, and most of the Somalis, the tribal distribution for the sample is very similar. To be consistent, the industrial figures include the businesses we failed to interview.

markets we surveyed: 5 to 10 per cent of shops in the Luo, Luhya, Kisii and Kamba markets were Kikuyu, but no other people had set up businesses in another tribal area. Kikuyu businessmen are to be found as far afield as Southern Tanzania.

TABLE 3   *Tribal distribution of ICDC loan recipients*

Tribe*	Male population	ICDC loans to April 1966† Industry	ICDC loans to April 1966† Commerce
Kikuyu	20%	64%	44%
Luo	14%	12%	11%
Luhya	13%	8%	9%
Kamba	11%	4%	13%
Kalenjin (Nandi, Kipsigis, etc.)	10%	—	3%
Kisii	6%	2%	6%
Mijikenda	5%	4%	1%
Meru	5%	2%	1%
Somali	4%	2%	6%
Embu	1%	—	3%
Swahili and Arab	1%	2%	1%
Taita	1%	—	2%
Others (Masai, Turkana, etc.)	9%	—	—
Total %	100%	100%	100%
Total no.	4,134,634	50	97

* The classification follows the 1962 census, from which the figures are taken, but has been simplified where the distinctions are not relevant to our comparison. Several important groups, like the Turkana and Masai, have not been distinguished, since these pastoral peoples have as yet taken little part in business; and all the Kalenjin-speaking groups have been put together, but not the closely related Kikuyu and Embu.
† Only loans which had been issued are included: in one or two instances, the sorting between industry and commerce has been altered, where the ICDC's classification seemed inappropriate as a description of the enterprise.

When the Uganda government opened a settlement scheme, designed to encourage progressive farming among the people of the region, local applicants were few, but Kikuyu from 400 miles away promptly took up the offer.[1] So the ICDC loans probably

[1] In general, according to the 1962 census, a higher proportion of Kikuyu live outside their homeland. 30·6 per cent of the Kikuyu were living outside Kiambu, Fort Hall, Nyeri and Embu Districts, which the census defines as their homeland. The highest proportions after the Kikuyu were for the Nandi (23·8 per cent) and Swahili/Shirazi (21·7 per cent). For the Luo it is 10·7 per cent, Luhya 17·2 per cent, Kisii and Kamba 12·4 per cent. See Volume III of the 1962 Census.

went mostly to Kikuyu because here too they were the keenest applicants—and at least by their own account, they scarcely enjoyed any political advantage.[1]

If the Kikuyu stand out as entrepreneurs, it seems to be partly because they are also more sensitive to the political and occupational frustrations we have already discussed. Their homeland was hemmed in by the pattern of European settlement. Blocked to east and west by the forests of Mount Kenya and the Aberdare range, they were prevented from expanding either north or south by the boundaries of the alienated land. Their resentment against the colonial régime was therefore greater, and their political opposition more determined than of any other tribe. At the same time, since they lived nearest to Nairobi and the European farms, they provided most of the labour. Pressure of population forced them to migrate: for though they inhabited some of the most productive farmland in East Africa, they could not satisfy the needs of their growing population on it. Parts of Kiambu District, where the families of over half the Kikuyu businessmen originated, are more densely settled than any other rural divisions in Kenya.[2] Some had grown up on estates in the White Highlands where their fathers were employed, and had never known the life of a traditional peasant economy. Thus the Kikuyu were surrounded by the achievements of modern commercial agriculture—the coffee plantations, the herds of dairy cattle, the European townships with their industries and sophisticated shops—yet their own part in them was always subordinate. They acquired a wider experience of the colonial civilization than other peoples, and a keener sense of their own exclusion from its opportunities. As we saw in Mahiga, this sense of relative deprivation even antedates the colonial era. The Kikuyu had already been used to looking outside their own society for an economic and social reference group in the days of the Masai trade.

[1] Twenty-six per cent of Kikuyu businessmen said their loans had been facilitated by political contacts, 22 per cent of the rest. In spite of their growing political isolation, the Luo businessmen seem to have been helped as often as the Kikuyu: three of the ten said they had made use of political contacts.

[2] For Kiambu as a whole the density to the square mile is 557 but in Limuru Division it is 1,228, in Kikuyu 1,525 and Kiambaal 1,703. Only two other divisions in Kenya (apart from townships) reach densities over 1,000—Vihiga in North Nyanza, a Luhya area, and Mombasa West, which is suburban. The densities of the two other wholly Kikuyu districts are 491 in Fort Hall and 428 in Nyeri. Only Kisii and North Nyanza, amongst the non-Kikuyu districts, are as thickly populated.

The Origins of Entrepreneurs

Entrepreneurship seems to arise from this complex interaction of national, tribal and personal frustrations with exploitable opportunities. Where the resources are too few, the frustrations cannot find an outlet in new enterprises—there is neither the capital, nor the market, nor the experience. The poor and uneducated, who have failed in their search for employment, are unlikely to find an opening in business either. Conversely, where the frustrations have not been deeply felt, business is likely to be a half-hearted pursuit, even when the means are to hand. The Kikuyu have been more aware of their deprivation than other Kenya peoples, more experienced in the ways of a modern economy, and as they began to exploit this experience in the development of their own farms, they have generated more resources for entrepreneurial ventures. Though there are entrepreneurs as able and ambitious amongst other tribes, the circumstances which create them must have come less often together.

The way in which thwarted political and educational aspirations merge into entrepreneurship stands out very clearly from the career of a Kikuyu, first teacher, then journalist and clerk, who—after restlessly searching for the scholarship which always eluded him—settled at last as a prosperous businessmen. Born in 1934, he was educated in Independent schools—the schools created by the Nationalist movement to challenge the ideology of colonial education: for a while he was taught by Kenyatta himself. He became a teacher in an Independent school, wrote a political pamphlet, published a newsheet. But when the Emergency was declared in 1952 his school was closed, the publisher of his pamphlet jailed, and the agents of his newsheet arrested. For two years he worked as a clerk in Nairobi, until he too was arrested and repatriated to his home district. For the next three years he exhausted his savings in vain attempts to secure permission to return to Nairobi. Then in 1958, as the Emergency began to relax, he took a job as a clerk in the local township. Within a year or two, his salary had risen from 300 to 800 shillings a month with a substantial bonus— wages that only a highly valued employee could hope to earn. He now began to invest his savings in business—a shop, a hotel, another shop—and encountered familiar difficulties: employees who stole, a brother who gave too much credit to relatives. After two years he abandoned his businesses and his well paid job to resume his search for education.

He had been promised a scholarship to India when he left school, but the Emergency had destroyed his hopes. Now he heard of chances of scholarships to America, and travelled to Nairobi in pursuit of them. Again he was disappointed: his political contacts let him down. Here he met another scholarship hunter, who became his companion and steady business partner. For a while they ran a bakery together, started by his brother, hoping to raise the money for fares to America. Bakeries are a difficult proposition, and the business failed. He returned home, resolved to study for a school certificate by correspondence course, and took up trading in second-hand clothes. But hope of studying overseas revived. Hearing that if he could reach the Russian ambassador in Ethiopia, he could get a scholarship in Russia, he set out to walk to Addis Ababa with his friend from Nairobi. But they were arrested by the Ethiopian police and repatriated.

By now his savings were once again exhausted, but he and his companion determined on a last attempt. They proposed to set out for Dar es Salaam, to reach the Russian ambassador there. First they would use the 60 shillings in post office savings which remained to them, then sell their wrist-watches and clothes, finally their car. If by then they had not reached their destination, they would settle wherever they ended up. In the event, when they reached a town near the coast, his brother persuaded them to try their chances in business: later, when they had made some profit, they could go on their way to Dar es Salaam. They had five shillings capital.

They began by trading in fish: they brought 70 for a shilling, fried them and sold them for seven shillings. Then they bought a net, hired a canoe, and started fishing. But finding this too tiring and unrewarding, they bought two more nets, and contracted with professional fishermen to share the catch with them, in return for the use of their nets. The trade began to prosper: they bought a butchery, rented a beer hall, opened a shop—and as the years went by, the Russian scholarship passed out of mind. By 1967 they had the shop, the beer hall, sugar and banana plantations, the butchery, a livestock trade, a 300 acre farm in the Rift Valley, and interests in three other businesses elsewhere. Their educational ambitions seemed finally displaced into an entrepreneurial career far from their homeland, and detached from the political commitment of their youth.

We can trace in the social background of African businessmen, then, a similar interaction of frustration and opportunity as appears amongst entrepreneurial groups elsewhere. But the pattern is less marked by explicit social differences, and so African businessmen are not an identifiable minority. The Asian immigrants to Kenya, contrastingly, also exploited a situation of both exclusion and opportunity, but because it was more clearly defined, they responded to it more consciously as a group. Asian, like African entrepreneurs, were reacting against the over-population of their homeland. They too encountered political discrimination under the colonial administration: they were not permitted to buy land either in the African reserves or the areas of European settlement, and their employment in public service or European companies was bound to remain subordinate to white superiors. Yet they had experience of commerce, and sources of finance, at a time when few Africans knew how to take advantage of the demand for trade created by imperial rule.[1]

No political solution to their exclusion was conceivable, however, as it was for Africans. They were bound to remain a minority, restricted to a narrow range of careers—in professions, skilled crafts and business. Hence they were thrown back upon their distinctness as communities with their own religion and culture. Each sect closed in upon itself in mutual protection, reinforcing its family and cultural loyalties. This internal social cohesion promoted a style of family business, which could pioneer commercial opportunities without external support, and remained segregated from the society it served. In our survey of Asian businesses in and around Nairobi, we found that 90 per cent of the jointly owned enterprises were shared exclusively between members of the same family or sect. Correspondingly, most of the businessmen did not believe that closer integration with African society was possible nor that the various Asian groups could work more closely together. And they overwhelmingly rejected the ideas of intermarriage between different Asian communities, or between races. Thus each community held to its social isolation as the inevitable counterpart of its internal cohesion.

African entrepreneurship, however, arises from frustrations

[1] A few wealthy Baganda did try to organize caravans between the Coast and Kampala at a very early date. But they ran out of money, the porters nearly starved, and the ventures ended disastrously. See Matson.

which are not specific to any self-conscious group. Though the businessmen were, as a whole, a distinguishable occupational category, they seemed scarcely aware of it themselves. And though they were politically committed, the movement against colonialism was too universal for this to draw them into mutual recognition. Thus their sense of exclusion was either very personal or very general. It attached to no identifiable community within society, small enough to support each other in the face of the majority. And so the assets which they could exploit in reaction against exclusion were also personal or general, not communal. They had gained experience and self-confidence in employment, and made useful friends amongst their companions at work; they could bring pressure to bear on an African government to extend economic privileges to its own citizens. But the pattern of frustration did not create or reinforce any loyalties adaptable to business organization.

This interpretation of the circumstances which turn men towards a business career still leaves an underlying question unresolved. For it would be meaningless to write of frustration, or a sense of deprivation, except in the context of purposes already set. If the businessmen were dissatisfied with employment, it was because they valued other achievements, and we cannot understand the origins of their entrepreneurial energy apart from the unfulfilled ambitions which generated this discontent. Though the values they held were, in part, a justification of their business activities, these values must also have shaped the ideals that they hoped to realize.

THE AFRICAN BUSINESS CREED

Two villages of peasant farmers share the same traditions, the same economy and the same Catholic religion. In one of them a Protestant happens to settle. Within a few years he has converted the whole village. A mission is established, with a clinic; the austere, white-walled church is stripped of crosses, pictures, statues—all the sentimental, superstitious, indulgent clutter of folklore glossed with Christian myth; the children go to school, so that they may read the New Testament in their own language. The village becomes more literate than the other, the children more ambitious, the parents proud of their moral enlightenment. They take their illnesses to the clinic and their savings to the bank, forsaking witchcraft, drinking and the marrying of many wives. And their economy begins to progress. Has the new religion, intruding by chance into this one community, added something essential to development? Or is it just that their soil is more fertile —and their church, perhaps, another expression of their sense of superior economic opportunities?[1]

In a parish of a Zambian chiefdom, a group of Jehovah's Witnesses stand out as the most progressive farmers, the most independent of traditional ties of kinship, and the most enterprising in the crafts they practise. Seeing themselves as set apart—members of the New World Society, who alone will survive Armageddon— they are sustained by a structure of belief and organization which justifies their worldly ambitions, as it justifies their spiritual striving. To prepare themselves to inherit Jehovah's Kingdom upon earth, and preach to the unconverted, they need to be literate, well dressed, progressive, proving their superiority as the chosen people, and their competence for tasks God has assigned them. A good suit and a well appointed home are signs of grace. But signs only—the progress towards spiritual maturity demands

[1] This example, of two Mexican villages, is taken from McClelland, 1961, pp. 406-11.

77

continuing effort. Is this insistent ambition for a higher standard of living an outcome of their faith? Or does it arise essentially from the frustrations of younger men—disappointed in their search for skilled employment, and precluded from senior lineage positions —who adopted this church because it speaks to their condition?[1]

Both these examples concern the power of religious ideas to stimulate economic development. They are fragments of contemporary evidence for a historical thesis, whose most famous exposition is Max Weber's interpretation of the rise of capitalism in Northern Europe. Weber argued that the spirit of capitalism grew out of Calvinism, evolving an ethic at once harshly ascetic and impressed by wordly achievement, and from this paradoxical blending of self-denial and self-justification derived its compulsive energy. The argument has a relevance beyond its historical context, for it reappears, softened into a secular morality, as a crucial prescription for economic growth. Entrepreneurship, it is claimed, will only arise within a social group which holds values similar to the Protestant ethic.

Calvin taught that men and women are damned or saved at the whim of an unintelligible God, and can do nothing about it. At first sight, no doctrine could be more discouraging to human effort. But the anxiety to prove oneself of the elect, to demonstrate by the quality of one's life the enjoyment of God's grace, engendered a moral outlook which saw relentless labour as a religious duty, and wealth as proof of virtue. This Protestant ethic, in Weber's interpretation, moralized acquisitiveness. God commanded that a man should follow his calling in this world, not for reward now or hereafter, but in celebration of divine glory. If he was called to business, and it prospered, his duty lay in furthering it to the utmost. The acquisition of profit thus became a rightful task, divorced from human greed, since however great his wealth, the businessman should still lead a plain, sober, unassuming life, as the servant of God. Such a morality was economically very productive: it commended specialization in one's calling, diligent labour, the acquisition of profit, and an ascetic self-denial which left no use for that profit but reinvestment in renewed effort, and no end to the pursuit of it. Puritan asceticism, and its belief that every man was called to his task, combined to promote the virtues of worldly success as a rigorous spiritual discipline. Hard work,

[1] See Long, especially Ch. VIII.

thrift, the rational exploitation of economic opportunity, plain living and remorseless accumulation were the service of God in this world, and a preparation for his favour in the next. Backed by this sense of divine command, the Puritan businessman could face risks, and disapproval, and the misery his achievements brought to others, with a stern self-righteousness.

If Protestantism accompanied and could be interpreted to justify the evolution of capitalist entrepreneurs, did it partly create them? Is there a particular pattern of values which—whether it derives from Christianity or other ideological roots—must first develop and mould the entrepreneurial character, before men appear who can redeem their unsatisfied ambitions in business? If so, ideology will influence the chances of entrepreneurship more fundamentally than a businessman's social or economic circumstances. This is the central argument of David McClelland, for though he uses the language of psychology, his 'need for achievement' (reified as *n* Achievement in his notation) is a secular interpretation of the Protestant personality. 'The connection seen by Max Weber between the Protestant Reformation and the rise of the entrepreneurial spirit', he writes, '. . . can now be understood as a special case, by no means limited to Protestantism, of a general increase in *n* Achievement produced by an ideological change.' He bases this conclusion on evidence, some from the art and literature of societies, some from experiment, and some from questionnaires, assembled to demonstrate the relationship between economic growth and the fostering of an individual need for personal achievement. Thus if tribes, social classes, nations, religious sects differ amongst themselves in the entrepreneurial energy of their members, it could be because they impart to their children a different ideology of personal achievement. McClelland therefore argues that moral propaganda is as crucial for promoting businesses as the provision of capital, training in skills, the organization of management and markets, or any of the other policies in common use now. 'The problem, of course, is to "develop character" by means that will not be rejected out of hand as an unwarranted intrusion into a national way of life. The solution lies in presenting openly the psychological evidence that certain motives and values are required for economic development. Then the individual is at least faced with a clear decision of what he wants to do—cling to the old values with their associated inefficiencies or

79

seek to acquire the new ones. . . . There is no real substitute for ideological fervour.' Elsewhere, he refers to 'the general acceptance of an achievement-oriented ideology as an absolute *sine qua non* of economic development'.[1]

So for McClelland, the example we quoted at the beginning of this chapter is crucial, for it provides a rare instance where the influence of a new ideology seems separable from other factors of change. But the evidence is ambiguous. Some—though not all—of the Protestant children scored higher in a game designed to measure the strength of their need for achievement. But we still do not know how much the prosperity of the village depended on the fertility of the soil, nor why it was so open to conversion. So, too, with the Jehovah's Witnesses in Zambia. Their background of experience was distinctive, and their economic energy may have been stimulated more by a sense of deprivation of conventional status than their conversion. Their emphasis upon their faith varied, besides, from situation to situation: where it suited their needs, they might still exploit traditional ties of kinship, returning to time-honoured values of their community. And from place to place, congregations adjusted their beliefs to their economic chances: in poorer regions, the Witnesses stressed the rewards to the faithful in the life to come, rather than the need to prepare oneself by practical progress here and now. For all its proselytizing energy and organization, their faith seemed as much a flexible rationalization of change as a cause of it.

The interaction of ideology and economy is therefore hard to determine, and perhaps so subtle and so complex that cause and effect can never be disentangled. The sense of frustration which drives men to become entrepreneurs is likely itself to express the conventional values of society, in whose terms they are excluded —they cannot be gentlemen, or officials, or chiefs. If they turn to other values, as they turn to business, in response to the same discontent, then the ethical rationalization of entrepreneurial behaviour can be seen more as a reflection and justification of economic changes than a cause of them. Yet men cannot manipulate their values at will: they must draw them from some authority greater than their immediate self-interest, and however they bend them to their purposes, they cannot break them without destroy-

[1] McClelland, 1961, pp. 391, 430, and 1963, p. 93. For an attempt to apply McClelland's thesis to an African society, see LeVine, 1966.

ing the legitimacy of their actions. At the conclusion of his famous essay, Weber tartly disclaimed any final judgment: 'The modern man is in general, even with the best will, unable to give religious ideas the significance for culture and national character which they deserve. But it is, of course, not my aim to substitute for a one-sided materialistic an equally one-sided spiritualistic causal interpretation of culture and history. Each is equally possible, but each, if it does not serve as a preparation, but as the conclusion of an investigation, accomplishes equally little in the interest of historical truth.'[1] Investigation has not as yet made the answer less equivocal. But at least we can discriminate more clearly now the different ways in which a system of values may facilitate entrepreneurship.

Firstly, when these values are embodied in an institution, they may define a group whose social cohesion can be turned to economic advantage. So, for instance, the Asian immigrants to East Africa created a commercial network out of caste and sect loyalties. The religious beliefs they held were not, in themselves, especially appropriate to entrepreneurship: but the sense of sharing a minority culture, if not the character of that culture, helped forward their business enterprise. The Jehovah's Witnesses in Zambia seem to have been attracted towards the church because it confirmed and consolidated a desire to break out from the constraints of traditional society and urban employment. It brought together like-minded men, who found here a creed which reinforced their mutual sympathy. It also set them apart. The Witnesses repudiated conventional politics as irrelevant to God's design, and refused to join the dominant party. The reprisals they risked by this drew them closer together, and provided a bond of trust in economic as well as religious life.

Secondly, a system of values can provide a coherent moral argument for entrepreneurial behaviour, which not only justifies business to the businessman, but gives the principles from which he acts a universal validity. 'Businessmen adhere to their particular kind of ideology because of the emotional conflicts, the anxieties, and the doubts engendered by the actions which their roles as businessmen compel them to take, and by the conflicting demands of other social roles which they must play in family and community', write the authors of *The American Business Creed*. 'Within the

[1] Weber, p. 183.

resources of cultural tradition and within the limits of what is publicly acceptable, the content of the ideology is shaped so as to resolve these conflicts, alleviate these anxieties, overcome these doubts. For the individual businessman, the function of the ideology is to help him maintain his psychological ability to meet the demands of his occupation. It follows that the ideology has functional importance also for those on whom the actions of businessmen impinge and for the whole society.'[1] The values are not merely a crude rationalization of self-interest, but a system which attempts to integrate business aims with the aims of society at large, defining the rights of businessmen, government, employees, shareholders, customers by the same principles. And since it is often easier to recognize a principle than to know where self-interest lies, the value system itself will acquire an influence upon behaviour apart from the business aims it justifies.

Lastly, moral beliefs may act autonomously on men's minds, forming a character which conceives entrepreneurship as his duty. He is brought up to respect himself for his personal achievements, and if he cannot dominate his circumstances, forming them to a design which bears his signature, he feels that he has not realized the meaning of his life.

These three functions—institutional, justificatory, imperative— are distinct, and a system of values which serves one may not fulfil the others. But in practice they are likely to merge into each other. The ideology which draws its members into mutual protection may also legitimize their economic relationships and as it does so, drive them on to achieve more, inculcating the same values in their children. Nor need these functions be fulfilled by an explicitly articulated value system. Racial and cultural loyalties may bind a group together, without constant emphasis on the beliefs they share; entrepreneurship may be legitimized by practical economic arguments, whose underlying values are barely stated; and it may be stimulated by a dominant culture, whose superiority is taken for granted. But each of these functions seems necessary. If no religion or ideology justifies and stimulates entrepreneurship, nor consolidates trust in business affairs, there must still be some moral argument to sustain them, even if the premisses on which it is based are not clearly expressed. And this argument can never be wholly derived from rational calculation of

[1] Sutton, Harris, Kaysen and Tobin, p. 11.

the interests of business itself, since these interests have no intrinsic moral persuasiveness, until they are set in a wider context of human purpose. There must, therefore, be an African business creed, and it must be a partly independent influence on the way business develops, whether these beliefs originally preceded entrepreneurship or derive from it.

The Protestantism of African business

The African conception of proper business conduct seems at first sight to arise unambiguously from the Protestant tradition, its pure and faithful heir. As the men we interviewed conceived an ideal businessman, he was hardworking and honourable, friendly and patient, unassuming and thrifty, contemptuous of extravagance, concentrating his attention on his business affairs, and, above all, proof against the inseparable temptations of the market place—drink, women, and the corrupting influence of idle, pleasure-loving friends. Some of them expressed the driving spirit of capitalism in its purest form. 'Business is the history of my life, I think', said a Kikuyu garage proprietor. 'In school, in the holidays, I used to buy chickens and eggs to sell. And when I played, I used to play at trade. Even when I had a job, I did business on the side —buying a bicycle today and selling it tomorrow—so I was sure business was my vocation. . . . The first qualities of a successful businessman are capability in what you are doing, sincerity and honesty—and dissatisfaction. You should never be satisfied, even if you have repaired twenty cars today. Satisfaction is a hindrance of progress. Whatever I do, my desire is to do more. If you're like that, you never see what you do, you never appreciate what you do, you never feel rich, because you are never satisfied. Most people in my experience get satisfied so quick, and that's a great hindrance to progress. I'm never satisfied with the hours I work, the money I bank every day, even with the office where I work. . . . A friend once told me the secret of his success was that in business you should be honest and sincere and hardworking, and never be satisfied. These are four things he told me, and finally to live on what you earn. He told me, too, "you can't work for money and spend money, you must work and spend later on". . . . A businessman should see that every penny he earns goes back into the business, and not to think to enjoy when he's starting business, but to

work. . . . Apart from church, I don't have any other social activities—I don't know how to dance. Unless I'm away from town, I
must go to church every week. . . . I don't smoke or drink, and I
am a pure vegetarian—not even eggs. On principle.'

Here is the sense of vocation, the self-denial, all the insatiable
energy and moral purposiveness of the Protestant spirit. If he
expressed it with especial emphasis, he was not uncharacteristic: as
a whole, the businessmen supported by the ICDC were active
Christians. Over half attended church regularly most Sundays,
16 per cent at least once a month, another 9 per cent several times a
year, while only 6 per cent disclaimed any formal religion. Over
half of them, too, said explicitly that their Christian convictions
had helped to form the character that had enabled them to succeed
in business.

> Because of my Christian convictions I stopped drinking,
> which was a menace to my life, and I stopped smoking. It has
> helped me to tell the truth, even when it is bitter. And it's
> helped me quite a lot getting along with other people, and
> understanding them.

> The discipline helps you, so that you are not a rogue and you
> fear God. If you have no religion you have no morals, and can
> easily dissipate your wealth.[T]

> You have to ask for God's guidance in everything you do,
> and the practice of prayer gives you peace. And so you can
> talk to your customers in a good way.[T]

> I was helped because I had this religion before I was in
> business, and it taught me to be honest and not to quarrel, or
> to despise others or use abusive language, or to be proud.[T]

Yet, for all their moral earnestness, it never occurred to them
during our interviews to vindicate their business activities by
Christian purposes. Rather the other way about: they justified
moral behaviour very pragmatically by its contribution to business
achievement. If you did not drink, you saved; if you were not
proud or quarrelsome, you would have customers; if you were
honest, your prices would be fair, and your partners would trust
you. The successful businessman was a model of practical virtue
and enlightened self-interest.

One thing is honesty, that counts for more than anything else. Secondly, one has to have very decent behaviour in society—that has much influence in business. If you are a drunkard, or abusive, or involve yourself in funny things of life, people lose confidence in you. Your standing in society matters very much in business. You must be a man of high integrity, and creative and sensitive. And self-confident— that's a most important thing.

A man with trust. Trust means looking after your business, co-operating with people and speaking nicely, and if you get a loan from Government not treating it as your property. If you pay it back, then they may give you more. . . .

He should be a humble man who knows how to talk to customers, he should never be proud, and he should be friendly to the people, but not to the extent of giving them things free. . . . He shouldn't pursue pleasure, or close his shop to attend to other things. He should open his shop in the morning, and stay there until five o'clock, even if there are no customers . . . because he is responsible for his business, and he should be continually thinking about it, and not going out at night.[T]

He must be someone who is patient, and doesn't want to buy expensive things at the beginning of his business when he has no money. He should be prepared to forgo all social activities like drinking and others, and concentrate on his work. It is necessary to know how to tackle your customers if they come drunk and insult you. You mustn't quarrel with them, but you should act like a preacher or judge in these situations and talk well to them. Business is in talking.

He must be thrifty and talk nicely to people—be diplomatic. He shouldn't be too generous, or he'll undermine his business. If you are a drunkard you can't be successful, or if you are a person who likes pleasure or women, who will want presents all the time. He must be a person who likes to work always, so that he keeps on working hard. And bad friends will spoil your business, distracting you from your work.[T]

Those people who are hardworking, talkative and imaginative, so that they can think and know what sort of goods people want. People who are honest and don't want to deceive others, and those who are trustworthy, so that they will treat a child honestly without giving him fewer goods for his money. . . . People who are loyal citizens, law-abiding and who don't waste time in court cases from drunken rows or breaking laws. And who don't drink to excess, because you might drink your profit away, or get your money stolen . . .ᵀ

Invariably, when we asked them to describe the qualities of a successful businessman, they emphasized such virtues as these far more often than morally indifferent traits. Thirty-eight per cent said he should be friendly—a good man, a man who likes people, and knows how to speak to them; 36 per cent mentioned integrity—an honest man who speaks the truth; 32 per cent that he must be hardworking, and 30 per cent that he must be sober and thrifty. The only ethically neutral qualities commonly suggested, in a fifth of the answers, were ability at handling accounts and experience. Thus success in business owed more to character, in their conception, than to special talents. Similarly, when we asked them why, of the businessmen they knew, some had done well and others failed, they most commonly attributed success to hard work and concentration, failure to idleness and extravagance. When we asked more generally about the reasons why businesses failed, they suggested incompetent accounting most often—it came up in half the answers—but extravagance, drink and women ran it close. Among the businessmen in the market centres, too, drinking too much, running after women, spending foolishly was mentioned by over half of them as a cause of failure, and more often than any other cause. 'There are many other reasons why people fail', said a shoemaker, 'but there is one which is very important, and includes them all. When you begin to think you are a wealthy man, and use your money carelessly, then you will certainly fail.ᵀ' Buying a car for pleasure, marrying another wife, but above all, drinking were fatal temptations. In their attitude towards drinking—the stupidity of drunkenness, the boastful hospitality of bar-room society, the grasping girls encountered there—the businessmen were at their most puritanical.

Over half of them said they never took alcohol at all, some drank only from social necessity, and only 38 per cent were prepared to drink sociably without reservation. A fifth disapproved of it for others as well as themselves, and used their influence to discourage it.

As for drinking, I tolerate it as much as I can, but I'm all against excessive drinking. I have very strong convictions against our people drinking heavily. Anybody here who is drinking at work would be reproved. I called in my machine operator the other day, because he was arrested by the police for drunkenness. I paid his fine for him, and had a good talk with him. And so far since then he has stopped drinking.

I've never drunk beer. I don't know what it tastes like. I was attracted towards the church because I hated drinking very much. If I were head of the Government, I'd ban drinks. I don't allow any of the tenants in the houses I own to brew beer. If they do, they are discharged at once.[T]

It wastes a lot of money, and I object very much to other people drinking and smoking. If we find a partner drinking too much, or an employee, we will consider sacking them. We haven't done so yet—but some of the partners drink secretly after work.[T1]

As a whole, the businessmen objected to drinking partly because it impoverished people and partly for the behaviour to which it led—the drunken quarrels, indignity and tragic accidents. It was a practical objection to the consequences, rather than a dogmatic objection to the principle: some went out of their way to emphasize that it did not arise from any religious injunction. And in general, in their attitude towards other vices, as well as drinking, their morality was more secular than religious. They used the arguments of Benjamin Franklin, Samuel Smiles or Dale Carnegie, not Calvin.

The ideal businessman was certainly a model of Protestant virtues—diligent, truthful, responsible, trustworthy, humble, prudent, thrifty and abstemious. But in each of them, they pointed to the economic advantage. They quoted from their own lives, and the experience of acquaintances, many instances to show how, when a man neglected them, he spoiled his chances.

---

[1] The partnership none the less sold beer, as part of its business. But the ethical objection gave the directors no serious difficulty. 'We sell beer as a company, not just ourselves—and anyway it is an employee who sells the beer,' they remarked with admirable casuistry.

I started another business when I was in Eldoret, a retail business in the Indian bazaar. My partner ruined it, he even ended up in prison. He was a drunkard and careless.

I met a friend—a former chairman of the Council—who had a wholesale business. He failed—he drank too much, during the day time, and was very rude to his customers. So he was not trusted, and he was dishonest, mostly because of the drinking.

We had a hotel next door which was bought by Africans— it had been a European hotel. There were four partners, but when they bought this hotel, they didn't co-operate amongst themselves. They started quarrelling over who would be the manager, and also taking money in bad ways. They only ran the hotel for six months. They couldn't afford to pay back their bank loan, and the hotel was sold. . . . They bought it for 60,000 shillings, and sold it for 12,000 shillings.

I can think of one, for example . . . the directors appointed themselves and gave themselves airs—sleeping in expensive hotels, travelling by air. In six months there was no business. They called themselves an import-export business—very high language. . . . Extravagance contributes a lot. A man starts in a big way—a secretary, a telephone, an office, a car— and ends in a small way.

Thus the wisdom of virtue was proved by events. They rationalized their creed of moral conduct by the demands of the career they had chosen. None of them ever suggested that this career was itself the expression of a moral duty—as the Jehovah's Witnesses in Zambia, by contrast, were consciously preparing themselves through business for the Kingdom of God on earth. They took the propriety of business for granted, and used its needs as a secular argument in support of the moral principles they had grown up with. This must have helped them to reconcile any uncomfortable incompatibility between entrepreneurial and Christian behaviour. But the claim that successful business must be ethically conducted is not the same as an assertion that business itself has a moral purpose, or serves any part of society's ideals.

Religion did not, therefore, fulfil the second of the functions we noticed, any more than the first. The businessmen's moral code seems too pragmatic, too much derived from arguments of self-interest, to serve as a legitimation of their enterprise. Still less did they draw any moral incentive from it, impelling them towards business achievements. The reasons they gave for taking up business were most often economic or vocational—they had seen an economic opportunity (43 per cent), been dissatisfied with employment (28 per cent), were attracted by the work (26 per cent), or wanted to use their training and experience (23 per cent). Most of the other reasons occasionally mentioned were of the same kind—unemployment (6 per cent), lack of education (5 per cent), poor prospects in farming (2 per cent). Only one altruistic motive came up at all commonly: 16 per cent said they had wanted to make a contribution to development.

In a society already industrialized, so pragmatic an approach to business would be unremarkable. A conventional career attracts men with conventional religious views, who do not need to validate their way of life by referring it explicitly to a system of values. Church-going—if that is the custom—and business are both accepted without question by the majority. But it is perhaps more puzzling that innovators, well aware that they were pioneers, should have been so little concerned with moral justification. As we shall see, for instance, they repudiated claims of kinship sanctioned by the traditional values of their culture. Yet their answer was simply to say: business is business, it cannot respond to these demands. They did not hold an explicit alternative interpretation of kinship obligations, merely circumscribed them to exclude their business affairs. Nor was it self-evident that business must necessarily agree with the needs of national development. In neighbouring Tanzania, the ruling party has specifically debarred businessmen from any political office, as potential capitalists too self-interested to be trusted agents of national policy. And there is at least some latent conflict between private business and the broadly socialist ideals which Kenya officially endorses. Yet only one of the businessmen we met seemed troubled by such questions. His own company was failing, and he had turned most of his energy to promoting a new secondary school:

Those who are ruthlessly hard-hearted, even to their own sons or their relatives, and who are very strict and don't believe in promises—they are the ones who get on. If you are sympathetic like me, you lose money. I find it hard to refuse people, and not only in business. But in business you need to be very unsympathetic to other people's problems. . . . For me, it's better to work as a co-operative, with proper management, and just get my wages as a manager, and not touch the money. These capitalist ideas of making money for oneself are corrupting the country. People are leaving government service just to work for themselves, their sons and daughters. And even though they make 200,000 shillings, they don't help the public. Where people are dying of hunger, and have no hospital, or no schools, they are just keeping their money in the bank.

In a poor country with growing inequalities, such views cannot be so uncommon that they may be dismissed out of mind. If businessmen claimed the right to grow richer than their neighbours, to exclude kinsfolk from the jobs they offered or the profits they made, to borrow from the scarce resources of their government, they could not assume that everyone must agree with them. And indeed, they were well aware of the jealousy and resentment their success aroused. So their lack of an explicit ideology of business needs to be explained. What gave them their undoubted confidence to go their own way, their determination and conviction that they were morally justified?

The acculturation of African business

Any interpretation can only be speculative when the values themselves are not articulated. But the explanation seems to lie in the nature of the colonial experience. For two generations, the society in which the businessmen grew up had been dominated by an alien civilization, whose superior power and achievements were overwhelming. Because Kenya was settled by the colonists, that civilization penetrated more deeply than in most African states. The Kikuyu especially, to whom most of the businessmen belong, worked for Europeans, grew up on their farms, were everywhere surrounded by their institutions. In these circumstances the alien civilization becomes, in a sense, a substitute for ideology. To an outsider, the way of life of the colonists appears to represent a coherent system of values, because its different aspects are all displayed in the same group of self-confident strangers. He is impressed by the manifest power of this way of life, rather than the intrinsic validity of the principles which sustain it. Since he wants to share its power, he seeks to master it, taking the underlying value system for granted. His interest is displaced from the value system to the form in which it is expressed. So the institutions and customs of a civilization become a frame of reference for an outsider in a way they cannot for its own members.

In this sense, both church-going and business derive from the same principle of behaviour: each is an aspect of European ways, as they appear to African eyes. Religion and economic life are related, because the civilization whose economic achievements the African businessman wants to emulate seems to depend on its religious institutions also. The nature of the relationship does not need to be articulated, so long as it appears in practice that both are part of the same highly successful way of life. So the underlying justification of business is not religious but nationalistic. A Kenya businessman judges himself and his society by the achievements of contemporary Britain, as he sees them. Whether or not they are ultimately desirable, he needs to prove that they are within his grasp: otherwise he remains humiliated by a power which has dominated him, and which he has never challenged.[1]

This explanation of the way African businessmen derive their system of values is supported by their conception of European business. We asked them what advantages they thought Europeans, and secondly Asians, had over Africans as businessmen, and whether Africans had any compensating advantages. They believed that Europeans possess the qualities of integrity, forethought, thrift and diligence which they admire—'firstly they are trustworthy; secondly they have long experience of business; thirdly since childhood they are taught to keep time, and that to

---

[1] In this interpretation, the difference between Kenya, which is sympathetic to private African enterprise, and Tanzania, which is not, would lie in the different nature of their colonial experience. There was little European settlement in Tanganyika, so the colonial presence was principally political, not commercial. Tanzania is perhaps for this reason more concerned with asserting political achievements. But these achievements are still referred, essentially, to Western European standards in the speeches and writings of its President. The appeal is to the liberal tradition of political thought derived from John Stuart Mill and the Fabians, rather than Marxism. Thus the response to colonization remains a challenge to the colonial power in its own terms, though history and circumstances throw a different aspect of its civilization into prominence.

waste time is to waste money; fourthly children are taught to be honest. These qualities are like a shield to their business, and they get big loans, because they are trusted.' The African businessmen saw these qualities as arising from the traditions of European civilization, and contributing to its economic success: the moral and material assets of European businessmen were inseparably merged in their way of life. Africans were at a disadvantage, above all because they lacked such a tradition, which they unconsciously distorted and idealized to fit their own case. They did not necessarily believe that it was superior to African traditions, but these were now obsolete. To find an identity in the modern world, they could only turn to the example of the civilization which had destroyed the relevance of their own inheritance, and learn from it as fast as they could:

> Education, civilization—they have seen their ancestors doing these things. For example, when I was at Ruiru, I got a rough working knowledge of farm machinery, just because for so many years I was working in a place where there were machines. Europeans can sit down and work out what will pay, they don't just go into business because they see others do it. . . . If a European is given something to do, and the same amount of money as an African, the European will do it better.

> It's education, and their way of life. It's more a commercial life. Whatever you do, you try to do it without wastages. For instance, even at home in the kitchen you measure the things you put into the pot. This extravagance of our people in business is partly because at home people don't measure when they are cooking, they just pick up a heap of bananas or whatever it is, and throw it in the pot.

> They have experience—open eyes: that is, foresight and knowledge to know what it likely to happen in future. They also have determination and courage: 'it's better for a man to be dead than to live just doing nothing'. They get help from their parents to start them off. By twenty-one, a European has had some money put in the bank for him, while an African would have absolutely nothing and would have to start from scratch.[T]

92

Europeans have troubled minds. Once a European finds a way to solve his problems, he sticks to his solution, and teaches his children. Once a person gets a job, he keeps it all his life. Europeans are short of land, and their population is increasing, so they have to go all over the world—to Kenya, to America—in search of ways to keep themselves alive. Since they don't have enough land, they have to find a solution to their problem. And Europeans respect the authority of their parents, and their customs. No one will break their customs and do the wrong thing, even if he has a lot of money. So in that way they can do something good. They have inherited good behaviour from their parents. But to Africans business is something quite new. We have never had any experience, or any training or information on how to run a business. The old African tradition of keeping cattle has gone. Since we can't follow our forefathers, and all that is gone, the greatest help would be to have institutions where we can be trained. If the children of Africans, Asians and Europeans can go to the same school, there is no reason why they shouldn't go to the same commercial training. Africans can do anything Europeans do, if only they get the training.[T]

Thus the African businessmen recognized experience as the outstanding European advantage—an experience which they passed on to their children as an integral part of their culture. Sixty per cent commented on this: only 38 per cent mentioned the obvious material advantages of European capital and access to credit, 21 per cent their integrity, and 12 per cent their business connections. As an electrical engineer succinctly put it, 'I'd compare Africans as children recently born in business. It's a new venture, and none can see beyond the wall. Europeans can see beyond the wall: Europeans have experience. Now Africans have the chance to learn.'

The reaction against Asian business

In part, they see Asian businessmen in the same light. Asians too have grown up in a commercial culture—'they have business in their veins'. 'They started business many years ago: the child is born into a house of business, and his father teaches him only that job.' But the African businessmen were more impressed by the solidarity of Asian families, and the way they helped each other commercially. Thirty-eight per cent mentioned the advantage of experience, 45 per cent their family connections:[1]

> The advantage is not in money. But they have relatives in business who will take them on and teach them, and they are humble enough to learn, because they are dependent on their relatives.[T]

> They also have the experience and capital background—and this main advantage of being able to run the business as a family concern, the whole business being run as a family. The father commands, and the children do as he says.

> What I know is, they are either all brothers, or all from the same family working together. Because they are related and trust each other their business grows much faster.[T]

> I think the secret of their success is this—what shall I say— community-mindedness. They help each other in their own community. They will meet in the evening to discuss what shall we do about this shop or this business. And if one of them wants to start a business, the people of his community will go to the wholesaler and guarantee him, so he can get even up to ninety days credit, and in that way his business will soon stand. But they will never help Africans in the same way.

Here, too, the African businessmen recognized that commercial success arose from the qualities of a way of life—a self-sufficient, patriachal life of hard work, simple fare, and single-minded dedication to the family business. But they could not identify with it, as they identified with European ways. They had grown up under the influence of British institutions, while Indian communities seemed closed in upon themselves, guarding their secrets. The businessmen regarded Europeans as, on the whole, helpful if

[1] Forty-seven per cent mentioned Asian access to capital and credit, and this was the commonest answer. But it is essentially the same point, since in African eyes this advantage stems from the family connections through which Asians obtain finance.

cautious teachers; Asians as rivals, out to frustrate African competition. And Asians were generally believed to be untrustworthy—
unfaithful in their promises, quoting different prices to different
customers, driving unscrupulous bargains. So there was nothing
to be learned from them. They would not share their experiences,
and their methods were suspect:

> They have nothing exemplary. There is nothing to be
> derived from the example of the way they conduct their
> business. Mainly this is because they don't deal honestly, and
> they believe in theft. They would buy things stolen from
> their brother's shop without scruple, and this is something
> which Africans and Europeans don't like.[T]

> Since I have worked for Indians for some time in this busi-
> ness, it is very difficult to find an Indian who wants an
> African to make progress in business. He may say it in words,
> but in action and in his heart he doesn't.[T]

> You can't find a man employed by Indians who can then
> start a business of the same type. You can learn from Euro-
> peans, but not from Asians. You can't find 100 men in Kenya
> who can speak Indian language. Even house-boys can speak
> English, even if they can't write it, learning from Europeans.
> But after twenty years you won't learn any Indian language,
> and it's the same in business.

> An Indian never trusts anyone, and he will always cheat. A
> man who has been employed by an Indian for many years
> won't have anything to show for it but perhaps two pairs of
> trousers. A man who has worked for a European will have a
> farm and some property.[T]

A quarter of the African businessmen mentioned the dishonesty of
Asians, and a quarter again their unhelpfulness to Africans. No
one contradicted these views. But none said Europeans were
dishonest or untrustworthy, and only one that they were unhelpful, while 11 per cent said the opposite, and 21 per cent spoke of
their integrity. Since these answers were given spontaneously, in
response to a question which did not invite comment on Asian or
European treatment of Africans, nor point to moral judgments,
they almost certainly represent feelings which are widely held. In

all the discussions we held with groups of African businessmen, resentment against Asians was unanimous and insistent.[1]

Yet some who criticized Asians most vehemently had also been helped by them, and their comments on both races were strikingly discordant with their experience. 'There are very few Africans who can get far without European backing', said a garage proprietor. 'A European sticks to his price, he doesn't bargain, and he doesn't speak with two tongues.' Yet he believed he had been cheated by a British official, who was supposed to be advising him. Asians, he considered, were 'robbers—crooks always, everywhere'. Yet a Sikh had installed all his machinery for him free of charge out of friendship. A photographer who bought his first camera through the help of an Indian friend still believed that 'these Indians are very bad people, they don't want you to learn'. In practice, more of the businessmen had learned their skills working for Asians than for Europeans; some of them employed Asians as book-keepers or mechanics, and seemed to trust them at least as much as their African workers; and though they complained of Asian wholesale prices, European prices were generally higher. Their resentment cannot therefore be understood simply as a reaction to ill treatment. It was also a rationalization of hostility

[1] Asian businessmen, of course, see themselves very differently. When we asked the sample we interviewed about their advantages, 41 per cent mentioned experience, but only 19 per cent capital, and 9 per cent the mutual help of Asian communities. A third believed they had no advantages at all. They attribute their commercial success overwhelmingly to hard work (85 per cent), and secondly to thrift (33 per cent). None suggested that they were cleverer bargainers, or more ruthless in competition. Nor did they share the idealized African view of European business. They hardly mentioned integrity, experience or any quality of character as European advantages —but chiefly the help they had from their overseas contacts (52 per cent) and, after that, capital (26 per cent). They recognize an obligation to train Africans: 39 per cent said they had given practical training, through employing Africans where they would learn skills, and most considered that the relationship had been successful. Twenty-eight per cent thought it fair for the Government to discriminate in favour of African businesses, because it was their country, after all, and they were economically backward. So in principle, they expressed themselves in sympathy with African progress, and accepted a responsibility to help them. In practice, though they commonly employed Africans in skilled manual jobs, very few employed any in clerical posts, and only one in management, where more was to be learned about running a business. Only 4 per cent had ever gone into partnership with an African, and most of these said it had not been successful. Since Asian businesses are characteristically family concerns, it would be difficult for them to take an outsider into the management of the business without radically altering its structure. In this sense, the African complaint against Asian exclusiveness is partly justified. It is much easier to bring African management staff into an impersonal bureaucracy like a large European company.

towards their principal competitors. Their idealization of European business served as an exemplary contrast, justifying the condemnation of Asian practices.

Asian competition was more widespread and more obtrusive than European, in capital and range of activities nearer the level African businessmen could aim for. They were dependent on Asian suppliers who also served their rivals, sometimes at a better price. But European business was remote, and could afford to be casually helpful, since African businesses were still a long way from threatening their interests. In search of a model for their own behaviour, it was natural for African businessmen to identify with the dominant commercial culture against the minority culture which most nearly threatened them. Within this frame of reference they singled out the difference between the two cultures where the Asians are morally most vulnerable—the conventions of pricing. British businesses in Kenya characteristically charged fixed prices. But in the tradition of the bazaar, price is a battle of wits between buyer and seller, where both may legitimately start from a wholly unreasonable proposition. In African eyes, this is a dishonest attempt to cheat the customer. 'They are more or less like thieves', said a printer, 'buying cheap and holding their stocks until prices are high. The goodness of the European is that he will show you how to get things at a good wholesale price. But the Indian will charge the highest prices he can, and never tell you if you could get it cheaper.' A third of the African businessmen specifically attacked Asian prices, and their language bristled with moral condemnation—robbers, liars, cunning as a hare, devious as a thief.

Yet their criticisms are both inconsistent and self-interested. They blame Asian businesses for charging too much: they blame them too for charging too little, undercutting their own prices in ruthless competition. Both, from their point of view, are unethical. In principle, they dislike bargaining and variable discounts, and adopt these practices reluctantly. Amongst the tactics of retail marketing, they generally repudiate price manipulation as a weapon of competition. They want the security of a system of fixed prices, where the weaker competitor, with less capital and a small turnover, and less experience, can buy and sell on the same terms as his established rival. This, they believe, is the European principle, and they give it the force of a moral example.

Thus the Asian presence reinforces the prestige of the dominant culture. African businessmen make Indians the target of all their frustrations, and accept Europeans as their ally, unconsciously distorting the qualities of each into simple opposites. Bad business conduct is the conduct which harms African business, and it is represented in their stereotype of the Indian shopkeeper. Right conduct is impartial, open, supportive, and its stereotype is the British colonial official, whose image stands, too, for his commercial compatriot. So moral justification is referred to a civilization rather than an ideology. 'Indians are the exception, because Africans are determined to copy the European way—honesty and fulfilment of promises.' But if there had been no Indians to play the devil's part, African businessmen could not have identified so wholeheartedly with European ways.

In all these views, they were clearly projecting their own anxieties. Their image of European families, passing from father to son the wisdom of experience and principles of rectitude, secure in their traditions, seems to express a yearning for continuity and certainty which African society has lost. Kinship and custom could not guide them in a modern commercial economy. The authority of a father, the loyalty of a relative, the obligations of a contract were all doubtful, in a limbo between the past and the future. The businessmen saw in European culture not only a sustained tradition, but a system of impersonal fair dealing which was explicit and predictable, and therefore trustworthy. So they rejected everything in their own inheritance—such as ties of family or tribe—which stood in the way of these principles of universal, rational justice.

From this standpoint, African society had nothing to contribute out of its resources of experience. Most of the businessmen could not see any asset which they could exploit, as Africans, to compensate for the advantages of their Asian and European competitors. They were ambivalent about the one possibility that occurred to them. Twenty-eight per cent did believe that African customers preferred to buy from their fellow Africans, so long as they could find the same stock and service there. But 33 per cent specifically denied it—people bought, indifferently, where they could get what they wanted at the best price; some were jealous of African businessmen; educated Africans, out of snobbery, preferred the Asian and European shops. From their commitment to the principle of commercial impartiality, some of the businessmen even questioned whether it was right to encourage such racial loyalties. 'If we start doing that, striking more to one side in this, so to speak, racist way—well, it's not a good way to go on.' African traditions, then, could not help them: in business they were as children newly born.

The motives of African businessmen, and the creed by which they interpret them, seem to arise directly from their circumstances. They are, as we saw earlier, characteristically drawn to business by vocational frustration. They are searching for a use for their talents which employment cannot offer them, since they lack education for the most influential jobs. And they hope that in time business will pay them better. But they also identify this personal discontent with the national impatience for economic development, and see in business their one chance to make a contribution, where their own efforts will count. Since they understand progress in terms of the achievements of the colonial power which dominated them, their conception of business is framed by the civilization they are striving to emulate. So their business creed is derived from the practices of European businessmen, as they interpret them, and have seen them amongst the predominantly middle-class British settlers who made their home in Kenya. They justify the puritan values of hard work, thrift, honesty and plain dealing, not by the religion which originally sustained them in the colonizing power, but by their material success. This is the conduct to imitate, because it leads to the achievements they envy. Not that their Christianity is insincere: but they take its ethical foundation on trust, as part of the civilization they are determined to master. So the principles of African business are derived pragmatically from the requirements of successful entrepreneurship, within the context of an economy dominated by advanced industrial nations.

The question remains, whether the ambition which drives African businessmen to emulate European achievements rests in a particular structure of personality, formed in childhood by the values of their teachers, and determining the way they responded to their situation. Certainly, the businessmen we met often expressed the spirit of the achieving personality, as David McClelland conceives it. They spoke admiringly of the 'bold heart of risk' that dares to take chances. They were restlessly dissatisfied with their successes. And they sacrificed their peace of mind, almost recklessly, to this insistent competitiveness:

Progress will come from competition. Suppose, for instance, I go to the New Stanley Hotel with another African. Coffee costs a shilling, a doughnut costs a shilling, and a meal costs seven shillings and fifty cents. I can't afford it, so I just have a coffee and a doughnut. But the other man orders a meal, and perhaps a bottle of wine at fifteen shillings. So I begin to ask, how did this man get money—he didn't inherit it, he didn't get it from heaven. And that will stimulate me to take an initiative, so that I can become rich too.[T]

Most of the time I am worried. I think of all that will happen to me if I don't succeed: but I have got a hope. The more the business grows, the more I worry, and the less time I have to rest. I'm never satisfied. Before I had the shop, I had time to drink and to rest, but once I took the shop, I was there every evening, checking the accounts and going straight to bed. I just hope that one day I will be more satisfied, when the business is established. . . .

Business is a gamble—you never know whether you'll have a profit or not. The most important thing is that if a customer asks for something, and you don't have it, from that moment you start worrying how to fulfil all the customers' needs—how to get more money, how to get more customers, why did I lose that customer, how to get more business. I went to the doctor for insomnia, and stomach trouble, and he says it's just from worrying about the business.

Business means risking everything you have in a venture that you are uncertain about. Even if you don't risk capital, you may lose a good job. When I started this company I was certain, but I wasn't 100 per cent certain. My wife and mother didn't like it a bit. They said you are borrowing from the Government, and you'll end in jail.

I always worry . . . it's inevitable. Long ago I had a grass house. Then when I bought a bicycle, I would be passed by someone on a *piki-piki* (motor scooter), so I thought I should get a motor bike. Even now I have a stone house and a car, but I could be better off, and planning future expansion keeps me awake.ᵀ

There is a compulsiveness about this quest for achievement which seems to express an underlying strain. Forty-four per cent of the businessmen said they suffered from indigestion, insomnia or other functional symptoms of anxiety. Did this anxiety arise, perhaps, from a restlessness of ambition more fundamental than the self-sustaining stimulus of a creative activity? And if so, was this character formed by values they had assimilated in childhood?

Some of the businessmen themselves spoke as if they saw a relationship between the values acquired in school and the entrepreneurial vitality of society. They were concerned that the rising generation would lack their pioneering determination, as the educational system channelled ambition more and more exclusively towards white-collar jobs. 'I worry about the lack of progress in Kenya, and that other countries won't respect us until they see the local people making an effort and progressing. Just now I am thinking of retiring, but I don't have a son ready to take over the shop. Those who have been in school want to work in offices. This is the first generation to start seriously in business, but our sons haven't caught the spirit.ᵀ' As we saw in the one school where we studied students' attitudes, there does seem to be an overwhelming preference for bureaucratic employment. The businessmen themselves were aware of their low prestige. 'Although I perform some useful service for the public, I haven't as high a standing as even a low civil servant', remarked a highly successful wholesaler and transporter, with several shops and a large flour mill. 'People don't respect businessmen.'

The status of occupations certainly reflects the values of society. But it seems doubtful whether values such as these fundamentally affect personality, especially in a society where families have not established an attachment to particular professions handed on from father to son. In any society, children strive for approval, and values seem more likely to determine the frame of reference in which they choose to be judged than the strength of their need to do well at something. If they cannot win approval within one frame, there is always a pool of different interpretations of success to which to refer their ambitions. Indeed, it is just those who have been thwarted of success in conventional terms who will be drawn towards entrepreneurship. These innovators will justify themselves by whatever systems of belief their history and circumstances put forward, reinterpreting them to fit their situation. They may repudiate some current values, or redefine them to suit their activities—emphasizing progressive modern ideas against tradition, for instance, or equating their purpose with national aspirations for development. And in a society changing as fast as Kenya, such rationalizations are liable to abrupt reinterpretations. So, for instance, businessmen deeply committed to the Mau Mau movement later accepted as a model the civilization they had so stubbornly resisted. In these circumstances, the values learned in childhood may be less of a determinant than the experiences of adult life, as men struggle to define their identity in an unstable world.

From this point of view, we can distinguish three separate elements in the formation of entrepreneurial character: childhood experience, explicit systems of values, and social circumstances. In a society in process of radical transformation, childhood training may not be informed by any articulate value system which continues in adult life to explain the sense of a man's purposes to himself. He is, rather, in search of beliefs to give meaning to his situation. In such a period of social evolution, articulate values seem more likely to derive from the pressures of present circumstances than from established beliefs. The words will come from the ideologies and moral traditions a man has heard about, but he will put them together, out of context, in a new attempt to express his place in life. Thus, Christianity, nationalism, socialism, racial antagonism all seem to influence the African business creed, but all seem to reflect an aspect of the colonial experience. And it is the experience itself which defines the achievements worth pursuing, as Kenya struggles to come to terms with the society it has inherited. The civilization of modern bourgeois industrial nations comes to stand for an ideology, as an idealized model of successful conduct. Though in the eyes of African businessmen it is a Christian civilization, they follow its principles not to save their souls, but their pride.

PART II
THE ORGANIZATION OF BUSINESS

5

MANAGEMENT

Any organized activity presupposes that those who take part understand their rights and duties, and abide by them. Who gives orders and what about, the basis of his authority, what he gives in return, the extent of responsibility have all to be established, arbitrated and enforced. Organization depends upon mutual confidence that these rules will be respected. In the last resort, this confidence derives from the power of sanctions to enforce the rules—and the nature of the sanctions will determine the nature of the organization. But it also rests on the assumption that the sanctions will not need to be called often into use. For unless the rules are followed without continual questioning or contempt, the co-ordination of activity becomes too precarious to be manageable. Even if every order is a threat, every task completed an unwilling concession to superior force, the despotism would scarcely function long if the threat of punishment had always to be realized. So the rules must be assimilated to the values of a social order which the members of the organization accept as fair, or at least as their unchallengeable destiny.

Wherever a radically new form of activity is introduced into a society, its organization is caught between incompatible demands. The more it is governed by familiar patterns of authority and obligation, the more readily will its rules be accepted. Yet unless the rules break with tradition, they are unlikely to conform to the activity itself. In this dilemma, entrepreneurs may act with great harshness, trusting to an ever-present fear of punishment to make the rules secure; or adapt innovation to established patterns of work; or pioneer a new philosophy of values to justify and generalize their rules of conduct. They may try all at once, as they grope pragmatically for a viable solution. So, for instance, the English cotton masters at the end of the eighteenth century would hang a strap by each child worker, a beating always within arms'

reach. Even humane men like Robert Owen devised an equally
obtrusive moral sanction—a board of variable coloured segments
beside each mill hand, whose sectors were adjusted week by
week to advertise the shortcomings of his character. At the same
time, much of the work in the early factories of the industrial
revolution was subcontracted to foremen, who adapted the traditions of cottage industry to the organization of factory groups.
And these expedients were justified or challenged in the context of
a running debate about the morality of industrial discipline, which
sought to universalize its principles and identify the best interests
of the workers themselves with it.

An African businessman, like an eighteenth century cotton
master, is caught in the same conflict between familiar and func-
tionally rational organization. The outcome of the English
experience—factory legislation, trade unionism, the conception
of labour as a commodity to be bought and sold, of managerial
authority as a reward earned by achievement—are known to him
from the laws introduced by colonial government, and the
principles of European firms. If he has ever worked for a European, his employment was seen in these terms. But he cannot
assume, as a master now himself, that the alien rules which governed relationships between European employer and African
worker will uphold him too. The traditions of economic organization in an African community are very different. He has to recreate
a viable pattern of working relationships which will be accepted as
fair treatment of one African by another, and which African society
will back with its own institutions.

The problem grows with the scale and complexity of the enterprise. In the simplest businesses, the only internal relationships are
between employer and his few undifferentiated employees; and
perhaps between partners. But as the business becomes more
sophisticated, the employees begin to range in a hierarchy of
responsibility, their tasks are more specialized, the co-ordination
of their work more exact; and the organization approaches a size
where regulation must be possible without the continual presence
of the owner. Thus the industrial enterprises the ICDC supported,
since they generally needed more workers and more technical
skills, faced more complex problems of management. Our analysis
concerns them especially—though the commercial firms shared
similar problems on a smaller scale, and their labour relations

followed a similar pattern. As we shall see, these firms resolved their problems by a style of management which, up to a point, served them well enough. But beyond that point they could grow no further, and even—seemingly unconsciously—frustrated their own chances of growth. They stood on a threshold of development in organization which they did not know how to cross. In this sense, their style of management was not a solution but an evasion of the underlying problem.

The pattern of organization

The pattern of organization of the African industrial enterprises we visited is typically a partnership or private company, with no more than twenty shareholders. The partners or directors will be of the same generation, and have known each other before they went into business together. Most likely they were schoolmates, or worked for the same firm, where the idea of pooling their experience in their own concern first occurred to them. Or they may have been in the same detention camp through the years of the Emergency. But they are probably not related. At least one of them is experienced in the techniques of the industry, and is likely to become the manager. As often as not, the management is shared between the directors, one supervising the work, another sales and accounts. Directors' meetings are regularly held, and a record kept. In the first years, no profits are distributed, but the managers are paid a salary—often less than they could be earning in employment, to conserve resources. While the business is establishing itself, the managing director may sacrifice a great deal, accepting only half or a quarter of what he earned before. If it is very little, it will be called an allowance, by way of apology.[1]

Even men who are the sole proprietors of their business sometimes pay themselves a salary, to discipline their spending. 'I used once just to take money and use it for my own needs', a garage owner explained. 'I found this very difficult to record, and I didn't

---

[1] Our description concentrates on the industrial concerns, because their organization is likely to be less simple than in commerce. The commercial firms were more often owned by a single proprietor, and only half of them had any managerial staff apart from the owner-manager—most commonly his wife. Only four of them—compared with nineteen of the industrial firms—were registered as companies. They also recruited their employees much more locally than the industrial firms, since they did not need specialized skills.

know how much I was taking. So I decided to pay myself a salary. It used to be 300 shillings (a month) before the business expanded.' He had since increased it to 1,200 shillings.

Besides the directors, the management staff may include a book-keeper, who has no share in the ownership of the business. In a small firm, this is the most difficult position to fill: they cannot easily afford a well qualified man, whom they can trust. So they take on a youngster with some education, and check his work themselves, or call in a more experienced person to look it over once a month. If they can afford it, they will have their accounts audited every year.

Skilled workers were also hard to find. When they started, some firms recruited a core of experienced employees from an established European or Asian business, offering them more money or appealing to their pariotism. If the African owners had bought out a European, they usually encouraged some of the experienced workers to stay—though again they might have to offer more money, since African management was mistrusted. Otherwise, recruitment generally followed a routine of sorting applications, interviews, tests and probationary employment, whose thoroughness depended on the difficulty of the work.

Some of the employees have been working in this dry-cleaning business, and some we have trained. They send applications, and then I interview them. I have a great pile of applications, from Nairobi and Thika and all over the place: written applications are a useful guide, because it's important in this business to be able to write. When I need an employee, I call one or two for interview. First I look at qualifications and testimonials, and whether he has been working in this sort of business. Later on I give him work and see how he can do it, and how he can attend to customers. I take them on temporarily for about two weeks, and decide whether they can work.

Half of the mechanics were the former owner's employees— I didn't discharge any. The others came with testimonials from their employers. I send them to the foreman for inter-view, and he gives them a test. It's easy to find people these days, but good mechanics are hard to find. Even I could employ three grade II's if I could get them.

They are recruited from other firms. They come to me and I test them. I give them a bit more pay. Most of them I know personally—there are very few workshops of this kind in Nairobi, so it is easy for me to get to know Africans there, and know their capabilities. I find out what they're getting and offer a bit more.

When the work is less skilled, the present employees will be asked to bring in recruits, or word is passed round the neighbourhood that jobs are going.

All are employed casually according to the work. The largest number we ever employed at one time was seven, for three months last year, making chemical measures for the Agricultural Department. It didn't need great skill. You can train a keen chap in two days to solder. They were all recruited locally. I went to the headman, and said I wanted some good chaps who wouldn't cause trouble or talk too much. I interviewed about fourteen, with my secretary. They were all young people about twenty. People with any experience are very, very few.

Carpenters, plumbers, masons—people like that—there are plenty in the country with experience, though they have never been to technical school. We just send people into the country and let them know there are vacancies, and they come just like that. We ask for references and go through recommendations. Then we see how a man does in a supervised job—we give him a week's trial. The foreman interviews them and then recommends to me. In the mines we don't select people. We tell the headman we need so many people to dig so much, and he finds them.

Since unemployment is widespread, recruits are easy to find so long as a high level of qualification or experience is unimportant. And technical competence can be quickly tested. But integrity is harder to judge—'and the one who is experienced is also experienced in stealing'. Theft is much the commonest source of trouble with employees not only amongst the industrial enterprises, but in commerce and the country markets, too. 'It was a long process and cost me a lot of money before I got the right people who would not steal,' as a Nairobi shopkeeper ruefully admitted. Over a third of the employers in the ICDC-supported businesses and a quarter in the market centres had experience of employees who stole. Few altogether trusted any of their workers, except their wives, and even then, a man with more than one wife needed to be on his guard. 'They both have children, and there isn't enough to go round, so there's jealousy and rivalry between them. If you bring them into the shop, they start taking things without caring what happens, because each thinks the other is getting more than her. With one wife you can survive.'T

Both the industrial and commercial firms, therefore, try to organize the work so that they do not need to trust their workers very far. Stocks are checked daily, deliveries tallied with materials issued, traps set for employees under suspicion. Anyone caught is warned, and dismissed if he takes no heed, sometimes publicly as an example. The stricter firms hand thieves over to the police.[1] Others recognize the temptation, and deal more mildly with pilfering, so long as the fault is admitted.

> I have a lot of trouble with theft by my workers. They take things—tools, saws, planes. I used not to take any notice, I never even bothered to inquire where the tools had gone. I just used to go out and buy another. But now I have decided that if anything is missing, the employee must pay. It was getting to be too much.T

> I have talked to them about being honest, and that I want to trust them when I am not here. And I also try to trick them by counting things here and checking when anything is missing. Sometimes when I know money has been sent here while I'm out, when I come back I just keep quiet and wait to see if they will tell me. Sometimes I send them out with my own money, and see if they return the change. But in fact, I have found them honest.T

> Mostly I call them together and talk to them against it. I had one mechanic I expelled for stealing parts. I expelled him publicly, as an example to the others. There are a number of ways they can steal. For instance, drivers can do two trips

[1] They are not necessarily more puritanical, but have learned that leniency can rebound: if a man is simply discharged, he may complain to the Labour Department that he has not been given due notice, and since no case has been pressed, he is technically justified.

when the customer has only paid for one, and the driver pockets the difference. It's hard to prevent. So I talk to them almost monthly about it, and tell them this is only a young business.

I forgive any other mistake, but not theft. If I find anyone, I report to the police. I take that very seriously. There's only been one case since I've been here. He was arrested and dismissed—he stole a customer's battery.

Pilfering apart, the commonest complaints are of absenteeism, slacking or drunkenness. They are all dealt with in much the same way. The offenders must make up time lost or accept a fine, are warned and finally dismissed if they do not improve. Control depends on close supervision, and a gradation of penalties designed to compensate the firm for the damage it has suffered rather than to punish the misbehaviour for the sake of principle. Many firms would keep an employee caught stealing or cheating, so long as he admitted his fault and paid back what he owed. Ideally, tasks are regulated within a few hours: stocks are checked at the end of the day, parts or materials issued only for the immediate job, and the time it should take estimated. If the outcome does not tally, the worker must make up the difference—stay late to finish his assignment, pay for the missing tools or the discrepancy between delivery and receipts, accept a cut in wages for the hours lost. Unless the trouble is persistent, he is only likely to be dismissed if he refuses to accept the penalty. And since jobs are hard to find, he will usually give in.

The system is simple, and protects the firm from serious harm. But it leaves the workers with little responsibility. This worried some of the businessmen we met. They wanted an immediate check on what was going on, but they also wanted a responsible, stable work force which would identify with the interests of the business. Yet without delegating authority, and exposing themselves to the risk of abuses, they could hardly expect the workers to share the problems of management. 'I try to encourage the workers to feel more responsible, though I haven't achieved that yet', said the manager of one of the largest companies. 'I find that if you give them some responsibility, and leave them on their own they do better. They take some pride in their work, and don't abuse it. . . . But the people here are illiterate, their mentality is very different from an educated person. Unless you keep chasing them they can't work well. They need constant supervision.' So management was faced with the universal dilemma of authority that seeks to share its aims without sharing its control, and characteristically resolved it by paternalism. Businessmen held meetings with their workers, tried to educate them to understand the need for discipline, hard work and wage restraint, lectured them about drinking and improvidence, and sometimes took a fatherly interest in their personal problems:

> I talk to them against drinking, and try to impress on them that hard work leads to success. No one has it written on his forehead that he'll never get rich. A great fault with most African employees is that they squander their money. If a European or Asian is employed he treats the work as his own, and after two years or so he has saved enough to start on his own. . . . They (the African employees) bring me their problems like buying land or sending children to school, and I give them advice. I want them to remember me as a man who helped them to acquire property. I don't want to see them remain poor. That's why at the end of the month I allow them to overdraw their salaries, or even give them more if there are special problems, and hope that they'll use it wisely.[T]

> Once in a while, in the evenings we discuss how they should behave. If we have noticed someone is not quite up to the mark, we tell the others not to behave like this, and him to improve. They bring their complaints to me then, not during the day. They are always welcome to come to me when they have financial difficulties.[T]

The businessmen's ideal of labour relations is not, then, based on bargaining, where each side ignores the interests of the other, and gives as little as it can. Nor is it modelled on a family, despite the hint of paternalism, since the employer does not pretend to be primarily concerned with the welfare of his employees. The closest model is perhaps the classroom. Like a school, the firm has its own internal system of rewards and punishments. Like school-children, the workers are closely supervised and treated as essentially irresponsible. Like a schoolmaster, the employer urges them to identify their own interests with the tasks he sets, and act with the sense of responsibility he does not trust them to hold. As in a school system, success is finally measured by objective criteria of performance. Of all the institutions of modern society, school is the most familiar—the longest established and most respected. Since education is everywhere popularly accepted as the principal means to personal success and national progress, it would be natural for businessmen, who see themselves as agents of the same purposes, to be influenced, too, by its ethic.

Consistent with this schoolmasterly approach, the managers had little time for trade unions. Only the industrial firms had any number of union members amongst their employees, and though they tolerated membership, they dealt brusquely with trouble.

There was one time when someone came here, and told me he was a trade union representative. We talked and talked, and he asked so many questions about insurance and compensation. Later he told some of our workers to join the union. He asked me to collect two shillings from each of the workers. This I told him I couldn't do, but if he came at the end of the month, he could collect himself. He held a meeting here one afternoon when we were all away, without our knowledge, and slapped one of the workers who refused to take part. Next time he came, I set the dogs on him—he ran away and never came back.

Once when I was away in Nairobi, a trade union official came and incited the workers to strike. About 160 bags of flour were wasted. When I came back, I gave a rise to the workers who lived around the township. Then I went to our country branch, and sacked about ten. The rest agreed to come back to work. After a while, I sacked the workers in the town I'd given a rise to, because there were lots of people wanting work who were prepared to accept less.T

We've had spots of trouble time and again—people complaining that we are very bad employers. They try to influence others, until we have to get rid of them. We had a go-slow strike last December. It was not confined to us, but to the whole industry. The strike was later disqualified by the Minister of Labour. But we'd sacked some people even before the Minister disqualified it. And afterwards we took some back.

While unemployment is so widespread, union organization fragmentary, and Government generally unsympathetic, employers can get away with such high-handed action. The businessmen see trade union interference as misguided—defending workers whose dismissal was fully justified, or claiming wages which would ruin the enterprise. They say they offer the best wages they can afford, and that it is in the employees' own interest to accept them. In practice, even when the pay is certainly below the going rate, a firm that puts its difficulties frankly seems able to keep the goodwill of the workers. 'I had to put them in a clear picture about the company. I talked straight, and told them the bitter truth. I asked them what they would do in my position. I talked frankly to them, and they agreed that they would have done the same as me. They knew the truth. If we were making money, I'd give finger and nails to see they got their proper pay.' The unions are therefore in too weak a position, and too inexperienced, to arouse much support, and only seven of the firms we visited reported any strikes or trade union intervention.

Most of the businesses, besides, did not believe that they were underpaying their workers. Fifty-four per cent considered their wages average for their area, and 24 per cent more than the average. The detailed figures they gave did, in fact, generally correspond with government rates, where these applied, and they only paid less from necessity. They paid more where skilled labour was scarce. 'No one would like to leave me,' as an instrument repairer said, 'because they couldn't get the same money elsewhere. It's the only way I could get good mechanics.'

But goodwill depends as much on the way wages are paid as their amount. In Kenya, it is the custom to pay monthly, and since even in Nairobi few manual workers earned in 1967 more than 200 shillings or so a month, an informal system of interim advances has grown up. An employee expects to be able to claim on the wages due to him when he is faced with exceptional expenditure—sickness, school fees, taxes, buying a cow or a piece of land—or just to get by from one pay day to the next. Nearly all the businesses in the ICDC sample, therefore, paid advances, usually on request. But the custom is awkward for a small concern that does not always have money in hand, and a quarter of the businesses appointed a fixed day in the middle of the month. 'Everyone used to come at his own time,' a furniture maker with seven workers explained, 'and I found it difficult to be withdrawing money every day like that. Now I have a guarantee of a date when they must come: it's fixed, so that they don't come and embarrass me in front of customers or at home. I find it is no use to lose a good man for financial difficulties, but they were coming to get money every day, and coming again the next day to say they had nothing for food. So I started this system—one day when everyone comes for his advance. Now they don't trouble me at all in between times.'

Even when it is regulated to a fixed date, and treated as routine, the system tends to bring out the paternalism latent in the relationship between employer and employee. The worker may receive as much as half his pay by explaining his financial difficulties and appealing to his employer's benevolence. It does not come to him automatically, as a right, but as a concession to his poverty. If his employer is easy-going, he may be continually overdrawn, so that he comes to look on him as a patron to whom he is indebted. At the same time, since he has to justify his claims for an allowance, he puts the employer in the position of financial monitor, whose advice must be respected.

But this touch of paternalism overlays an essentially contractual system of employment. Workers are recruited impersonally, to suit the job, at rates which reflect the state of the labour market. The employer's concern with the welfare of his employees extends no further than the interests of the business: he does not want to lose good men through intolerance or lack of sympathy with their financial difficulties. Though he would like them to share his sense of responsibility for the success of the enterprise, he tries to regulate his organization so that he does not need to trust them far.

In practice, these principles seemed fairly successful. Just over a third of the businessmen supported by the ICDC complained of theft, and a fifth of idling and drunkenness at work, but other difficulties were uncommon. Two-fifths said they had no trouble with their workers at all. The market businesses, though they paid much lower wages, had even fewer problems. Over a quarter of them paid less than 50 shillings a month, and nearly three-quarters less than 100 shillings to at least some of their employees, yet 61 per cent said they had no trouble. Since most had only one or two employees, if any, supervision was much easier for them, and the work much simpler. But they seem to have followed the same general principles as the larger firms. Only a quarter, for instance, said they would choose an employee on a friend's recommendation rather than by impartial evidence of competence. They recruited workers for their experience and qualifications, and dismissed them readily if, after due warning and advice, they were unsatisfactory.

Yet the whole pattern of management has a crucial weakness, which grows with the business. It depends on the close personal supervision of the owner-managers. There is scarcely any trusted salaried managerial staff who have no share in the business—and the few we found were usually Asian or European. The problem of delegating responsibility to trustworthy employees has not been solved, but evaded. And this leads most businessmen to proliferate small-scale organizations compatible with the proprietary style of management in which they feel secure. All but a tenth of the businessmen supported by the ICDC had other economic interests, either farm or business, in whose running they were involved. But as these interests grow and diversify, personal supervision becomes more and more arduous, and the lack of responsible subordinates more crippling. Thus the outcome of their inability to delegate is a scattering of energy and resources which only compounds the problem.

This diffusion of interests is also an aspect of the evolution of business as a distinct career. Until recently, it was mostly an activity of farmers seeking new ways to employ savings, and the idea that it required single-minded attention was foreign to them. The insecurity of businessmen struggling to master unfamiliar anxieties of management draws them back towards the land, and this too inhibits their entrepreneurial development.

The concern for land

Of all the interests which can distract a manager from the supervision of his business, farming is the most compelling. Land is more than another economic asset to exploit: it is the final security and proof of success. For most men—labourer, politician, civil servant, businessman alike—land is still the goal towards which every endeavour leads at last. 'We Africans, whatever we do or want, we must have land', said one of the most successful businessmen. 'Without land you are useless. Money gets finished, but you never finish soil. Without land you are nobody. Your business may collapse, land is always there. You can always get money from the soil.' Out of his profits he had bought a fifty-acre dairy farm, and re-established himself on the land from which his parents had been excluded. For him, business was not an alternative to farming, but a means of reclaiming his heritage. Only in the last few years has business begun to appear, even to a few, as an exclusive economic interest: most men still hesitate to cut themselves off from the land.

Until 1956, when the consolidation and registration of individual land titles began, virtually every African family had, in principle, a right to cultivate land somewhere. But since the colonial government did not encourage commercial farming amongst Africans, the land provided little cash income. Shopkeeping, like employment, made money for school fees, taxes, building materials and farm improvements; it was essentially a subsidiary activity, where—with luck—a small capital outlay would generate a more regular return than farm produce sold in the local market. Even when cash crops were introduced in the 1950s shopkeeping and trading still seem to have been complementary rather than alternatives to investment in the land. Not only was the income less seasonal, but the return was quicker. So a sum of money, too small to make a substantial improvement to the farm, might be put into commerce to grow. If the business was successful, its profits could be reinvested in the land later. At least, it might meet most cash outlays, and allow the farm profits to be ploughed back. So there has grown up a symbiotic relationship between farming and rural shopkeeping, where the most progressive farmers are often the most successful businessmen, distributing their resources between the two activities to achieve the fastest accumulation. But the farm remains their first love.

At the same time, land consolidation has driven more and more families off the land altogether. The fragmented holdings were redistributed, so as to assemble them in units large enough for planned commercial farming, and then registered under individual, not family, titles. The owner was forbidden to subdivide the property again below an economically viable acreage. Families which had cultivated clan land, or whose rights were not well represented—because they had settled elsewhere, were jailed under the Emergency regulations, or possessed only marginal holdings—were liable to be dispossessed. As children grew up, they could no longer look forward to a share of their father's land as a right. Consolidation and registration began in the Kikuyu country in 1956, and by 1965 had spread to most parts of Kenya except the Coastal Province, the Kamba country, and the pastoral areas, covering over 1,500,000 acres.

Though registration deprived many of land, Independence created new opportunities to buy. The colonial restrictions on the purchase of land were swept aside. Settlement schemes and the departure of the European farmers opened the White Highlands to African ownership, and anyone who could find the capital for a down payment had a unique opportunity to acquire some of the most beautiful and fertile farmland in the world. For those with the capital to invest, companies and co-operatives were formed sometimes with several hundred shareholders, to buy out European farmers anxious to sell. Land was exceptionally cheap: in 1964, prices were little more than half their value four years later. So successful businessmen, whether they had land already or not were tempted to acquire new holdings. A wholesaler whom we interviewed, for instance, had ten acres in four small-holdings inherited from his father and his father-in-law, and a 250-acre dairy and wheat farm, purchased with the help of a £2,000 government loan. A carpenter had bought three acres for his son, in his original homeland, five acres about his house, and shares worth £100 in two large commercial farms in the Rift Valley. A hotel keeper had bought eighty acres of tobacco land with a partner, and then thirty acres of his own near his home. And some of the Nairobi businessmen had settled on substantial farms on the outskirts of the city, once European-owned, commuting daily to their offices.

So business has not so far deflected ambition from its traditional goal. On the whole, the more successful a man is in business, the more land he acquires. In the market centres, altogether two thirds of the businessmen owned some land of their own, and 30 per cent of them more than five acres—which, in the most fertile parts of Kenya, is enough to provide food and a small cash income for a family. Amongst the businessmen whose profit reached 300 shillings a month, nearly half had more than five acres and less than a quarter none. Fewer still of the businessmen supported by the ICDC were still without land altogether, and a much higher proportion had holdings above 20 acres. As the scale of business grows, so does the farm (Table 4).

TABLE 4   *Landholding of businessmen*

Acreage	Market businessmen Profit under 300/–	Profit 300/– or more	All	ICDC-supported businessmen
none*	32%	20%	31%	14%
less than 3 acres	13%	9%	12%	11%
3–5 acres	19%	19%	18%	15%
6–10 acres	16%	17%	16%	18%
11–20 acres	7%	15%	8%	9%
over 20 acres	6%	14%	8%	32%
no estimate†	7%	6%	7%	1%
Total %	100%	100%	100%	100%
Total no.‡	441	176	848	87

* Including those who owned only minor shareholdings in farming companies or co-operatives.
† Where land has not been consolidated and registered, the owner may not know the acreage even approximately.
‡ Total of the third column is larger than the first two combined, since it includes businessmen who did not estimate their profit, and one market where the amount of profit was not asked.

Three-quarters of these farms, even when they were only a few acres, grew some cash crops as well as food for subsistence. A third of the more prosperous businessmen, both in the markets and the ICDC sample, also grazed exotic cattle. So the farms could not simply be left to traditional methods of cultivation. We asked the ICDC-supported businessmen who managed their land: a few looked after it themselves, or left it to a partner in the property, but two-thirds entrusted the day-to-day supervision to their wives, sometimes with the help of paid labour. They were therefore usually still much concerned in the management of their farms, following the accustomed division of tasks by which women do most of the work in the fields, and men are responsible especially for the planning, care and marketing of cash crops and dairy produce.

The more substantial businessmen tend, then, to be more substantial farmers too, owning more land than most men who have no means of livelihood other than their farms. And as they make more money, they will go on adding to it. Over half the businessmen supported by the ICDC said they would like to buy more land, and a third had already invested some of their business profits in it.

For all this, there are signs that the attachment to land may weaken, as men gain confidence in business, and realize that they cannot exploit its possibilities without concentrating their energies. We asked the businessmen in the market centres which was more important to them, their farm or their business, and which made more profit. Thirty-eight per cent said their business was both more profitable and more important, 30 per cent said their farm. But another 19 per cent said they cared more for their farm, even though it was less profitable than the business. So although the majority made more from business than farming, the farm was still more often their first concern. As the businesses become more profitable, however, the balance of loyalties shifts. Almost half the businessmen who made more than 300 shillings a month found more money and interest in business, and only a quarter preferred farming on both counts. Those who made less than 300 shillings were more equally divided—slightly less than a third for the farm, slightly more than a third for the business, on the grounds of both profit and importance to them, and they were more likely to prefer their farms even when they made less money.[1] It seems that even while business is still small in scale a man who finds he can make money from it begins to become more attached to it, and to see himself more as a businessman than farmer.

A few of the ICDC-supported businessmen explicitly repudiated farming, and identified themselves wholeheartedly with their new economic role. A Nairobi chemist, for example, said: 'If I had any land, I would have sold it to raise money for the business. I'm not interested in land. You can't do two things at once; when you combine them, you can't concentrate on one properly. I could invest in a co-operative farm, but I'm not thinking of it. Those

[1] There were also about 7 per cent who said their farms and businesses were equally profitable and important to them, and a few who did not give a clear answer. Only 2 or 3 per cent in both groups cared more for the business if it made less than the farm, while 21 per cent of the less prosperous and 15 per cent of the more prosperous still attached more importance to their farm, though it made less money.

who want to be farmers, let them be farmers, those who want to be in business, let them be in business.' A baker, who had inherited a small-holding, had worked out that the cost of exploiting it was more than the effort was worth. 'Traditionally I have got land, but I don't farm. I have been given it by my father, but I don't do anything with it—it's about four acres. I don't think it's economical. At this moment it's not being used, I don't find time to do anything with it. It's easier to buy food. I have sometimes had a tenant there, but not at present. I'm really interested in business, not in farming. In 1951 I was farming, and I had a lot of maize. But when I calculated what I was paying for labourers and supervision, I found I'd be better off just buying maize. If you are in business, you must just be in business. After all, what we are after is money. Money in the bank is your best friend. Why take it out and put it into farming, which requires a lot of supervision if it is to make money?'

As farming becomes increasingly commercial, and land is held under personal title which can be freely bought and sold, it loses its intrinsic worth. Money, not soil, is the final security. At first, commerce is merely a means of supplementing farm capital or domestic income, then a rival to farming, and at last may supplant it, as the implications of costing the farm like any other economic asset become apparent. This rationalization is inhibited by the profound appeal of land a man can call his own, the soil he can crumble in his fingers, and pass on to his children as their inheritance. Yet business too has an excitement, a sense of unexplored opportunity, which begins to claim an undivided loyalty. Industry, especially, which challenged the European and Asia dominance of the most modern sector of the economy, attracted men who were losing their attachment to the land.

Although, as a whole, the businessmen supported by the ICDC were acquisitive landowners, there was a marked difference between industry and commerce. Seventeen per cent of the industrialists owned no land at all, another 15 per cent less than three acres, and only 21 per cent more than twenty acres: while in commerce, only 10 per cent had no land, 5 per cent less than three acres, and 45 per cent more than twenty acres. Over a third of the commercial men, too, owned more than one farm, but only 4 per cent in industry. And in spite of their smaller and fewer holdings, the industrialists were as likely to be satisfied with what they had:

44 per cent did not plan to buy any more land, compared with 38 per cent of the commercial businessmen.

These differences are related to the distance of their business from their homeland. Only a fifth of the industrial concerns were established in the location[1] where their owner was born, but 38 per cent of the shops, and men who have moved away from their native community were less likely to own land. Indeed, none who had stayed at home was without a farm at all, compared with a fifth of the others, whose holdings were also generally smaller. So industry, in drawing people away from home, had also drawn them away from the land. The most progressive of the industrial businessmen were least likely to own any land at all, while in commerce, success in business and farming went together.

Commerce and industry seem then to follow characteristically different patterns. Retailing and wholesaling is still predominantly rural, in the hands of men who have held to their local ties, and established themselves as prosperous farmers and businessmen within their native community. For them, the two activities are complementary rather than competitive, and close enough to be supervised together. But industry is more urban, gravitating towards the larger townships and their hinterland, and attracts men whose birthplace holds them less. Their parents were landless, perhaps, or passed what little they had to another child, or brought their children up on a European farm where they were working. The industrial businessman cannot easily supervise a farm far away, and if he buys, he will more likely look for a former European property which promises—if only he can find a way to manage it—a handsome return to his capital.

The diversity of business interests

Both in commerce and industry, over a third of the businessmen also owned, largely or wholly, businesses other than the one we studied, and this diffusion of resources and attention seems a greater risk than farming. Here too retailers and wholesalers were more likely to spread their interests: as well as owning more farm-

[1] A location is the smallest administrative unit, with a population of usually 5,000 to 20,000. Above that is the division (approaching 100,000 in the most populous areas) and the district, which may have over half a million. Finally, Kenya is divided into provinces of several million. About half the businessmen were still living in their native district in commerce and industry alike.

land, they owned more businesses, their businesses had more branches, and they invested more of their business profits in other activities. On every count, they were less inclined to concentrate their activities (Table 5).

TABLE 5   *Diversity of interests amongst industrial and commercial businessmen*

Percentage of businessmen	Industry	Commerce
owning* a farm (3 acres or more)	68%	85%
owning* other businesses	34%	41%
investing business profits† in farm	4%	35%
investing business profits† in other businesses	13%	25%
with branches to business studied	25%	40%

* Including joint ownership but not minor shareholding.
† That is, profits of the business studied.

But in both groups, the diffusion of interests seems to damage the chances of any one concern. It is more difficult to manage than the distraction of a farm. As we saw, most men leave their farms in charge of their wives, who have been brought up to farm work as their natural occupation, and who share their husband's interest. Even if the farm is not fully exploited, capital is secure in the fertile soil. But businesses are left in the hands of partners or employees, usually unrelated to them, who may readily cheat them if they do not watch their interest closely.[1] And mismanagement can lose them their whole investment with nothing left to show. As one business goes down, they may be tempted to rescue it with funds from another, and bring down all their enterprises together. Both capital and supervision are spread dangerously thin.

The ablest businessmen seem to recognize the risk, for the owners of the concerns which had made money and grown were much more likely than the rest to concentrate their efforts. *The chances of profitable expansion are far more clearly associated with this concentration of attention than with other assets like capital, training, professional book-keeping, which might be expected to influence their progress.* Unlike farming, where progress in business and land-holding

[1] Amongst the businessmen with other business interests, 9 per cent managed them themselves, 42 per cent left them in the hands of an unrelated partner, 15 per cent to a partner of their family, 30 per cent to a salaried employee, 6 per cent to wives, 3 per cent to another relative. (These figures add to more than 100 per cent, because some men had several other interests, which might be managed differently.)

go together, successful shopkeepers are here as single-minded as the industrialists, and tend as often to avoid the distraction of other business interests. All together, 79 per cent of the most progressive businessmen owned no other business, 52 per cent of the rest: or—looked at the other way—half the businesses where the owner had no other interest were highly successful, a quarter of the others.

Why do so many businessmen disperse their attention, when all the signs suggest that it damages their chances? They blame the lack of progress of a business on shortage of capital, they dream of new branches, more ambitious lines of production, import agencies, nationwide distribution, yet put their spare resources elsewhere. It is easy to understand why men should want a farm, which is also a home and security against failure and retirement, but why another business, when the one they have has scarcely begun to realize their hopes for it? The explanation seems to lie in the underlying weakness of their style of management. As we discussed in an earlier section, they tend to organize their businesses so that responsibility is concentrated in their own hands, the employees closely supervised. There is no trusted subordinate management, apart from the owners, and occasionally their wives. But a business organized in this way is constricted to what the owner-manager can keep under his eye. So long as he personally checks the stock, deliveries and cash, and is continually amongst his workers, guiding and overseeing them, he can maintain a system of working relationships which depends on only a minimum of trust. But to expand, he must delegate. Someone able enough to take responsibility is also able to cheat him or appropriate his business experience for a rival venture of his own. 'These educated people are terrible,' as one man remarked, 'they can steal with a pen.' So the businessman looks for a subordinate who will fear him—a man who cannot compete with him. And this will usually mean someone with less education and ambition, who cannot handle an organization of any size, nor exercise authority over many workers. 'African businessmen', as one of them admitted, 'if they employ a person who has got experience, they don't trust him very much, because they are always so suspicious about money. That comes from poverty. So they lose experienced people because they are suspicious. Also they don't give good salaries so that people will work for them for many years.'

When a businessman has spare resources to invest, he prefers to start another small concern, which he can staff with a manager whose qualifications and expectations do not threaten him, than to expand his present business beyond the critical limit of direct supervision. The proliferation of small business interests arises from an inability to delegate authority, which is partly inexperience, partly lack of suitable candidates, but partly too a failure of nerve. Businessmen dare not risk entrusting management to a responsible employee, because they lack confidence in such a relationship between Africans. They accept the professional integrity of an Asian accountant or European manager, but scarcely amongst themselves. And so they shy away from providing opportunities for Africans to prove themselves.

Two or three small concerns seem, then, more manageable than one large one, because they do not require the creation of new levels of responsibility and a new kind of organization. Usually the businesses will be owned in partnership, so that one partner is always in direct control of each; or if a shop is left to an employee, it will be of a size where the owner can maintain so close a supervision that the manager remains dependent on, and dominated by, his patron. Yet this side-stepping of the critical difficulty in the growth of an enterprise not only frustrates the development of substantial African businesses, but weakens them at their present stage, since the owners cannot be everywhere at once, and he loses his grip. 'You've got a business and you stay two or three months, and see that your business is good', warned a butcher. 'Then you go and start another business, and by the end of the year the business is not good, because you can't manage it, or you employ a manager and you don't know what he is doing.' A baker remarked, 'I know of quite a lot of people in my part who accumulated quite a lot of money. But they were trying to do so many things at the same time, they never kept proper accounts, and had to leave other people to run things. They had very good businesses but they were doing so many things, jumping from here to there, that they failed. They are now some of the poorest people in my area.' Even when businesses are left in the hands of a partner, the other owners are not relieved of responsibility, because they do not trust each other to guard their interests. And mistrust leads to a self-protective milking of the partnership's resources, which justifies and reinforces it. 'In most of these partnerships or co-ops, people tend to feel that they are being cheated or not treated fairly, so they take money from the company, going underhand, and this leads to failure. They don't trust each other.' The businessman with many interests finds his time and energy stretched to the limit. Trusting neither family, nor partners, nor experienced employees, his attention is claimed by a variety of small concerns, each in itself easy enough to supervise and control, but which together overtax his resources. So African businessmen, confronted by a scale or organization they do not know how to handle, disperse their talents, and endanger what they have already achieved without tackling the crucial obstacle to their ambitions.

There is one way out of this impasse, which one or two of the larger firms were already considering: to employ a European manager. The solution is attractive, because it avoids the hard task of pioneering a vocation of employed management within African society. But unless the European manager is to train his African replacement, his presence only perpetuates dependence on foreign skills which are scarce and expensive, and inhibits the development of indigenous enterprise. The qualities of Europeans are, besides, idealized: some who respond to the demand are likely to be doubtfully competent—men who have drifted aimlessly into overseas employment where the competition is less, or who take the job as a temporary expedient.[1]

An illustrative summary

To summarize these problems of management, let us follow the career of a hypothetical entrepreneur, putting together characteristic events from the lives of the men we interviewed.

Suppose a young man—disappointed of a place in secondary

[1] This has already become apparent in Nigeria. 'Hiring expatriate personnel involves other drawbacks besides direct expense. Some of the most successful Nigerian entreperneurs say that their experience with foreign personnel has not been favourable. They maintain that expatriates working for African firms do not exert the same degree of effort, are not as conscientious, are not as interested in the success of the business as those working for European-owned firms. . . . Furthermore, an indigenously owned firm, having limited connections overseas, finds it much more difficult to appraise the real qualifications of a potential employee and so may hire persons not having all the skills and qualifications they claim. Two prominent Nigerian businessmen have told me of such experiences. One has declared himself so dissatisfied with foreign personnel that he refrains from expanding his business— which he maintains he can do successfully with additional managerial personnel— rather than employ Europeans again in managerial positions' (Schatz, 1963).

school, and tired of aimlessly roaming country lanes—finds a job in a garage as a spanner-boy. Working beside a Sikh mechanic, watching and listening, he begins to learn how to use tools. Soon he is repairing bicycles in his spare time, slipping a spanner into his pocket as he leaves work. This is the simplest of all businesses. There are no costs: he works anywhere he can, his customers bring whatever parts their bicycles need, and labour is free, since he does not value his own leisure. Takings and profit are all one. Then, perhaps, he quarrels with his employer. Tools are missing, he is told to pay for them from his wages, he takes offence. Humiliated by his subservience as an employee, he sets up as a bicycle repairer in the market place at home. He has saved just enough to pay a month's rent for a space on the verandah of a shop, a bottle of rubber solution, patches and wrenches. Most careers in business will end here. Confusing money in hand with money gained, the bicycle repairer treats a friend too many in the bar and leaves himself with nothing for the rent. Or he gives credit to a schoolteacher, unluckily transferred, and his cousin, who does not intend to pay, on the principle that kinsmen are in business to support their relatives. Or the harvest is poor and bicycles lie untended, waiting for better rains to put them on the road again.

But suppose the bicycle repairer is shrewder, more fortunate and more determined. The enterprise moves from verandah to shop, accumulates a small stock of spare parts, branches into makeshift repairs to local cars. And he takes on his younger brother. The business now needs some simple records and super-vision. At first, the owner does not realize that he has become a manager, until the emptiness of his cash box begins to puzzle him. The younger brother has been borrowing from the takings, and selling goods on credit to his personal friends. Meanwhile, the owner has been spending less and less time in the shop. He has formed a partnership with three of his clansmen to open a grocery store in the market, invested his savings, and manages the two concerns together. He has a wife now—who sometimes minds the store when he is called away—and an acre or two of land. The trouble with his brother grows more serious. The elder tries to check stock and takings, insists that each sale is recorded, but the younger is becoming increasingly irresponsible—gets drunk, turns up late or not at all, is rude to the customers. Resentful of subordination, jealous and frustrated, the younger brother forgets his sense of failure by drinking more and airing his grievances before their father. Finally the elder gives him the bicycle-repairing business for his own, in the hope that once he is his own master, he will pull himself together. It soon collapses: but thereafter the elder brother promises himself never to trust relatives in business again.

There is trouble with the grocery store, too. It has been making so little profit, the partners are not satisfied, and the figures pencilled in an exercise book by the manager hardly tally with the stock. The manager's wife has been taking goods for her household, which is reasonable enough, since the manager draws no salary; some credit is outstanding, which may perhaps be recovered. But discussion between the partners is heavy with mistrust, and there is talk of taking matters to court. In the end, they agree to sell up the business, share the proceeds between them, and dissolve the partnership. The bicycle repairer turned grocer is back in employment again.

Years later, now an experienced mechanic, he turns to business again. The English owners of the garage where he works are anxious to sell. The European farming community is dwindling away, as Independence opens the highlands to African ownership, and the garage is going cheap. Four of the senior African employees form a partnership to buy it, pool their savings, and approach the Government for a loan. But their resources are still too few. So through their friends and acquaintances, they offer shares in a company, and at the inaugural meeting, the four partners are duly elected to be its directors. The company begins well. Profits are ploughed back to install new equipment, and visiting shareholders are impressed with the signs of progress. But there is one serious misunderstanding: the shareholders expect preference. They are disconcerted to be refused credit, like any outsider, when their accounts are overdue; and resentful when their nominees are rejected for employment. Fortunately, most of the shareholders are more concerned with the success of the enterprise than personal privileges, and a policy of businesslike impartiality is decided on. But as the business grows, more fundamental weaknesses begin to appear.

The interests of the company become increasingly diverse. It has bought land by the garage for a hotel and bar, invested in a bus company in exchange for a petrol and maintenance contract, and bought a couple of Peugeot taxis. The directors, besides, have made personal investments—partnerships in a wholesale business or a cattle ranch, farms in their homelands, a bakery. As prominent businessmen, their participation is sought by every venture. The manager is harder and harder to find at his desk, as the promotion of new enterprises and the supervision of his own and the company's affairs draw him on an endless round of meetings. He is buying supplies in Nairobi in the morning, attending a director's meeting 100 miles away in the afternoon, nursing a sick cow in the evening. The next day he is in Nairobi again to discuss an ambitious new company, or negotiating to buy another acre of land. His formidable energy is stretched to the limit. His business anxieties haunt him now: he cannot relax, sleeps badly, suffers from indigestion. But they will not let him go. He has learned from his early failures that he can trust no one, and must supervise everything himself. Yet it is an impossible task, and the company is beginning to crack.

One year, for the first time, the garage shows no profit. The two taxis, poorly serviced and old before their time, are costing far more than they make. Customers are complaining of shoddy repairs in the workshop. The bus company has been badly managed, with conductors pocketing fares and clerks fiddling the petrol accounts. The hotel is too pretentious, attracting only the local administrative élite, who are offended if refused credit, but casual about paying their bills. The company's accounts are disturbing, but not very informative. Good enough to show the profits of the buoyant years, they never explained them, and cannot now explain where they have gone. The managing director is looking for an Asian accountant, to put their affairs in order. As he swallows a whisky to make him sleep, he wonders in the small hours of the night whether to retire to his farm, and hand it all over to an English manager. He would pay him a generous salary, if only he could find one—far more than he pays himself.

Each of the incidents in this imaginary career has a real counterpart in the life-histories of businessmen we met—though not in just this form, nor all together in so encyclopaedic a tale of mistakes and misfortunes. The incompetent and irresponsible relative, the quarrelsome and mistrustful partnership, the shareholders who demand privileges, the over-extension of business interests are each familiar traps lying in wait for the unwary entrepreneur. Each is set by mistrust, or misplaced trust, and sprung by the intrusion into a business of extraneous conceptions of relationship.

In the story of the bicycle repairer, he moved further and further away from familiar patterns of working relationships at each stage in his business career. At first, he turned naturally to his brother and his wife; then to his clansmen; then to his workmates; and finally to anyone willing to buy shares in his company. Step by step, he chose his associates more exclusively for their particular value to his business—their skills or their capital—and established the relationships more formally. And he was forced to do so, because familiar patterns of association were not adaptable, and made claims upon the business which belonged to another order of relationships. His brother claimed equality, and was jealous; his wife claimed her housekeeping goods, as she would gather food from the farm; the shareholders claimed the privileges of a mutual welfare society. Yet, as he isolated the business from these extraneous demands, he also isolated himself. Disillusioned with familiar associations, he was unable to find any other basis of mutual trust, and gathered all responsibility into his own hands. The burden was beginning to exhaust him.

The limitations of African management derive from this isolation. An innovator has to distinguish his principles of organization from familiar ways, insisting on his different demands. But by detaching his principles from conventional expectations, he does not automatically reintegrate them in a new system of mutually accepted relationships. Rather, he creates a situation where unfamiliarity and misunderstanding generate a pervasive mistrust. He reacts to insecurity by bringing everything under his personal control. But this autonomy is constricting, and can stultify a successful transition to new forms of socially established relationship. Thus the two stages of social innovation—repudiation of custom, and its supplanting by new customs—are not mutually reinforcing. The first stage creates tensions and anxieties which may inhibit the evolution of the second, and the process of change is then abortive.

There is, however, a crucial aspect of the way African businessmen conceived management which we have so far only implied. Their principles of organization, being essentially contractual, did not draw upon family ties. Yet family businesses have often been successful mediators of entrepreneurship. Kinship, as the most adaptable and abiding of all principles of human co-operation, can bridge profound social transitions, providing a continuity in relationships which eases the insecurity of change, and broadens the group within which a self-protective autonomy is sought. Indian immigrants, for instance, pioneered commerce in East Africa by exploiting and adapting their traditions of family and caste loyalties. Why could the African family, too, not adapt to the needs of new economic structures, evolving a form of business which broke less completely with the past?

6

THE FAMILY IN BUSINESS

African traditions of family obligation have often been blamed for
stultifying entrepreneurship—kinsmen plunder the business of its
profits, demand jobs though they are not competent, and squander
its assets. The strength of the family group to assert its collective
well-being over the prosperity of its individual members is
believed to rob personal ambition of its reward and incentive. Yet
equally, if once the family can identify its welfare with the progress
of a business, this sense of family duty—upheld by custom and
pervading every circumstance of life—turns into a powerful
support. All the diffuse and unspoken obligations which bind
kinsfolk together then also bind them to the business. In small
concerns and great financial dynasties alike, the incorporation of a
business as the mainstay of a family's continuing prosperity gives
the enterprise a strength of purpose which transcends a single
generation or a single household. It draws on a deeply fostered
loyalty which, even when it is grudgingly extorted, no impersonal
contract of employment can match. Thus if the interests of the
business and the family can be made to converge, these consolidated relationships will withstand the uncertainties of a changing
environment more confidently than either apart. But this identi-
fication of family and business will only evolve spontaneously
where the structure of kinship, as custom defines it, conforms to
the necessary distribution of authority in business. Otherwise,
business itself may seem a disloyal activity, and the entrepreneur is
caught between his sense of family and his sense of economic
rationality. However he may try to educate his relatives in the
principles of a viable enterprise, he may be forced further and
further from any hope of reconciliation as he defends the business
from their demands.

This was the characteristic situation of the businessmen we met.

They were drawn towards an ideal of family co-operation, of mutual trust and security for themselves and their children. Yet they also valued efficiency, eager to create enterprises that would stand comparison with a sophisticated European firm; and here kinship seemed to have no place. Even if business was ultimately to serve the family—paying school fees for younger brothers, nephews, children, providing security for the future—the family had first to subordinate its interests to the business. The difficulty of resolving the dilemma left them uneasy, and sensitive to pressures which they still felt they must withstand.

This ambivalence is clearly illustrated in the remarks of the managing director of a company which owned a shop, a farm and a timberyard, as he turned over in his mind the call of his business, his family, and wider obligations to society:

You may have a man from your family who can't be trusted at all, and someone from outside who is completely trustworthy. We don't really take account of whether people are relatives or shareholders in employing people. We just look for anyone who can do the work. For instance, suppose you had a shop. Even if you had two sons, if you don't trust them well you can leave them, and employ someone from outside. But if you trust your children you'll employ them. . . . I would like to involve my family in jobs in the business, but at present it isn't possible. But I invited my brothers to buy shares, and bought shares for my daughter—she being the first born, I want her to do well. According to our traditions, if the first child goes crooked, the others will go wrong too. So I bought the shares just to make her happy: this is for her. I'd like to work with my family. On the whole, family would do better, because we would tackle the problems of the business together. And they would be more concerned if anything happened to me, for instance if I had an accident in my car. But it's true that someone who is not a brother may do better. If you consider many aspects of the business, and things at home, it may be difficult to teach a brother new things. He may not be willing to learn, since you have grown up together. A friend may be more interested in learning, to keep the friendship. All the same, in general I'd prefer to employ my family and my friends. But if I see someone

sitting doing nothing, being lazy, I'd be very angry. If someone is lazy then the business loses money and it's your own
fault. I don't want anyone in the business, friend or relative,
who doesn't work. We can co-operate in other things, but
not in business. And, also, I can't sack someone just to employ
a relative. . . . The Bible says 'love your neighbour as
yourself'. From this I have learned to take people into the
business, whether they are my brothers, or of my religion, or
others. Anyone can learn to measure planks—my brother
could do it—but I want to help others, not only my family.[T]

At every point in the discussion, as he began to follow his sense
of family, he was called back by an equal loyalty to the business. In
practice, the structure of the company was hardly based on kinship.
Two of the seven directors were cousins, and his brothers and his
daughter were amongst the other thirty shareholders. But of their
eighteen employees, only two were related to any of the directors,
and the rules of work were explicit, tough and functional:

If for instance someone is sent out to buy anything, he must
bring receipts for everything he has bought. And at the end of
each month we make a stock check, and then check against
the receipt for sales. There's an agreement with the workers,
that if they lose anything which is their responsibility, they
must pay for it. Even if it is five cents you have to pay. For
instance, if a salesman loses three shillings in his accounts, he
has to pay. If you lose more than your salary, you lose all your
pay and have to find the rest. This is made absolutely clear to
everyone when they are taken on. I had to pay a small sum
myself when I had a discrepancy in my accounts. It is the same
with credit. The company as such doesn't allow credit. It is
entirely the salesman's responsibility if he wants to give
credit to his friends. If the customer doesn't pay, then he has
to repay the debt himself. All the salesmen are warned of this
when they are taken on. If the salesman doesn't have the
money himself to take the debtor to court, the company will
pay the court costs for him, and recover them from the court's
award. But if the case fails, then the salesman has to pay the
court costs back to the company himself.

If someone is late, a deduction is made from his pay, or if
there is much work he may be able to make up for time later.

But if someone rings beforehand to say he will be late, particularly if he lives at a distance, then he may be excused. All the work is supervised, and people are warned if they are not doing their work properly, and this is reported to the directors. We keep a record. We have sacked several people—and one of them was a shareholder. The workers are told when we take them on that the director concerned will be supervising their work.[T]

The discipline of the organization was, then, regulated by a contract of service, carefully explained to each recruit, and binding on everyone—director, shareholder, cousin or brother alike. And this conception of business relationships represents the preference of most African businessmen—not so much because the ideal of corporate family enterprise has never attracted them, but because they seldom find a way to assimilate kinship successfully within a hierarchy of managerial authority.

As a whole, only a fifth of the businessmen in the market centres and 9 per cent of the men supported by the ICDC preferred their relatives as employees or business associates, and believed that they would be more trustworthy than outsiders. This minority view argued, firstly, that kinsfolk most deserved the help a business could offer, and would repay it loyally. 'It's an advantage as to progress, and to help their financial difficulties and their education. It's better to help the family than people outside. And your family work more efficiently, with all their hearts. They do better than outsiders.' Secondly, relatives would identify with the business. 'They look after the property you've got, knowing it is *our* property.' And lastly, the family interest was seen as an assurance of continuity. 'If my sons weren't with me and I died now, my property would get lost.' But the sense of family unity, which makes the property of one the property of all was more often argued as an objection than an asset: a relative treats your business as his own, puts his hand in the till, comes and goes as he likes. And above all, he will not take orders:

You see, if you bring your family into business, and if he feels that he is not getting enough—if he feels he is not getting money as I am getting, because he sees the money coming in, and doesn't realize all the expenses—then he won't work well, and make argument. So I think it's not good. That's my feeling. All the same, I couldn't refuse. But if he didn't work well, I'd have to get rid of him. He'll have to learn that the business is mine.

No relatives have joined me in the business yet. I don't find any advantage there—unless when I am thinking of expanding the business, I might ask them to contribute finance. But as employees, relatives might be disobedient, and refuse to sweep the floor, for instance, and can't be so reliable. Once I employ my brother here, he thinks I can't order him about, I can't sack him, I'll have mercy on him—an older or a younger brother, it doesn't make any difference.

It is my experience, when you have your relatives working with you they feel part of the job, and either come late, or give excuses, or expect you to be fairer to them than to others. I think they are not good as partners either. I don't know—it's my own view—I get on better with others than with my family.

You may take someone as a tractor driver who knows the job alright, but then the relatedness comes into his mind, and he won't work well. He begins to think this is something different from a job because he is your brother.

There are two types of people. One is a stranger, who when he is employed is very careful in the business and respects the manager. The second is a relative, who comes and because he knows the business belongs to his brother, tends to relax and be proud and careless. From my experience I find people from far off or from outside the family are more reliable, because they fear and respect me more.[T]

So it is hard to establish a relationship of employer and employee, because on the one side, there is 'a sort of jealous consciousness' which makes the employee resentful of his kinsman's authority, and on the other, a fear of embarrassment which inhibits the employer from exercising that authority—'I wouldn't like to employ relatives because they might spoil the work, and then if I accused them I'd feel ashamed because of this family relationship'. The tension is compounded by all the differences which beset any family, and endure with the bitter tenacity of intimate conflicts—quarrels over land, the ingratitude of the young, inheritance, envy:

Relatives know so much about you. If your parents were poor they will know how you came up, and they'll despise you. They say they have helped to make you rich, and they will try to ruin your business. This can even go to the extent of relatives boycotting your shop, rather than make you rich by buying from you. And if your father was poor, even if you can do well, they don't want to work for you. . . . If you do take on someone you've been brought up with, he knows your parents and background too well. There may have been quarrels because of differences over land, and these will be brought up in the business. For example, if you sack a relative his parents may complain that you hate him, and then they bring up old family quarrels. To avoid all this it's better not to employ relatives.[T]

For such reasons as these, a third of the market businessmen, and nearly half the businessmen supported by the ICDC, said they preferred not to employ or be associated with relatives.

This mistrust of relatives grows out of experience, as much as any generally recognized maxim. Each businessman who repeated in much the same phrases his fear of the jealousy and insubordination of kinsmen seemed to express a personal discovery, often describing how they had been let down:

Relatives are less reliable—we know this, because we have tried to employ them. They were more than non-relatives to start with. But they would borrow money, and if we deducted it from someone's salary, he complained. They ended owing us 3,000 shillings—that's my cousin—so we moved them slowly by slowly to other work, so they couldn't realize what we were doing, and they left the work.

Originally I used to work with my relatives. There were two, I employed one as a turn-boy once, and he used to just sit and watch the others. When the driver and the others complained, he told them that the work was theirs. I told him this attitude wouldn't do, and I sacked him. Afterwards he came back, but he was just as bad. Another was a mechanic. He used to go off home and stay for a fortnight, and when he came back, he expected to be paid just as if he had been working. When I refused he bore me a grudge, so I sacked him.

The best workers were not related to me at all. One was my brother, in fact, and when I went to Nairobi he became troublesome, wasn't working, and abused the other workers. So I dismissed him—which caused a lot of trouble with my relatives, but in the end I convinced them that work must come first.

My brother sold the piece of land meant for me. Then he went to learn driving. People used to ask me, why don't you employ your brother as a driver? So I took him on, but he never came to report to me, and almost wrecked the lorry. He was putting paraffin in the engine, and when the fan-belt broke he tied it up with a piece of sisal, and he forgot to put oil in the engine. He never told me anything. At last I had to go and get the lorry back, and it was almost scrap. None of my brothers have agreed to be trained in the job. Some of them are jealous—they think I am just working for myself.[T]

In business never deal with relatives—that's my experience—because they feel they've got the same rights as you. For instance the Mombasa branch—it just went down and down. There was money coming in, I'm fairly sure of that, but my brother said there was none. But with my brother in Kampala the experience has been very good. This brother is very young and fears me. The other was big-headed. But on the whole you're better not with relatives.

The highest proportion of businessmen, however, did not believe that relatives were likely to be either more or less reliable than outsiders. It depended on character and competence: the relationship itself was unimportant. If a brother or cousin was hardworking and able, they saw no reason to refuse him. But they were not prepared to dismiss some other worker to make room for him. For these men, family was simply irrelevant. A few were more ambivalent: 'If he's a good person, he's more reliable than other people, because he feels he belongs to that business. He knows that if he's in difficulties he can be assisted by the business. But if he is not so good, then it's worse than with someone else, because you can't control him. He'll take what he likes from the business, and you'll never know.' Nearly half of both samples of businessmen held these views, as Table 6 shows:

TABLE 6   *Attitude to relatives in business*

	Market businessmen	*ICDC-supported businessmen*
Prefers relatives	19%	9%
Prefers non-relatives	35%	46%
Indifferent or ambivalent	46%	45%
Total %	100%	100%
Total no.*	824	85

* Excluding those who did not answer, or answered unclearly.

Most businessmen clearly did not want to base their working relationships on family connections: kinship was either irrelevant or a nuisance. And principle influenced practice—those who mistrusted relatives employed them least often; those who preferred them employed most. But despite their opinions, they were drawn into association with kinsmen more often than they said they wished to be. Even though, amongst the businessmen in the market centres who employed anyone at all, those who mistrusted relatives were less likely to employ them, nearly a third still did so —compared with three-quarters of those who preferred relatives and about two-fifths of the indifferent. Amongst the ICDC-supported businessmen the divergence of principle and practice is wider: 68 per cent of those who mistrusted relatives were associated with at least one of them as employee, partner or shareholder, in one or another of their businesses. The proportion is less than for those who preferred relatives (86 per cent) or those who were indifferent (81 per cent); and they also employed fewer.[1] But clearly the family still had a hold even on the businessmen who feared the risks of kinship.

On the whole, however, though family ties were common enough in both partnerships and employment, they were not dominant, and they intruded least into the more sophisticated businesses. In the market centres—apart from two-thirds of the businesses owned by a single proprietor—46 per cent were partnerships exclusively of relatives, 9 per cent included both relatives and outsiders, and in 45 per cent the partners were not

[1] Three-quarters of the businessmen who preferred relatives were associated with two or more of them in business. But amongst those who mistrusted relatives, only a quarter had as many as two relatives working with them.

related at all. So purely family partnerships accounted for only 15 per cent of all the businesses together. A little over half the businesses had employees, and of these 57 per cent employed no relatives, 19 per cent both relatives and others, and 24 per cent relatives only.

Of the 87 ICDC-supported businesses, 40 were owned by a single proprietor, 27 were partnerships, 16 private companies, two public companies and two co-operatives. Amongst the jointly owned businesses, in 28 none of the owners were related, in six all related, and in 13 mixed. Businesses in which members of the same family predominated accounted for only a fifth of those which were jointly owned. The commonest ties between business associates were not family, but having worked or been at school together. At first sight, however, family relationships were much more frequent between the owners and the workers in their business: 52 per cent employed at least one relative, 30 per cent more than one. But the businesses often had ten or twenty employees, and relatives remained a small proportion of the work force—3 per cent of the 850 in the industrial enterprises, and 14 per cent of the 550 in commerce (a third of whom were the owners' wives). Nor was this due to lack of family applicants. Half the industrial and most of the commercial businessmen had been approached by members of their family for jobs. Two-thirds of them had turned down all requests, and most of the others had rebuffed some. 'I have refused many, and it is indeed very embarrassing', as the director of a prominent company confessed. 'I handle the situation as it comes. It's sometimes very hard to refuse. But I prefer them taking a job elsewhere, even to help them with money. In principle, I don't like it. If it had been a family business, that would be another matter.' If the business was owned in partnership, they could argue that family favouritism would upset the other owners; or they asked what jobs their relatives thought they could do, and then pointed out that no such work was available; or protested that they could not sack a competent worker to make room for a relative. These reasons were not always taken without resentment. But the businessmen seem to have found that, if they were firm, their principles were reluctantly accepted in the end. Essentially, they were trying to insist on the difference between the modern and the traditional economy. As a clothing manufacturer put it: 'At home on the

farm, the work is done by the family. Here it is a matter of skill.'
And a characteristic comment recurred again and again in our
interviews: 'If I employ relatives, they will think it is my farm. . . .'

For the most part, then, the businesses were family businesses
only in the sense that they often employed relatives, and—if they
were jointly owned—often included relatives amongst the partners
or shareholders. But they were not characteristically organized to
further the interests of the family, as an aim of the enterprise. The
claims of kinship were generally held to be subordinate to the
interests of the business, and allowable only where they seemed
compatible with it. This bias towards businesslike impartiality
included friends and fellow tribesmen too. We asked the businessmen in the market centres to choose, for example, between two
hypothetical employees: 'Suppose two men came to you for a job.
One is recommended by a friend of yours, as a hardworking man
who could do the job. The other is a stranger, but he has more
education and experience. Which would you choose, the first or
the second?' Only a quarter chose the friend of a friend, and 58 per
cent the stranger. The rest argued cannily that neither personal
recommendation nor paper qualifications were to be trusted, and
said they would test both applicants themselves. The businessmen
wanted experienced workers, who could be expected to prove
competent: friends might well not know what the job required,
and as likely as not were exploiting friendship to secure a favour.
So personal recommendations were suspect both for their
judgment and their motive.

Small rural businesses depend on local employees, since they
cannot provide accommodation for outsiders. Their workers will
naturally be of the same tribe as their employer. But the ICDC-
supported businesses were often established in tribally mixed
townships, and could sometimes house their employees on their
plots. They were less bound to employ their fellow tribesmen. In
practice, 37 per cent had workers of different tribes, and a third of
these businesses also included workers of different races—an
Italian mechanic, an English labour foreman, Asian clerk or
accountant. And though the rest were all of one tribe, only a fifth
of the businesses recruited all their labour from the community
round about them. Amongst the 47 jointly owned businesses, six
included partners or directors of different races, six of different
tribes only, and six of different districts. Yet, even though most of

the businesses were tribally homogeneous, 86 per cent of the businessmen still repudiated any tribal preferences. All that mattered was competence for the job. Even the dozen who did prefer local recruits were influenced more by commercial arguments than tribal loyalty: 'Customers prefer to meet local people they know in the shop', or more ruthlessly, 'People from here haven't the experience to demand higher salaries. We get trouble over pay from outsiders.'

In everything the businessmen said about family or tribal loyalties—whether they were discussing employment, partnership, or the claims of kinship, whether their businesses were large or small, owned individually or in company—their answers reflected the interests of the business far more than the interests of family or tribe. They did not always see these interests as conflicting, but few saw kinship as a likely asset to business relationships. Although family partnerships are common, and many businessmen employ relatives at one time or another, they did not conceive this as the creation of family concerns. They seemed less influenced by family loyalty than by the convenience of looking for help amongst the people they knew best. Once recruited, relatives were not expected to claim upon the relationship. They were chosen for their usefulness to the business. If the family were the readiest place to look for hardworking, honest and competent associates, this did not mean that the business had any duty to be useful to the family. Rather, the family as a source or recruits was on trial: and the evidence showed that it was not, as a rule, particularly reliable. Business was a new kind of activity, part of the modern economy which Kenya was trying to create. It could not be bound by the working relationships familiar to a community of peasant farmers. Once this was acknowledged, relatives might be considered on their merits.

The kinship is repudiated

If this creed is dominant, why should African society repudiate the family business so generally? These principles are held by young and old, educated and uneducated alike. In the market centres, age, years of schooling, birth order, the size or profit of the business had none of them any discernible influence on the businessmen's attitudes towards family. Nor did they influence what businessmen did, except that the more profitable enterprises slightly less often employed relatives. The figures for the ICDC-supported business do suggest that both younger and more educated men mistrust relatives more, but the differences are all between the mistrustful and the indifferent; the small minority who prefer relatives remains the same. So it does not seem as if these attitudes stem from the influence of progressive modernizers.

Nor are they imitated from the model of successful small-scale enterprises most familiar to Kenya Africans. Most of the garages, sawmills, dry cleaners, workshops, builders, wholesalers and retail shops were established in Kenya by immigrants from India. At the time of our enquiry, these Asian firms still dominated wholesaling and small-scale manufacturing or service industry, and African business had to compete with them. They employed many African workers, and an African craftsman was more likely to have served his apprenticeship with an Asian than a European employer. Yet African businessmen seem to have been altogether uninfluenced by the Asian example. For Asian businessmen endorse just those principles of family and communal loyalty which their African counterparts reject. We interviewed a 10 per cent sample of Asian businessmen in Nairobi, and the Asian shopkeepers in two townships about twenty miles outside. Both their attitudes and practices were characteristically different from the African businessmen. Most of them preferred family associates in business, and seldom formed partnerships with anyone outside the family circle (Table 7).

TABLE 7   *Attitudes to family of African and Asian businessmen*

	% preferring relatives in business	% of employers employing relatives	% of joint ownerships between relatives only
	(100% =)	(100% =)	(100% =)
Market businessmen	19% (824)	43% (466)	46% (268)
ICDC-supported businessmen	9% (85)	52% (87)	13% (47)
Asian businessmen	60% (278)	63% (252)	82% (154)

These differences can be partly explained by the greater poverty of African society. Family businesses are only possible when the family can provide most of the capital and managerial skill it needs. The Indian immigrants who pioneered business in East Africa came from a commercial class in Gujerat where, without looking beyond their family circle, they could find both money and reliable assistants. Their children in turn grew up in the shop: serving behind the counter became as natural a part of their childhood as herding goats to an African boy. Even youngsters of fourteen might be sent on responsible commercial assignments, trading on their own far from home. The poorer the community, and the more recent its experience of business, the wider an entrepreneur must forage for his resources. If he does not depend on the family, he contracts few obligations to it. He must respect more the interests of those on whom he does depend—the government agencies or banks to which he turns for loans, his partners or shareholders, the experienced foreman from another tribe who alone understands the technical operations of the enterprise.

This interpretation is born out by the differences between the market businesses and the businesses supported by the ICDC, and especially by the differences amongst the ICDC-supported businesses between industry and commerce. The industrial enterprises were the most highly capitalized and the most specialized. In establishing their businesses, the industrialists needed to find partners with relevant assets to contribute—a suitable site, technical knowledge, experience of the market—which their families could not provide. In fact, none of the jointly owned industrial firms were exclusively family affairs, and in two-thirds of them none of the partners or directors were related at all. By contrast, a third of the commercial partnerships included kinsmen only. Similarly, no specialized technical skills are needed to run a wholesale or retail shop, but a garage breaks down without experienced mechanics. Qualified men were hard to find. An African garage proprietor, for instance, willing to pay generously for a competent mechanic of any tribe or race, is not likely to see family loyalties as relevant to his situation. The industrial businessmen were, therefore, more often mistrustful of relatives, and less likely to employ them. They were also far less often approached by their family, which suggests that relatives themselves recognized the need for specialized qualifications. So only 36 per cent of the industrial firms, compared with 70 per cent in commerce, employed any members of the owners' families. Conversely, half the industrialists employed workers of tribes and races other than their own, compared with less than a quarter of the shopkeepers, and hardly any of them defended tribal preferences in principle.

Though the scarcity of resources can account in part for the African rejection of family businesses, it does not explain why even the small rural shopkeepers, who need little capital or specialized skill, still seem characteristically different in both principle and practice from their Asian counterparts. The Asians, as a minority excluded from agriculture by colonial policy, could bring much stronger sanctions to bear in their business relationships. A man who cheated his family or caste could be ostracized from commercial employment, and had few other sources of livelihood to turn to. It was as if an African had been expelled from the community where his rights to land lay. But so long as business remains a peripheral activity within African communities, the sanctions an African employer can apply to his kinsmen are relatively weak. If he sacks them, they can find jobs elsewhere, or return to farming. Since the business itself is not a family interest, but an individual achievement or a concern in which outsiders too are involved, the family has no reason to support the businessman's side of the argument. Indeed, jealousies and long-standing disputes may bias family opinion the other way. So, unlike an Asian community, an African kin group does not identify its own welfare with the welfare of commerce, because commerce is marginal to the landholding on which the family concentrates its concern.

Even so, the weakness of sanctions does not explain why many businessmen felt they had less control over relatives than outsiders. If the family will not intervene to reinforce an employer's authority over his kinsman, then the threat of dismissal is neither more nor less serious than if kinship were not involved. But the businessmen foresaw, not only that the family might resent the sacking of relatives and inhibit the exercise of their authority as employers, but also that jealousy and insubordination were likely. If Asian families do not face the same tensions, the explanation seems to lie in a fundamentally different tradition. The Hindu joint family lived together in one household, and farmed its land corporately. But this has never been the pattern of the domestic economy amongst the agricultural peoples of East Africa. However great the authority of the family head, each married son was entitled to his share of the family lands, each wife entitled to her hut. As a Kikuyu businessman put it, 'The Asian way of life is different. They live together in one house. They never quarrel. Our tradition is different. When you marry you have your own home. You may live near your father, but he has to build a house for you of your own. I live in the same block with my brother, but we hardly meet socially—only when we have to discuss family affairs.'

The management of the family estate in East Africa has been governed by the principle of sharing out equal portions, generation by generation.[1] For a married man to work for his brother is intrinsically humiliating, unless he has his own stake in the enterprise. At best, the arrangement is a form of apprenticeship, until he is ready to launch out on his own. Similarly, once his son is married, a father cannot expect him to accept the status of an employee, unless he also gives him his own share in the enterprise: and then the father faces the difficulty of providing the equivalent for his other sons. A tradition of dividing and subdividing family property works for land, if land is not too scarce, but not for a firm whose viability depends on the continuing integration of its activities. The Hindu tradition of corporate family activity therefore fits business much more readily. Sons and brothers do not claim a share in the enterprise, in the sense of any personal right. They are simply part of it, their contribution and their interests absorbed into the whole. African custom is fundamentally much more individualistic: according to his status, each member has explicit personal claims upon the family's economic assets.

[1] Each society had, of course, its own customs of inheritance. But as a general simplification, land was formally divided between a man's sons at his death, more or less equally, and the process of division began in practice earlier, as soon as each son married and established his own household. For instance, to take three Kenya examples, amongst the Kikuyu, 'After the death of the father the land passed on to his sons. . . . The eldest son who had assumed the title of *moramati* (titular or trustee) had no more rights than his brothers, except the title; he could not sell the land without the agreement of his brothers who had the same full cultivation rights on the pieces of land which they cultivated as well as those which were cultivated by their respective mothers' (Kenyatta, p. 32). Amongst the Gusii, when the head of the homestead died, if his sons were already married, 'Division of the land, at least among the houses, proceeds apace and can result in the formation of separate homesteads within a few years. . . . With the division of land amongst the brothers, each locating his homestead on his share, a full cycle has been completed' (LeVine, 1964, pp. 72–3). Amongst the Taita, 'Over time, a substantial proportion of a father's land is divided among his future heirs, since every son has the right to have land assigned to his first wife for cultivation' (Harris, p. 141).

So family relationships in business are likely to be uneasy, unless there is a sense of equal partnership and mutual responsibility. At the same time, any conflicts over the division of land will spill over into business associations, aggravating jealousies and mistrust. As the density of population increases, it becomes harder and harder to respect the custom of equal shares, without sub-dividing holdings to the point where they are no longer economically viable. Inevitably, some must be dispossessed of their traditional rights. Throughout the fertile, highly populated regions of Kenya, a profound revision of customary land-holding is taking place, as some are forced to surrender their claims upon family estate. Where land has been consolidated, and registered under individual titles, as in Kikuyu country, the process has been rationalized. The owner becomes legally entitled to designate his heir—and he is forced to choose, since the law also forbids sub-division into uneconomic units. Even where consolidation and registration have not yet taken place, it is often no longer practicable to insist upon a worthwhile share. Land-holding is therefore evolving from family to individual entitlement. The process is bound to generate conflict, as the struggle to retain a portion of the family land works itself out—a widow's children are ignored in the redistribution of consolidated farms; an elder brother sells the land a younger brother believes should have been his own; sons are disinherited. And as the process works itself out, amicably or in bitterness, kinship loses its hold over the allocation of economic opportunities: farming, as much as industry or commerce, becomes a private business.

If this is so, attitudes towards family should be influenced by population density. People from regions where the pressure on land is greatest would be more likely to have experienced family conflicts, and to question whether the traditional claims of kinship can still be honoured anywhere.[1] The regional differences between the market businesses seem to support this implication. The density of population varied from about 70 people to an acre, on the fertile spur of mountains settled by the Kalenjin, to 600 to 1,000

[1] We suggested earlier that the family concern with land prevented it from associating its collective interest with business. This might imply that the more landless families there are, the more the family will identify with business, and support sanctions against insubordinate relatives employed there. In the long run this may be so. But meanwhile, land shortage seems to create conflicts without leading family interests to converge on a new institution of mutual welfare—except, perhaps, education.

in Kikuyu country and Western Kenya. Nearly half the Kalenjin businessmen thought relatives more reliable than outsiders as business associates, but the proportion declines to less than a fifth amongst Kikuyu, Kisii, Luhyia and Luo, where pressure on the land is severe. Amongst the peoples from areas of intermediate densities—Taita, Kamba and the coastal tribes—between a quarter and a third preferred family associates. Employment follows roughly the same pattern: two-thirds of the Kalenjin employers took on relatives (slightly more amongst the Taita and coastal tribes), about half the Kamba, and a third or less of the Kikuyu, Kisii, and Luo employers. Although the correspondence of density and attitudes is not perfect, there seems to be a relationship between them, allowing for the crudeness of population per acre as a measure of land shortage and differences in traditional custom from one people to another.[1]

The East African family is, then, characteristically under too great a strain, too poor in resources, and too bound by the principle of sharing out to offer a system of relationships readily adaptable to the organization of a business. The family estate is not a corporate interest, but an entitlement from which each, in due time, can claim his portion. A father's duty is not to rule, but to provide. So the intrusion of kinship into business confuses managerial authority by claims to equality and independence. Unable to meet these demands, the employer provokes jealousy and insubordination, and faces the embarrassing task of disciplining his kinsmen. He would prefer not to become involved with family at all, or at least to make sure that any relative who joins him understands the relationship as a business arrangement, governed by the same rules of competence, discipline and effort that would apply to any other worker. He can afford to question the claims of kinship, because he is not usually beholden to the family. It has not financed or promoted his enterprise, and it no longer even controls his chances of acquiring land. If he is successful in business, he can buy a much more substantial farm than any

[1] Differences in traditional systems of kinship are probably also important influences on the attitudes towards family in business, but to understand them would have called for a far more extensive enquiry into the traditions of each people than we could have undertaken. Crude as the measures are, density of population does seem to be associated with attitudes. It is hard to see otherwise why, for instance, Kikuyu attitudes and practices towards family in business should be more like the Luo than the Kamba or Taita, whose language and traditions are more closely related to their own.

that is likely to come to him through the family estate. He is free to judge kinsmen on their worth.

Family businesses may still evolve in the future. As more and more families become dispossessed of land, as children grow up to look on business as their natural environment, as a commercial class consolidates, business may come to be the centre of a family's prosperity, its sense of identity and continuity. But for the present, business is too new. Most businessmen are the first generation in their family to turn to commerce or industry for a livelihood, and their children are still young. Even if the ideal of founding a family enterprise appeals to them, for the time being the relatives from whom they can recruit business associates are mostly of the same generation, where the rivalries are greatest, the sense of authority and continuity least. In the market centres, for instance, nearly two-thirds of the family relationships involved in business partnerships were between brothers or brothers-in-law: only 12 per cent were between father and son or son-in-law. In the ICDC-supported businesses, 41 per cent were between brothers, 36 per cent relationships by marriage, but only one involved relatives of different generations. Similarly, 30 per cent of the relatives employed in the market businesses were brothers or brothers-in-law (and occasionally sisters), 17 per cent cousins, 9 per cent wives: sons or sons-in-law account for only 22 per cent. In the ICDC-aided industries, two-thirds of the relatives employed were brothers or brothers-in-law, 19 per cent wives, sons or sons-in-law only 15 per cent. In commerce the pattern was different: there a third of the employees were wives, 22 per cent brothers. But the sons were still only 11 per cent.[1] When the businessmen spoke of

[1] In more detail, the distribution of relatives in business, according to the relationship, was:

	Brother or sister	Wife's brother or sister	Son or daughter	Daughter's husband	Cousin	Uncle/ nephew	Wife	Other relation- ships	(Total no. of relatives in business)
Markets:									
Partnerships	49%	12%	10%	2%	15%	8%	–	4%	(168)
Employees	24%	6%	20%	2%	17%	14%	9%	8%	(234)
ICDC									
Employees in industry:	51%	11%	11%	4%	–	4%	19%	–	(27)
Employees in commerce:	21%	1%	11%	–	12%	7%	32%	16%	(76)

relatives in business, they were thinking of brothers, wives and cousins, not of father and son.

As the men we met grow older, they may begin to look towards their children to carry on what they have achieved, and train them for their inheritance. A few spoke of this hopefully. More often they expected their children to establish their independence, and exploit the education the business had paid for in occupations of more prestige. A pattern of relationship where a son works for his father until he retires, and only then inherits all his achievement, is alien to East African traditions. Wealth is not held intact from generation to generation, but distributed in education, bride-wealth, land to establish each son in his manhood. Grandchildren, not property, embody the family's immortality. The evolution of family businesses must therefore depend on a profound change in the conception of a father's authority. Such a change may well come in time, as the family adapts to shifts in the structure of opportunities. Meanwhile, the prevailing idea of business organization tends to confirm principles in which kinship has no place.

7

CUSTOMERS AND COMPETITORS

We have tried to show how lack of confidence in partners and workers forces an entrepreneur to rely on direct personal control, constricting the scale of his organization; and why family ties cannot compensate for this mistrust and link business relationships to long-standing loyalties. The same lack of confidence also troubles the external dealings of the business. It is caught between the mistrust of its suppliers and its own mistrust of its customers. As a struggling African concern in an economy dominated by Europeans and Asians, it has to accept stricter terms of business than established competitors of other races, because its competence and probity are on trial. Yet it cannot readily pass this strict dealing on to its African customers, since the system of exchange in a community of peasant farmers is governed by a different understanding from a modern commercial economy. The business risks losing their goodwill by demands which they would interpret as harsh and rigid. Thus the unevenness of social change creates sharp disjunctions in the conventions of economic exchange between just those sectors of the economy which an African entrepreneur is bound to cross. He has to overcome the disparity between the expectations of rural Africa, and of national or international commercial networks. But he works with very slender resources. He has little time to learn from his mistakes, to convince his customers of the financial constraints upon his service, or earn enough respect from bankers and suppliers to make them ease their conditions.

Take, for instance, the experience of a prosperous farmer from a backward region, who started a business as a plough contractor. His people did not practise ploughing, and he had never seen it until he ran away from home to join the army—the first African from his district ever to enlist. 'When I was in the army I went to Somaliland. I used to walk about when I was off duty, and one day

I came across a woman and a child, who were ploughing with two oxen. They had ploughed a big plot of ground. This stuck in my mind, and when I came home I took up the example, and thought I would do the same.' At first he ploughed with cattle, but found it too slow. So he bought a tractor with a government loan, and began hiring it out to his neighbours. Then the troubles began. The driver was inexperienced, and the tractor needed constant repair—'And the trouble is, when you own something and don't know how it works, it's very hard to be master over the man who operates it.' He had to pay cash for fuel and maintenance, which came to much more than he expected, but could not exact the same terms from his customers. 'Often I didn't know whether I'd get paid or not. I'd do the work properly, and then the man who hired me would jump here and there, making excuses. If I did a job worth thirty shillings, people would pay five or ten, and then I'd let them forget the rest, for fear of not getting work from them another time. I never took people to court. I was afraid they'd turn against modern ideas and the use of hired tractors, because they'd associate it with court cases.ᵀ' Against these odds, the business failed. To maintain his equipment he had to deal on impersonal commercial terms with an Asian garage and a European motor agent. His customers treated his services as they would any help from one farmer to his neighbour, as an obligation to be repaid when they could. Yet as an attempt to pioneer new methods it was ultimately successful. 'There was very little hiring at the beginning, because people didn't know how useful a tractor could be, and it was expensive. But now people realize its value, and there would be much work. Even though I failed, I have made the whole district to understand. There is one co-op tractor, but there would be need for more, even up to twelve. Even people are booking it in advance. And nowadays people are more willing to pay.ᵀ' But for himself, he was still too heavily in debt for the original loan to gain the reward of his innovation.

Most African businesses, like this plough contractor, have to mediate between sectors of the economy in which their own standing, and the demands upon them, are profoundly different. Their customers are Africans—even among the ICDC-supported businesses, only about a quarter sold to other races too, and in the market centres hardly at all. But their suppliers are mostly Asian or European. Three-quarters of the ICDC-supported businesses bought entirely from Asian and European agents, only 8 per cent entirely from Africans.[1] In the market centres—where butchers and hotel keepers buy largely from the local farmers—18 per cent got all their supplies from Africans, but a third still depended exclusively on Asian wholesalers and the delivery vans of European companies. Patel or Shah's store in the nearest township remained their chief source of groceries, cloth and hardware. Within this economic network which supplied them, they were marginal—too insecure to be trusted with much credit, buying too little to be offered the best terms. But within their own community they appeared prosperous and fortunate. They were expected to be open-handed, as befitted an important man—generous towards the hard up, the provider of his kinsfolk, the patron of his drinking circle.

These contradictory pressures hemmed a small African enterprise between customers and competitors whose influence could each, in different ways, ruin its chances of growth, and constricted the profitable opportunities it could hope to exploit. If it sought a wide market, it faced larger established firms who traded on more favourable terms. But if it served a local community beyond the reach of powerful competition, it had great difficulty in manipulating demand without hazarding its slender margin of profit. Here the problems of credit were crucial: if it refused credit, stonily ignoring the hardships of a community where cash in hand was always scarce, it gave up its best chances of attracting customers, but if it did extend credit it risked crippling losses, since it could bring few sanctions to bear to ensure that it was paid.

The dilemma of credit

The customers of an African business are likely to include the poorer employees, whose monthly wage soon goes in rent, electricity, water rate, school fees, taxes, urgent debts, leaving little change from 100 or 200 shillings to carry them to the next pay day. A dry cleaner estimated: 'About 50 per cent of our customers are

[1] Half the commercial businesses do, however, get some supplies from state agencies, such as the Kenya National Trading Corporation, or the Kenya Meat Commission, which—since they are government-owned—could be considered as African suppliers also. But these agencies are European-managed, and deal on strictly commercial terms.

poor people, and from these we get more business—people with one or two suits. People who are better off just put their suits in a wardrobe and don't come so often. I don't know, I may be wrong, but I'm against having different classes of service at different prices. I think our customers are more the ordinary man.' But the ordinary man, employee of farmer, lives on his expectations—the next wage packet, the next harvest. Without credit, he can buy very little. Yet his poverty makes him least likely to pay his debts. Most African businesses, therefore, give credit, lose money by it, and regard it as one of the commonest reasons for failure.

Three-quarters of the market businesses and 62 per cent of the ICDC-supported businessmen gave credit to some of their customers. They tried to discriminate, restricting it to schoolteachers and government employees with regular salaries, to frequent customers who had proved trustworthy in the past. But in spite of their precautions, all of these business with ICDC loans, and 64 per cent in the markets, had still suffered substantial bad debts. The losses might be no more than 100 shillings, or as much as 10,000, but even apparently trivial sums may represent a month's earnings. Most of these businesses were probably losing at least 10 per cent of their annual profits through bad debts.

There was little they could do to recover them. Defaulters could not be traced, or the debt was not adequately recorded, or a continual promise to pay seemed more hopeful than legal pressure. Losses of several thousand shillings might be made up of amounts so small that prosecution would take more time and money than it was worth, for a court order which might never be enforced. Even when the amount warranted it, many businessmen hestitated to act, for fear of unpopularity. 'Up to 1965, I've got 10,000 shillings of bad debts', a wholesaler admitted. 'But you know, these are my people. I can't take them to court. I just ask them to pay. You just have to try politely to persuade them. If you take them to court, they may become your enemy.' And a metalworker said: 'I have taken some to the advocates. But on the whole, it's not advisable to take people to court, you'll lose your reputation. People will say you're too harsh, and start spreading rumours that you're the kind of man who will take someone to a lawyer as soon as he's a week late paying his bills. And that way you'll lose your customers. It is better for them to make you a promise, however little it is, and however long it takes.ᵀ' In practice, only a fifth of market businesses and two-fifths of the ICDC-supported businesses with outstanding debts had ever prosecuted any of their defaulters.

In themselves, these difficulties are common to retail businesses anywhere in the world. Apart from the fear that prosecution will lose the goodwill of the community, the other reasons against pursuing debts are probably as persuasive in the most sophisticated economies, where the extension of credit is more liberal, and the rate of default as high. The Asian businesses we questioned in and near Nairobi gave credit just as often, and suffered just as much from bad debts, as the African shopkeepers in the rural markets. They were more likely to prosecute—45 per cent with debts to collect had taken court action as against 19 per cent in the markets—but even here they differed little from the businessmen with ICDC loans. They were, however, in a much stronger position to withstand these losses. They dominated commerce, doing a much larger volume of business, including lines which their African competitors did not carry. They could buy more cheaply, too, and so adjust their prices to compensate for loss. Above all, they could obtain more generous credit from their suppliers, partly because they were well established, and partly because they were dealing with men of their own community. In our sample, 42 per cent of the Asian businesses in Nairobi bought on between 30 and 90 days credit and 19 per cent on longer terms: but only 15 per cent of the ICDC-supported businesses could get credit for more than a month, and half of them bought entirely for cash.[1] An Asian shopkeeper in difficulties may be able to re-finance his debts, appealing to a relative or fellow caste-member in the wholesale trade to guarantee his credit, but an African businessman has no personal ties within the commercial network on which he can claim. He represents a threat to the immigrant community which has created and lives by this network, grudgingly tolerated and alien to it. So unless his customers pay him promptly, he faces continual impoverishment: cash in hand to replenish his stock is always less than his sales, and so long as his suppliers' terms are inflexible, the business can only go down. Even when the customer can be trusted to pay in time, the delay may put the business in

[1] We did not ask the market businessmen about credit from suppliers, but their chances would certainly be less than the retailers with ICDC loans, amongst whom 69 per cent bought only for cash, and 12 per cent obtained over one month's credit. Some African business who bought for cash could have got credit, but the prices were then raised to a level which they reckoned they could not afford.

,eopardy: a government department, for instance, may take so long to pass an invoice through the bureaucracy that the business meanwhile loses further orders, its stock exhausted, and more materials unobtainable until the government work is paid.

African businessmen are well aware of these dangers. The commonest advice they would offer to a newcomer to business is to give no credit, or only with great caution. A picture, popular with businessmen, hangs above the counter of shops all over the country, printed in Britain or America many years ago. The left side shows a harassed young man, hair tousled, his papers scattered about his desk in despairing confusing: beneath is the legend 'I have given credit'. On the right, a complacent gentleman with a sleekly rounded belly under his watch-chain poses before his safe: underneath it says 'for credit come tomorrow'. African businessmen appreciate the moral. They spoke of bad debts—and personal extravagance—more often than any other cause as the reasons why businesses fail.[1]

Nor did they generally believe that credit was necessary. Beside the risk of bad debts, they thought credit drove customers away as often as it attracted them. 'In my opinion,' a wholesaler remarked, 'giving credit is like chasing customers away, so that in the end people lose their customers and their money.' A butcher quoted an Arab saying: if you want to see a man's face again, give him a free meal, if you don't, give him credit. The defaulting customer slinks past his creditor's door to the shop where, even if he has to pay cash, he is not confronted with his debts. 'People come with a very good voice, very persuasive,' as a sawmiller put it, 'and when you approach them they don't reject it, they are willing to sign to agree to pay. But they don't. I don't know why they ignore. . . .' In these embarrassing circumstances, naturally they dodged out of sight when they saw him coming, and took their business elsewhere.

Two-thirds of the rural shopkeepers, therefore, answered that

---

[1] Forty-seven per cent of the rural shopkeepers gave bad debts as a reason for failure, 53 per cent extravagance. The next most popular reasons were failure to keep proper accounts (31 per cent) and lack of capital (20 per cent). Half advised a newcomer against credit. After that, the most frequent advice was to cultivate good relationships with customers (26 per cent), keep accounts, start with enough capital, and avoid drink and women—each mentioned by about a fifth of the businessmen. The ICDC-supported businessmen put less emphasis on bad debts. Other difficulties, as we shall see, were more crucial to them.

credit was unnecessary, when we put the question to them specifically, and only 14 per cent mentioned credit spontaneously amongst
the ways of attracting customers. They relied mostly on a friendly
and unassuming manner (52 per cent) and, after that, on good
service (26 per cent). Yet there is a striking inconsistency: half the
businessmen, while they did not believe in credit, continued to
give it. Why, when the risks were so great, the benefit so question-
able, their own financial margins so cramped, did so many go on
with a practice most of them said they could well do without?

A businessman, especially if he runs a retail business in his own
community, is obviously vulnerable to the pressures of social
obligation. His wealth is exposed on his shelves, in the goods
people want: and it seems far more than it is, since the elderly
widow who needs a packet of sugar she cannot pay for, or the
cousin who has spent all his wages on school fees, sees the goods
themselves, not the few cents profit the shopkeeper makes on
them. A shop in the local market is as visible a symbol of success
as the senior civil servant's Mercedes Benz, and far more open to
exploitation, though it may earn its owner less than a labourers'
wage. Nobody believes that the shopkeeper is struggling to make
a bare living. When he demands cash, the district officer is
offended, the poor accuse him of meanness, and his family rebuke
his selfishness. And since he depends on the goodwill of them all,
he cannot easily resist.

Yet many do resist. They let the district officer take his custom
elsewhere, and try to explain the constraints of business to their
family. For better or worse, sometimes with understanding and
sometimes with bitterness, they insist that business is impartial
and strict:

> If they come for shoe repairs, even if it is only fifty cents,
> they must pay. But if they come for a cup of tea, I'll take
> them out to tea and treat them. Originally people didn't
> understand about business, and expected things free. Some
> businesses failed because of this. But when the business fails
> people laugh at you. Nowadays people know that business is
> business.[T]

> That's a big fight. In this part of the country, relatives very
> much intend that things should be given free. So we just have
> to dodge them out of the way. I always tell them, if you want

any free thing you should come to my home. This is a business place, not a place where things are given free.

They want their clothes cleaned free. I tell them the machine is to be paid, the workers are to be paid. They complain and hate me, but I don't mind. When our father died he gave land to each of us, and since then we have been independent, and gone our own ways.ᵀ

Thus the businessmen tried to deflect the obligation of kinship from the business to themselves, segregating it as a system of economic relationships governed by its own rules, where family loyalties had no right to intrude. Often, by agreeing to discuss requests only at home, away from their office, they underlined the distinction between their personal income and the assets of the business, drawing a physical boundary between their commercial and their family role. Sometimes they carried this symbolic distinction to almost obsessional extremes: if they were willing to make a present of goods, they would hand out the money at home, so that their relative could then go to the shop and purchase them like any other customer. Especially if the businessman paid himself only a modest salary from the enterprise, he forced his family to appeal to himself, not to a row of well stocked shelves, and insulated the business from claims he could not personally ignore.

Most applied the same principle to their household needs, as a printer, for instance, paid his business for his children's exercise books, which he had ruled and bound himself. Two-thirds of the market businessmen said they paid for every article they took from the shop for their own use.[1] So the differentiation of businessman from family man was followed uncompromisingly even into their personal expediture. The right of the business to insist impartially on strictly commercial terms was therefore more persuasive, because the owner too subjected himself to them. And he could afford to be more obdurate behind the counter, because he made it clear that this was the role an efficient, progressive business, contributing to the development of the nation, imposed upon him. At his own table, over a cup of tea, he could respond as a kinsman.

This attitude towards gifts to the family applied equally to credit—and between relatives, presents or credit are likely to come

---

[1] Since 7 per cent did not deal in household goods, only a quarter were actually taking goods without debiting their personal account.

to the same, in practice. Sixty per cent of the market businessmen said they gave no credit to relatives, and 20 per cent only on the same terms as any other customer: a tenth allowed them credit sometimes, 8 per cent as a rule, and the rest had no relatives in the neighbourhood, or sold nothing that they would want. So despite the pressures, most businessmen struggled determinedly to resist them. Even if they were not always as firm as they made out, they do not seem to have been forced into giving credit against their better judgment by social expectations they could not counter. The inconsistency between principle and practice seems to arise, not after all from a conflict between the demands of business and society, but from a dilemma of commercial strategy.

Whatever the risks of credit, a new business has somehow to establish itself against competitors with larger resources and regular customers. While its turnover is small, it can hardly offer better prices or wider stock: even to meet its competitors' price, it may have to accept the barest margin of profit, since it cannot buy on such easy terms. Credit—especially for a retailer, who cannot make a better article—is almost his only means of winning a foothold. As his business gains ground, he can begin to discriminate, but even then, he cannot afford to alienate regular customers whom he has trusted in the past. The rejection of all credit is an ideal towards which a business can progress, but seldom reach. Few ever secure such a hold on their market that they can set their own terms. So businessmen are caught between the need to expand and the crippling losses that may ruin them, if they take the only means in their power. The belief that credit is unnecessary seems to reflect a yearning to escape from this dilemma, to achieve a commercial advantage where a business need no longer be troubled by questions of personal trust. But this only ignores an issue which the business cannot avoid in practice.

The problem of credit has the same roots as the problem of management we discussed in the preceding chapters. A habit of personal integrity does not automatically transfer from familiar to new situations. People do not at first recognize that the obligations imposed by new kinds of relationship are as necessary and binding as the old. Why should a man be prosecuted for a debt he intends to pay, just because he cannot for the time being find the money? Why should he be treated as a thief, because he helps himself from his employer's abundant stock? Why should he be fined, because personal affairs keep him away from work? The offence seems excusable, the sanctions exorbitant. And so long as business is a small part of the African economy, the community does not identify its own interest closely with it, or concern itself to protect it. Business is exploitable, especially as people are ambivalent whether they want it to succeed. Success arouses jealousy as well as emulation. There is a sour satisfaction in seeing the ambitious dragged down again to the common level. So a habit of commercial integrity is not internalized or reinforced by popular disapproval. The temptation to default is not inhibited by a sense of guilt, or fear of disrepute. As one of the businessmen we met remarked, 'At this stage of our development it is unfortunate, because instead of people thinking that they will lose their reputations by not paying their debts, they rejoice that they can get away with so much money from a trader. Until people begin to value their reputations, you'll still have a few businessmen losing several thousands. . . . It will take time for people to have a general sense of responsibility towards their spending. But this is just the transitional stage in our development, and it will stop, because it wasn't so traditionally and neither is it lasting.^T' But meanwhile, security relies more on external sanctions, and these are cumbersome. A business cannot be forever sacking its employees or prosecuting its customers.

In these circumstances, entrepreneurs try to isolate their business as an independent system of relationships, so that it need not appeal to a commercial morality the community has not assimilated. Just as they give their employees no responsibility they can abuse, so they would like to give no credit which customers can abuse. But both expedients have the same consequences. By turning away from the social implications of innovation, they leave unresolved one of the greatest problems of growth. Sooner or later, commercially rational behaviour must either give way or indoctrinate society with its own principles.

The most successful businesses are not, therefore, the least likely to give credit. The most prosperous and growing concerns deal by credit almost as often as the humblest. It is the businesses in between, which have settled into a small profitable trade and then stick there, which most commonly insist on cash—or those in such difficulties that they can no longer afford the risk. Three-quarters of the profitable and expanding ICDC-supported businesses gave credit, and so did 79 per cent of the least profitable shops in the markets. But between these extremes, the less successful ICDC-supported businesses and the more profitable shops in the markets were comparatively cautious: 55 per cent and 62 per cent gave credit. Although a policy of dealing only in cash may be safe, and practicable for an established concern, it also frustrates growth.

The ambitious businessmen had to find ways of controlling credit, not repudiating it. They experimented with hire purchase, deposit accounts, cash discounts, arranged with employers to collect debts on pay day on the spot, asked for bank certificates, or made enquiries about a customer's credit standing. These expedients represent three essential strategies for containing risk: covering losses from default by spreading the cost over higher credit charges, and so giving the customer an inducement to pay cash; providing more automatic sanctions against default—by, for instance, insisting on a deposit which the customer forfeits with the goods if he does not pay the balance; and creating an intelligence network, through which the reputation and resources of a customer can be discovered. In these ways, the risks become more equally shared. The credit customer pays more, and if he defaults, he may lose either money or the chance of credit in future from any business where he is known. So he too acquires an interest in behaving with commercial integrity, not only for himself, but for others. For the more widely the habit of integrity spreads, the cheaper and easier credit becomes.[1]

The constraints on African retailing

None of these means are very practicable if most purchases are small, however, and business depends on a passing trade. A rural shopkeeper who mostly serves the crowds who gather on market days may not be able to protect himself effectively against risk. So he can only attract customers by his prices and stock, and here his competitive position is weak, since his access to supplies on good terms is limited by the size of his turnover. He cannot

---

[1] It would also ease the problem of credit if employers adopted the practice of paying their workers weekly instead of monthly. This would help to solve, too, the problem of advances mentioned on pp. 114–15.

attract trade from the Indian bazaar in the nearest township, and outgrow his beginnings. Amongst the ICDC-supported businesses, less than a third of the retailers gave credit at all, but correspondingly, few were really thriving and expanding concerns. Unless a businessman can escape from the constraints of rural retailing, where the dilemma of credit is insoluble, his chances of growing are slight.

This helps to explain why country markets are surrounded by rows of small general stores, all carrying much the same goods at similar prices. If credit is too risky, and the margin of profit too small to allow for price cutting, the shopkeeper can only compete by the quality of his personal service, or by varying his stock. When we asked the market businessmen how they tried to attract customers, half of them mentioned a friendly, patient and attentive manner, and just over a quarter good service. Besides these, no other means were suggested by more than 15 per cent of the businessmen—and 15 per cent said they did not try, it was all a matter of luck. Only 12 per cent tried to charge less than their competitors in the market: 17 per cent had made an agreement to fix their prices at the same level, and 51 per cent tried to keep their prices in line without any formal undertaking. The rest either had no competition, or dealt in goods with prices fixed by law, or simply did not know what others charged. Since most businessmen allowed customers to bargain over some goods, and reduce the price (though not usually below cost) of articles that did not sell, the similarity of their prices does not result from mutual protection. They were all trading on the barest margin of profit by which they could survive, and to undercut the market would have ruined themselves long before it drove their competitors out of business.

Even to vary their range of stock raised difficulties. They bought from local wholesalers who retailed the same goods at much the same prices, and who, since their margin of profit is so much higher, could carry a much fuller stock. One African businessman explained the difficulty by this model: 'The Indian, the African and the European are three people. The Indian has a shop on the right, the European has a shop on the left. The African has his shop in the middle. The Asian and the European have many things in their shops, but the African has only two boxes of soap and one sack of potatoes. No customer can enter such a shop, because it does not have what he wants, but the people on either side have it. Therefore it will compel the African to go to these shops on either side to get the things to sell in his own shop. And he will not have enough capital to buy from these shops in large enough quantities. If he had the capital, and knew where to get his supplies, then he could compete favourably. Then all that remains is knowledge of business.ᵀ' But meanwhile, he cannot earn the capital to escape his dependence on these much stronger competitors. He can only move out of range. So an African shopkeeper's trade is limited to those household goods which his neighbours would rather buy locally than in the nearest township, where they would find a wider choice at better prices. In effect, the cost of the bus fare, and the time the journey wastes, determine both his profit margin and his stock. The more important or infrequent the purchase, the more likely that it will be made in town. The rural retailer is left with a limited range of saleable goods, much like the shop next door, and the one next door to that. Only a fifth of the market businesses we interviewed claimed any special asset or goods—a refrigerator for cold drinks, a radio, more varieties of cloth, insecticides—which were not common to others of its kind.

So neither by credit, nor price cutting, nor widening their range could they do much to increase their turnover, to the point where they could afford the cost of transport to buy in quantity at true wholesale prices, from the same source as the middlemen who supplied them. At the same time, they were too suspicious of each other, and too competitive within the constraints of their situation, to take any co-operative action to overcome the obstacle. We suggested at several meetings with rural shopkeepers that they might pool their buying, sending a lorry once a month to Nairobi to obtain supplies for them all. But they considered it impracticable: people ran short at different times, and would not trust themselves to such a system, even if they could agree on how it should be organized.

Alternatively, a man with much more capital at the outset, and a ruthless determination to drive the other shopkeepers out of business, might be able to capture the whole retail trade in the market. But in practice successful and ambitious retailers prefer to take up wholesaling where, like their Asian predecessors, they supply the African shopkeepers round about and sell to the public too. And this combination of wholesaling with retailing proves to be the most promising line an African businessman can follow. It includes a higher proportion of profitable concerns than any other activity supported by ICDC loans. But its advantage does not lie simply in the size of its market. The crucial factor is the size of the market in relation to the scale of competition, and this delicate balance of opportunity largely determines the chances of African business.

The extent of competition

The new difficulties which arise, once a business begins to look for a wider market than the local community, stand out with formidable clarity from the experience of African bakers. Suppose a hotel keeper has made a small income from selling bread and cakes in his home market. Seeing that bread is growing more popular, he applies to the ICDC for a loan to install a modern oven and a dough mixer, to supply the shops and hotels round about. But as he opens up this new market, he also alerts competition. European or Asian bakers begin to extend their range into the neighbourhood, trucking their bread even fifty or a hundred miles along the highways. These rivals have more sophisticated equipment and a much greater volume of production. Their bread is sliced, wrapped, more expertly baked—and cheaper. They can well afford to sell below cost for a while, to overwhelm local competition. The African is soon faced with bankruptcy, or a further substantial investment to match this quality. If he is to invest more, he must also expand his market further, into less and less familiar territory. All but one of the bakers we met had either failed or were still struggling to survive, and they complained bitterly about the competition:

> The trouble is, we don't wrap in wax paper, it's too expensive. So shopkeepers aren't interested to buy our bread, because it gets dry too quickly. I wanted to start like Elliot's (one of the largest European bakers in Nairobi, a hundred miles away) wrapping the bread in wax paper, but the paper costs 4,000 shillings, and that would last only a few days. I don't know why these Nairobi bakers are allowed to come here, when Government has given us a loan to develop our business. If they go on like that, our business can't grow.

They were not coming before, I don't know why they are coming now. If Government wants us to compete with Elliot's, they should give us the money for everything—paper, machines, and so on. Bakers like Elliot's should stay in the big towns.

There is a lot of competition from the Asians who make bread in Kisumu. Since they have machines, they make a lot of bread, and better bread. They bring it by van, thirty miles. If they want to get your customers, they cut the price by two or three cents. In fact, with these Asians it's mostly undercutting. There's a government-fixed maximum price, but everywhere in the country you'll find prices vary. . . . With business people, they'll do everything they can to get you out of the market, and the weapon they use is to reduce the price. The competition is getting worse all the time. . . . We have complained about price cutting to the local authorities, but the answer we get is that they can't interfere if someone wants to sell at a lower price.

Both these speakers had a sophisticated knowledge of baking—one had studied the techniques in Britain, at his own expense—but they were faced with the daunting task of establishing a small business in markets where only an aggressive firm with resources equal to its competitors stood much chance of gaining ground.

The one African baker who did succeed in driving out his rivals was helped by the isolation of his district and the political mood of independence, which he vigorously exploited. At first he distributed his bread from a village outside the nearest township, where there were two long-standing Indian bakeries. By setting out at three in the morning, his salesmen could reach the surrounding markets more quickly than the Indian firms; and during the heavy rains, the town bakers could not get into the countryside at all. Not content with this, he moved his own business to the town, and set about his rivals with every weapon to hand. He entertained the local political leaders of both parties, promised his support to each, and recruited their youth wingers to campaign throughout the district in praise of his bread. The new premises opened to a flourish of beer parties, free bread and generous credit. Finally, he bought over the Indian bakers' drivers and salesmen, with their experience and goodwill, and left his rivals to struggle hopelessly for a while with offers of credit and cut prices. The campaign was expensive, but effective. The African baker ended in command of the market for fifty miles around. But the strategy only triumphed because the district, though prosperous, lies a long way off the main roads, far from the cities. He did not have to face the much more forbidding competition which perplexed the other African bakers, though they baked better bread.

The bakers' difficulties were shared by all African businesses which, like them, manufactured a standard product—sawmillers, a radio manufacturer, plastic moulder, bolt maker, canner. For all these, costs are less and quality higher the more they can make, and the size of the market is limited only by the durability of the goods, and the cost of transporting them. Since most of the densely settled parts of Kenya lie within two hundred miles of each other, even perishable goods like bread can be supplied from a few manufacturing centres. An African producer has to compete in a national or international market from the outset. He cannot begin with a small trade in familiar country. As soon as he installs machinery, and becomes more than a village cook or craftsman, he faces the uninhibited competition of sophisticated modern industry. No one else, like the triumphant baker, was able to fight for a corner of the market out of its reach. So amongst the businesses with ICDC loans, the 17 manufacturers of standard products were nearly all in difficulties: only three were doing well, two were making some profit, and the rest had either failed or seemed likely to fail. Even the few successful firms included several sawmills which, to withstand the competition of established European and Asian mills, had decided to amalgamate into a much larger enterprise, with another far more substantial government loan. Although they were already making some profit, the owners themselves recognized that the nature of the market offered small undertakings a poor chance of growth.

A small business is much more likely to succeed when the potential market for its service is restricted. If the cost of transport is too high, or the journey too long and expensive for the customer, the business is protected from distant competition. No one takes his car twenty miles to be repaired when the work can be done competently round the corner; or sends his suit out of town to be cleaned when there is a laundry at the end of the road. If he wants furniture or a water tank to his own specification, he goes to the nearest skilled craftsman, where he can discuss his needs, hurry the work along and get it home cheaply. If he needs a small stock for his shop, he cannot afford to go further than the nearest wholesaler. In such undertakings, the largest enterprise has no decisive advantage. A chain of dry-cleaning branches cannot compete with a single shop, if its nearest plant is further from the market and takes longer to return the clothes: a newcomer has a much better chance. He may be astute enough to pick a worthwhile market which has not been exploited—as a cinema cashier, for instance, planning to set up in dry cleaning, surveyed the country before he chose an important town without any plant of its own and was promptly overwhelmed with business. But even if he starts out beside established concerns, his competitors are more of a size he can hope to match.

The extent of competition, therefore, is related to the kind of business. None of the retailers amongst the businesses with ICDC loans faced competition from outside their district, 4 per cent of the wholesalers, 10 per cent of the service industries, and 20 per cent of the carpenters, tinsmiths, tailor and shoemaker who made to customer's order. For two-fifths or more of all these businesses, their only competition was local. But *none* of the manufacturers of standard goods had only local competition to contend with, while half had to compete with businesses from outside the district. The nature of their market made them far more vulnerable, and their chances of realizing a profit were barely half those of any other kind of business.

The success of African businesses seems to depend, above all, on this scale of competitive opportunity. At one extreme are the country shopkeepers, whose market for everyday groceries is largely isolated from outside competition, but whose isolation also constrains their trade within narrow boundaries. Because they have to buy for cash at high prices, they cannot by credit, variety, or under-selling achieve a competitive advantage, and the trade of the market scatters along the lines of barely distinguishable general stores. At the opposite extreme are the manufacturers whose market is unlimited. Such a market attracts national or international companies, against whose resources and sophistication a small African enterprise is powerless. The profitable and growing firms stand in between. Their customers range beyond the immediate neighbourhood: a wholesaler may supply the shops for ten or twenty miles around; a dry cleaner may cover all the nearby markets with his agents; a garage caters to all the tractors, buses, lorries and saloons within the district; a furniture maker can meet the needs of all the local schools. Yet their service is still localized. These firms can compete on more or less equal terms. Though they start with less capital than their established Indian rivals, they may be able to exploit racial loyalties to win customers, so long as their prices are no higher: the most successful dry-cleaning firm, launched on the eve of Independence, at first attracted customers because there was no other African in the business. They have the goodwill, too, of many Europeans anxious to express their sympathy with African ambitions. They are willing to live very cheaply, and plough all the profits back into the business. Though they are just as troubled by the risks of credit as a petty shopkeeper, they mostly deal with more prosperous, better-known customers and larger single purchases. The debts are individually more worth collecting, and more likely to justify the expense of lawyers' letters and a few exemplary prosecutions. Since their service does not gain greatly from economies of scale, they can install the equipment to provide a competitive quality. And within the range of their market, they can afford to advertise—distributing leaflets in the neighbourhood, exhibiting slides in the local cinemas, publicizing their opening as a civic occasion. So, one way or another, they have room to manoeuvre.

The most promising ICDC-supported businesses were, then, the wholesalers, the service industries, and the manufacturers to customers' specifications. As the size of the potential market widens, the proportion of profitable and growing firms rises, and then abruptly declines again, as the small African business begins to flounder out of its depth (Table 8).

A business is not, of course, guaranteed a profit because it enters a market in the middle range. As the table shows, the chances for service industries were only half and half. Even in a field where African businessmen had done best, miscalculation of the competition or the potential custom could easily prove fatal. A very efficient dry cleaner, for instance, established his business in a growing town served only by one other Indian firm. Then a European business opened, and the town council was threatening to license yet another competitor. At the same time, though the town was an important centre, it served a farming and industrial population with relatively few African white-collar workers to whom clean clothes mattered. In these circumstances, the African business barely covered its costs. The owner could only hope that if it survived long enough to repay its loan capital, it would eventually make a profit.

TABLE 8   *Success of different kinds of business*

	Retail only	Wholesale (& retail)	Service industry	Manufacturers to order	Mfrs. standard product
Profitable & expanding	19%	46%	47%	70%	18%
Profitable (not expanding)	50%	37%	5%	–	12%
Doubtful	25%	17%	21%	30%	35%
Failing or failed	6%	—	27%	—	35%
Total %	100%	100%	100%	100%	100%
Total no.*	16	24	19	10	17

* One large transport company which fits into none of these categories has been excluded.

Whatever their activities, only the businesses which judged the opportunities most shrewdly, or most luckily, and went after them aggressively were likely to succeed. As a whole, the profitable and expanding businesses advertised, cut their prices, raised their quality, exploited personal contacts and racial or political appeals more often than the rest. None of them—unlike a quarter of the less promising enterprises—admitted to being helpless in the face of their competitors' advantages. But they were also more likely to have found an opening where there were no serious rivals.

The promotion of opportunities

Could government policy extend the markets open to small African enterprises? With every allowance for determination and good judgment, the range of promising activities was more limited than either the businessmen or the ICDC seem to have foreseen. The ICDC was even in danger of concentrating its resources, apparently unaware, just where the chances were least hopeful. Under the revised development plan for 1966–70, £4m. were to be spent on industrial estates. The first of these—designed as a cluster of workshops with a technical centre to advise and and assist them—was intended for African engineering firms which 'must replace imported articles or process local raw materials, i.e. bring about foreign exchange earnings'. This is just the kind of activity where a small African business has least hope of success—the manufacture of standard articles in competition with imports or large national companies. Free advice and technical assistance can scarcely overcome the crippling handicap of small scale production. Understandably, the ICDC found great difficulty in persuading African entrepreneurs to take up leases on the estate. Even if no restriction were placed on the kind of business, an industrial estate tends to be too isolated from the shopping centres to attract customers, and does not suit a garage, dry cleaner, furniture maker or tinsmith—nor the small baker or sawmiller who can only survive if he retails part of his output directly. Since the ICDC was planning to spend only £1m. on other help to African businesses, it was in danger of allocating four-fifths of its resources to the most unpromising field it could have chosen.[1]

If industrial estates are not the answer, how is the range of African business to be extended? By 1967, the opportunities in wholesaling and service industries were already becoming scarcer. The first-comers had not exploited a buoyant and expanding market, but replaced or ousted European or Asian firms, or found an area that was poorly served. As these openings were filled, the competition between African businesses became sharper. Following the success of a few outstanding enterprises, the enthusiasm for dry cleaning was rapidly outrunning the demand, while wholesalers in the heart of the most prosperous agricultural district were slashing their prices in a fierce determination to dominate their African rivals. The IDCD support for industrial projects was dwindling for lack of clearly viable proposals.

The market for African businesses could be increased, most obviously, by protection, but on the whole the economic policies of the Kenya government were against it. While the ICDC argued that the cost was justified to bring in African entrepreneurs, other

[1] Although the ICDC believed that 'many countries have adopted this system with good success', the experience of industrial estates in both India and Nigeria has been discouraging. It is difficult to attract the right kind of entrepreneur, the technical assistance is ignored, rents—even when subsidized—are too high and frequently unpaid, and the estates not fully occupied. See Davenport, pp. 38–42, and Schatz, 1964.

departments were more concerned with the effect on prices, revenue and employment. The immediate issue was not so much protection against international competition as the protection of African firms against European or Asian competitors in Kenya, and here the Government was inconsistent. Though it protected African commerce—even more than was needed—the Government was curiously indifferent to African industry. African wholesalers, for instance, could probably not have pushed their way against established Asian firms without the manipulation of sugar distribution. Since the allocation of sugar is controlled by a government monopoly, the trade was simply redirected to African distributors. Other staple articles were brought increasingly under the same government direction, through the Kenya National Trading Corporation. Pressure was brought to bear on private companies to follow a similar policy. One African businessman threatened successfully to organize a boycott of a company's goods, unless it took the local agency out of Indian hands. Both local and national government began to discriminate openly against Indians, on the grounds that they were not citizens, and withdrew or curtailed their licence to trade. By contrast, Government was content to allocate the potential market for manufactured goods to whoever seemed best able to exploit it. The 1966–70 Development Plan, for instance, provided £4½m. of state capital to attract overseas investors—only half a million less than the ICDC was to spend on promoting African enterprise. At the time of our study, the appeal of African bakers for restrictive licensing was ignored; African sawmillers were denied allocations of timber from the national forests; and government departments or local councils rarely gave preference to African firms, putting their requirements out to tender with strict impartiality. Yet small-scale bakers and sawmillers were far more exposed to powerful competition, and in need of more deliberate encouragement than wholesalers or retailers. Though there is little to be said for protecting incompetent businesses, an efficient small firm may deserve some help to establish itself in the face of large alien competitors. If county councils restricted licences to bakers from outside the county, where African firms were competent to meet the demand; if African businessmen were given advice on tendering, and a chance to reconsider close but unsuccessful bids; if government departments sought out African suppliers wherever possible, and did not abandon them abruptly, without discussion, as soon as a better price offered; if the allocation of forest timber were co-ordinated with the ICDC's support for African sawmills—then several able African entrepreneurs, at present struggling against long odds, would stand a much better chance of justifying the money Government had invested in them. None of these policies was consistently followed at the time of our enquiry. Though the more the market is manipulated to favour African business, the greater the risk that political stridency will count for more than competence, such help would be less partisan than the advantages already handed to African commerce.

On the whole, in both commerce and industry, the Government seem to have been more concerned with participation than with protecting entrepreneurs. It wanted Africans to share in the whole-sale and retail trade as it wanted foreign companies to appoint African directors, train African staff and sell shares to the African public. It seemed willing to leave the economic initiative in the hands of government experts and overseas investors, so long as the benefits were widely spread. From this point of view, the promotion of African business was primarily a substitution of African for Asian or European ownership in small concerns, where there was little scope for redistributing shares and staff positions. As time went by, and the racial substitution progressed, the opportunities to foster genuinely competitive, self-reliant African entrepreneurs with a few thousand shillings capital became harder and harder to find. The profitable openings seemed nearly all to lie in local markets, or markets which could reasonably be localized by restrictive licensing. To go beyond this, African enterprise would have to organize on a much larger scale.

There is, however, one other kind of viable small industry: the manufacture of goods whose market is still small, but national or even international in extent. The animal figures and salad servers of the Wakamba woodcarving industry fill the curio shops of Fifth Avenue and Hampstead as abundantly as the pavements of Nairobi. In a world eager for the exotic, anything that works the wild life of Africa, its unique woods and stones, into clothes or household furniture or souvenirs has a chance to sell. Few Africans understand this market, or know how to exploit it. The tourist, looking for something distinctively Kenyan, carries home most often the creation of an inventive English housewife, or an

Indian shopkeeper's line in lampshades of zebra's feet. It is not that African craftsmen lack the skill or imagination, as the Wakamba and Kisii soapstone carvings show, but they have almost no experience of selling outside their local community. This inexperience handicaps them as seriously in more important markets than the tourist trade—agricultural tools, cheap furniture, clothes, footwear, building materials, metal work, stationery, food processing. In all these categories, there are goods which African craftsmen have made, cheap and serviceable enough to sell against competition. Anything bulky and easy to make from materials readily available, where the transport costs of finished articles are proportionately high, and the process of production too simple to need expensive machinery is within the scope of a small business. But we met several African entrepreneurs who had designed articles with much technical ingenuity and simplicity, and yet had no idea how to sell them. A blacksmith, for instance, had made a hoe, a metal-framed wardrobe covered in plastic, a jig for stamping corner pieces for suitcases, but his only means of marketing them was to bicycle round the local shops in his spare time. He did not even know the names of the African wholesalers nearby in Nairobi, who might have tested whether they would sell.

Help in marketing, therefore, might prove more productive than any other single support for African businessmen. They need an agency to put them in touch with distributors; introduce them to companies needing local supplies; find them addresses and contacts overseas for the export of local crafts; urge government departments, the police, army, schools and hospitals to make use of African businesses whenever they could; and by exploring the demand, to keep African businessmen continually informed of the potential markets they might exploit. The essential value of such an agency would lie in the direct personal relationships it could foster between the African manufacturer and his customers. Most African businessmen do not know where to begin, and without status in the commercial hierarchy, their few enquiries are casually treated. They ask to see the sales manager—who might be sympathetic—but can get no further than the foreman or office clerk, who dismisses them out of hand. Or they write letters in awkward English, which receive no reply. Where African businessmen have succeeded in establishing a foothold in the commercial world, they often owe it to a European friend, whose personal respect has served to introduce them. A marketing service would act as such a friend. It would not itself sell anything: to take from African businessmen the final responsibility for marketing their goods would only perpetuate their isolation. But it would make them known, and create the network of personal contacts outside their local community which they so greatly lack.

The problem of marketing is an aspect of a fundamental obstacle, which blocks the way of African businessmen wherever they turn: the disparity between the scale of the economy in which they compete and the extent of the relationships they know how to handle. The mistrust which inhibits the delegation of responsibility, and cramps the size of the organizations they can manage; the vulnerability of small enterprises to competitors whose economies of scale overwhelm their chances; the isolation which prevents them from reaching national markets—all the difficulties we have reviewed in the preceding chapters arise because the economic and social worlds of African businessmen do not fit. They are not supported in their economic life by any corresponding network of acquaintance, information, or custom.

Even an African shopkeeper trading in a country market stands at the end of a chain of distribution which extends through the local agent to the wholesaler in Nairobi or Mombasa. Within this commercial system he must buy on the strictest and most impersonal terms, since his trade is smallest. He is socially as well as economically marginal, and has no choice but to compete in this system on its own terms. As he assimilates its values, his manner of business becomes alienated from the expectations of his family and friends. As he differentiates economic affairs from kinship and community, insisting on the contractual nature of commercial obligations, he is forced to segregate his business unambiguously from his social relationships. His economic life becomes more strictly and single-mindedly isolated than that of an Indian or European businessman, whose family and social ties accommodate and facilitate their business dealings. He lacks the freemasonry of commerce, the clubs, golf courses, convenient marriages which mediate trust and open opportunities. So at home as abroad, he finds no social counterpart to his economic role. The community to which he belongs does not fully understand or accept his business principles, while the commercial world to which he belongs excludes him socially. This incompatibility drives him into a self-sufficient way of business, where he can operate without social support. He trusts no one, not even himself. He defends his business from the temptation to drink or provision his household at its expense, as he defends it from all the other extraneous claims. But such extreme segregation confines him to the range of activities he can personally control. He dissipates his energy in small-scale enterprises, unable to delegate authority. He prevents traditional obligations from intruding into business and disrupting its commercial integrity. But just because he assimilates the principles of businesslike efficiency so wholeheartedly, they become a wall which imprisons as well as protects.

African businessmen stand at the focal point of change, where all the pressures towards a modern, national economy encounter the jealous, hesitant, defensive response of the local communities. Their mistrustful self-sufficiency and isolation are the counterpart of their pioneering. If they had not been bold and inventive men, disrupting established ways and struggling to reintegrate them about new opportunities, none of the problems we have discussed would have arisen. And these problems are difficult to solve, because they reflect a pervasive insecurity of relationships, as people struggle to master the conflicting problems of wholesale transformation. African entrepreneurship has to be seen, not merely as an aspect of economic management, but of society as a whole—a crucial factor in the adaptation to change.

Against this background, we turn now to the two aspects of African business which have attracted most notice from Government—the provision of capital, and training of skills. These are the principal means by which the Kenya government has tried to promote African businesses. In the light of our analysis, how relevant are special loan schemes, management courses, education, to the development of entrepreneurship?

PART III
AIDING THE DEVELOPMENT
OF BUSINESSES

8

ACCESS TO CAPITAL

Amongst all the African businessmen we interviewed—whether in industry or commerce, whether government-aided or eking out a livelihood in a country market—lack of capital was, they said, their greatest difficulty. More than two-thirds of them mentioned it. Few of the country shopkeepers thought any other problem worth noticing. So there was a general demand for more, larger, less conditional or less security-minded government loans. Sixty per cent of the businessmen supported by the ICDC believed that Government should lend more—at least to the right people. So did 85 per cent of the businessmen in the market centres. Loans seemed to all of them the most obviously important help that Government could give. Governments themselves seem to accept this role. In Kenya, Uganda, India, the United States—wherever the promotion of small businesses have become an aim of policy— loans have been the first and most important inducement. But there are inherent difficulties in any public loan scheme designed to outflank the caution of private financing.

Governments lend money when they want to encourage developments too risky to attract commercial capital at a price the borrowers could afford. But they are seldom ready to accept the logical inference: if the risks are too high and the returns too meagre for private lenders, a government lending agency is likely to lose money too. Their loan schemes are usually designed to be self-sustaining, and even if there is some subsidy of interest rates or administrative costs, the businesses they support are expected to be viable without continual protection. If so, why were these businesses unable to raise capital in the commercial market to begin with? If the loan scheme intends to foster commercially viable enterprises which other investors shun, it can only succeed in a distorted market, where prejudice or ignorance have exaggerated the fears of private lenders. Only where the risks are in reality less than is generally believed, or a small abatement of interest rates makes a crucial difference, can a government lending agency pay its way without imitating its private counterparts. There is a no man's land between straightforward commercial investment and subsidy where Government may need to intervene to give new kinds of business a chance of proving their viability—as, for instance, an African government is likely to be more open to the possibilities of African business than a European bank, without necessarily being foolhardy. But this kind of intervention is very finely balanced between backing losers and backing the favourite.

Development funds are scarce and cannot be squandered on ill conceived or incompetently managed businesses: equally, they should not be wasted on projects which private investors are willing to support. The more Government helps businessmen who lack the security and experience to attract private capital, the greater the risks it runs, since there are no reliable precedents to guide its judgment. But the more precautions it takes, the more like a commercial lender it becomes, and the scheme will then be redundant. It may set out boldly in search of new talent, make some expensive mistakes, and end conservatively, lending against adequate security to well proved projects which would have attracted finance anyway. If a government loan scheme is not to be either unprofitable or pointless, it has to work out ways of choosing applicants and guarding against default different from conventional commercial practice but equally reliable. And if it succeeds, it has then to withdraw: for once it has demonstrated the reliability of its clients, its pioneering purpose is fulfilled. Otherwise the government scheme, instead of opening opportunities where private finance will follow, in time institutionalizes a permanent division of responsibility between private and public lending, which inhibits the integration of these new businesses into the financial system.

The Kenya government could not have escaped these problems. In 1961, when it launched its small business loan scheme under the Industrial Development Corporation with a revolving fund of £50,000, there was no alternative to government intervention. The segregation of the colonial economy into racially distinct sectors left Africans altogether isolated from the system of banking and commercial credit. Socially, they had no contact with European bank managers or their Asian staff, and economically, they had no assets a bank would accept against which to secure a loan. Their most valuable possession was the land they farmed, but until land consolidation began in the Kikuyu country in the 1950s, these customary rights could not be negotiated. Even after the registration of individual titles to consolidated farms, restrictions on land ownership in the African reserves encumbered their transfer. The banks had always regarded help to the African economy as a government concern, seeing their own function rather as facilitating international movements of capital; while the colonial administrations treated Africans as wards, to be protected against financial risks they could not sustain. One businessman told us that when he built his first shop in Nairobi, no loans to Africans of more than 2,000 shillings were recoverable through the courts, unless the transaction had first been approved by the District Commissioner. Two years before the independence of Kenya, the only sources of credit open to African businessmen were small government loans administered through local boards and, more importantly, the personal savings of their acquaintances. In these circumstances, a new instrument of government credit to pioneer more substantial African businesses seemed essential.

At the outset, the ICDC did not always insist upon security for its loans. It helped to finance several highly successful concerns, but its unsecured loans also included a disproportion of failures— five out of twenty, as against only two of the other sixty-seven. Prudently, it began to take more precautions. Reporting on the first two years of the Small Industries Revolving Loan Fund, the ICDC admitted 'considerable difficulties were encountered in establishing proper procedures for processing loan applications and following procedures to supervise the proper use of the funds and assistance given by the Corporation. Whereas there are still difficulties with some of the earlier loans of the Corporation, some of which may be wholly or partly irrecoverable, the arrangements for later loans are working satisfactorily.'[1] But these arrangements, though they protected the Corporation, could be extremely frustrating to the applicants. As it struggled to resolve the inherent dilemma of all such schemes, and pioneer new kinds of loans without being imprudent, its procedures tended to become so

[1] Industrial and Commercial Development Corporation, Report and Accounts for the years 1963/4 and 1964/5.

slow and the conditions so restrictive that they impeded the essential purpose.

In the first place, the discussions were often very expensive to the applicant in time and money—sometimes so long drawn out that when the loan was at last received, it came too late. One unlucky travel agent, for instance, told us: 'We asked for a loan of 100,000 shillings to buy new cars and expand. It took two years. It was very frustrating—the bureaucratic machinery, the red tape, running up and down to Nairobi, inquiries this way and that. We even said, if you don't do something soon, we are collapsing. And in the end, when we were collapsing, they approved a loan for a quarter of the amount we asked for. It was useless—too little and too late, the business went into liquidation before the loan was paid. . . . And there was so much expense—flying to Nairobi, letters, trunk calls.' A fifth of the industrial loans took over two years to process, another fifth over a year, and though the commercial loans were usually quicker, only a quarter of either were settled within six months.

Besides the six to twelve months of constant enquiry characteristically involved, continual visits to the ICDC office could cost an out-of-town businessman a lot of money. Some spent as much as 10 per cent or even 20 per cent of the value of the loan in getting it—only to receive at last a sum much less than they had asked for, inadequate to the original purpose. A carpenter, for instance, applied for 20,000 shillings, and when fifteen months later, and 2,000 shillings out of pocket, he was granted half what he asked for, he could no longer afford the equipment he had planned, which had meanwhile gone up in price.

Instead, he bought more stock. But here too he got poor value for his trouble, since the loan was to be paid against invoices at a designated supplier. 'I had to go to Nairobi eleven times to get the loan. It cost me 2,000 shillings in travel and hotel expenses. You would go to their offices, and they would tell you to come back the next day, and all the time your hotel bills mount up. It was all so much trouble I was going to give up, but I was persuaded to take the loan up by a European friend, because I'd already spent so much in expenses trying to get it. But the loan wasn't satisfactory, because I was given an invoice to a certain agent, and the agent could charge any price he liked, since he knew I had to buy from him.'ᵀ This tying of loans to specific items of equipment was the ICDC's usual practice. Only 9 per cent of the loans were paid in cash, while 80 per cent were paid entirely against invoices for goods ordered, and the rest in credit guarantees or by these means combined. Though the ICDC was then protected against any other use of its funds than had been agreed, the system was awkwardly inflexible.

The ICDC was not altogether to blame for the delays and expenses which businessmen incurred. It claimed that applicants seldom produced market surveys, bank statements or feasibility studies, and when asked to present more detailed information, would go instead to their Member of Parliament to raise support for their application. Their visits to the ICDC officers were often abortive and unnecessary, since they did not bring the particulars requested. The ICDC maintained, too, that it never required any business to buy from a supplier the business had not chosen. But these misunderstandings in themselves reflect the cumbersome and bureaucratic nature of the procedures. At the same time, an accountable public agency could hardly have acted otherwise without laying itself open to accusations of irresponsibility.

The most serious drawback for the industrial concerns, however, was not the red tape, but the ICDC's preference for loans for equipment over loans for working capital. From the Corporation's point of view, equipment could be evaluated and specified against the prospects of the enterprise, and recovered in case of default. It involved less risk. But without working capital a business could be left without the ready money for supplies, transportation, or advertising to exploit the equipment it had installed. Meanwhile, it was required to start repaying instalments of the loan used to buy it.[1]

The shortage of working capital was sometimes made worse because the business had already used up its own savings to buy land or put up buildings which the ICDC would accept as security. So, for instance, one firm had been encouraged to invest 100,000 shillings in new premises, as an asset to secure a loan. The partners borrowed heavily from their friends, finished the building, and received a loan for equipment. But by then they were so short of money, they were forced to sell their van, and had no means of

---

[1] The ICDC was not, in principle, against lending working capital. But it was not prepared to lend money for both equipment and working capital, on the grounds that the business itself would then not be sharing any of the risk.

getting their goods to market. Competition was keen, and they failed to get very good results—perhaps out of inexperience—from the secondhand machinery they had installed. With no margin to learn from their mistakes, or to develop a market, the business soon ran into crippling losses. 'Since we put up the new building, we have been so heavily in debt that we had no profit to reinvest in keeping the business going. If we had built more slowly, we'd have incurred less debt, and might have got on better. But the district officer impressed on us that if we put up a good building quickly, we'd get a loan and good machinery, and we'd make a good profit.T'

Most businesses never became so fatally indebted, though several lost valuable orders for lack of ready money to buy material. But it is easy to imagine how the conditions imposed by the ICDC for its own protection could frustrate its own ultimate purpose—the promotion of new enterprise. Suppose a pit-sawyer, for example, approaches the Corporation with the idea of converting his business into a sawmill. He has the lease of a suitable plot, but wants 50,000 shillings for machinery and another 50,000 shillings for timber and working capital. The ICDC responds with requests for further details, and an account of his present assets. He then decides to improve his chances of a loan by building a workshop. The negotiations drag on, and his savings are further depleted by repeated visits to the Corporation's office. Eventually, a loan is agreed for the machinery, but not the working capital: and instead of the equipment he had in mind, he is recommended to buy cheaper, secondhand machines. So the loan is, after all, only 35,000 shillings. Then—to imagine the worst that may happen—there are delays in fixing the machines, because the sawmiller is running out of funds. When they are at last in place they do not work reliably or economically, since the operator is inexperienced and the parts worn. Each time they go wrong a mechanic has to be sent for from Nairobi. But these interruptions are less of a handicap, because there is no money to buy timber to keep them busy. Meanwhile the six months' moratorium is up, and the first instalment of the loan is due for repayment. After a while the ICDC writes a stern letter pointing out the arrears. The sawmiller has never sought the ICDC's advice when it could still have helped him, for fear of exposing his difficulties and provoking the Corporation to press for its payments. By now his affairs are irretrievable.

He petitions for help and further funds, the ICDC threatens to sue. He may be genuinely confused about the legal responsibilities he has undertaken, offering to return the equipment in discharge of the loan, and unable to understand why the ICDC will only offer to help him sell it at a depreciated price. He sees the loan as part of a mutual co-operation in development, but the ICDC repudiates any responsibility for success or failure, insisting on the contractual commitment to repay, regardless of circumstances.

No business we visited suffered all these misfortunes together in quite this way, and no business failed only because of the conditions attached to the ICDC loan. Inexperience, competition, quarrels between partners, refusal of a licence to cut forest timber would compound the difficulties. But 11 of the 35 industrial enterprises from whom loan repayments were due had fallen into arrears, and two had agreed a postponement with the Corporation. They included, besides some failures, several with a promising future which had decided to risk retaliation from the ICDC so as to have enough in hand for urgent improvements in their position. They went ahead with new installations at the expense of their commitments, and so presented the ICDC with an awkward choice. As a public corporation, accountable for its management, it could not casually overlook default. The less reliable its debtors were allowed to become, the less money it could lend to other applicants. Considered simply as a financing organization, its direct responsibility was to get its money back, and re-lend to businessmen who would honour their undertaking. But at the same time, it destroyed its own achievements by foreclosing businesses which with more time and more money stood a good chance of proving their viability. In practice, the ICDC grumbled and waited. But it did not, perhaps, recognize the underlying difficulty. A loan for equipment, at 8 per cent interest, to be repaid in monthly instalments over three to five years from six months after the loan is formally issued,[1] leaves no margin whatever for unforeseen snags or setbacks, and presupposes that the business has enough working capital to use the equipment profitably from the moment it is provided. This is expecting a lot of a new business in relatively inexperienced hands.

[1] Commercial loans were normally for three years, industrial for five, with six months grace before the first instalment was to be repaid. The interest was originally 6 per cent, later raised to 8 per cent—1 or 2 per cent less than the rate charged by commercial banks.

The industrial concerns undertook a harder commitment than the wholesalers or retailers, who could use their loans to buy stock like sugar which was quickly sold. Even here, the ICDC attached conditions which sometimes made the loan difficult to exploit effectively. Since it was usually paid against invoices to a particular supplier, an unscrupulous agent occasionally took advantage of the situation to overcharge; or the business could not find a supplier willing to accept the arrangement; or it was unable to buy the variety of stock it needed. But the businessmen were mostly disappointed by the size of the loan. While the ICDC varied its industrial loans according to the applicant's proposal, its commercial loans were usually 20,000 shillings irrespective of what was asked. If the business had planned to take up wholesaling, or convert from general retailing to a more specialized line of goods, the money was often too little:

I asked for 100,000 shillings to buy fifty different items, and stock goods which are rare in the small shops roundabout, and to supply other traders. But 20,000 shillings was not enough, and I bought from only two suppliers. This was not my intention, and it did not meet my needs. For example, the sugar company wanted a deposit of 14,000 shillings on an order for 20,000 shillings worth of sugar, and the 6,000 shillings I had left couldn't be used for many items. I was not very happy about the loan, but nevertheless it was a step towards some of my plans.

The loan they gave me is very small. For someone to be successful getting a loan is a real problem, because of the need to mortgage something. The difficulty of African retailers is that 90 per cent of them have no security, and so can't get loans. My worry is that instead of helping people to grow, loans will only be used to build up the already built. One man that I compete with can get an overdraft for 700,000 shillings, because of his contacts. How can I compete with that?

Three-quarters of the commercial businesses received less than they asked for, and the commercial loans were also substantially smaller than to industry. In 1965 to 1966, the ICDC approved 125 loans for commerce, worth on average just under 19,000 shillings; and 25 to industry, worth about 40,000 shillings. Since a distributor for maize flour or sugar cannot buy in quantities worth less than 10,000 shillings to 20,000 shillings, the loans amounted typically to one or two orders, which raised the stock, but did not radically change the nature of the business. Many of the established shops and wholesalers had a turnover which should have enabled them to get credit of these amounts without the help of Government. The commercial loans had, therefore, less potential influence on economic development than the industrial loans.

The disparity between industry and commerce shows clearly when the ICDC's share of the total investment in businesses of each sector are compared. Apart from hire purchase and profits ploughed back, the average investment in the industrial enterprises from all external sources was about 70,000 shillings, and 53,000 shillings in commerce (excluding one company very much larger than the rest).[1] Of this capital, the ICDC provided an average of 65 per cent in industry and 50 per cent in commerce. But its proportionate share ranged widely, as the following table shows (Table 9):

TABLE 9   *The ICDC's contribution to capital invested*

ICDC's proportion of all external financing	Number of firms*		
	Industry	Commerce	All
Up to a quarter	4	7	11
Over a quarter to half	9	13	22
Over half to three-quarters	14	11	25
Over three-quarters	18	7	25

* Four businesses have been excluded either because they went out of business before the ICDC loan was issued, or because it had not yet been issued.

[1] The distribution of businesses according to the amount invested was:

Total external finance in Kenya shillings	Industrial enterprises	Commercial enterprises	All
10– 24 thousand	12	10	22
25– 49	12	21	33
50– 74	7	3	10
75– 99	4	–	4
100–149	5	3	8
150–199	4	–	4
200–299	–	1	1
300–499	3	1	4
500–999	–	–	–
1 million or more	–	1	1
Total number	47	40	87

The variation is related to the size of the total investment as well as the category of business. The ICDC contributed 76 per cent of the capital in industrial concerns established with less than 50,000 shillings, only 50 per cent in concerns with over 100,000 shillings, and 53 per cent in the middle range: in commerce, the corresponding figures were 58, 19 and 25 per cent. Thus the ICDC was making a relatively small contribution to the most ambitious commercial undertakings, although these were probably the only enterprises in the commercial sector which were really innovative.

Most of the industrial firms depended heavily on ICDC finance. In spite of the delays and the frustrating restrictions, they had little choice at that time, when African competence in industry was virtually untested. We did not come across any substantial African industrial enterprise which had not applied for an ICDC loan. But many of the commercial firms which relied most on the ICDC could be matched by others which had never applied to the Corporation, and done as well. The commercial loans do not on the whole seem to have served any purpose which private finance could not have been expected to meet. Even in industry, the long term advantages of government financing are doubtful.

The virtues of the ICDC loan scheme are obvious and attractive. It lends to African businessmen who cannot easily gain the confidence of banks, suppliers or credit financiers, because they are not known to them, and have no means of proving their reliability. It charges the lowest rate of interest that will cover its costs. It has technical experts to investigate the feasibility of projects, and —as best it can, with a small staff—offers advice to the businesses it supports. But as we found, and other countries have found, a government scheme of this kind also has inherent drawbacks, even when it is intelligently run. It takes a long time to approve loans. Its concern with security and recoverable assets distorts the allocation of resources between equipment and working capital. Its precautions against misuse of funds tie the borrower inflexibly to purchases he cannot freely choose. Its desire to spread its help as widely as it can pares down each loan to a minimum which leaves no margin for difficulties, and even creates them by encouraging investment in secondhand or cheap equipment hard to use efficiently. Caught between the obligation to pioneer new enterprises, and to pay its way, replenishing its fund of loan capital, it can push an able firm with a good market into sustained growth, or ruin a man by giving just enough to make the attempt but not enough to hold him up while he learns from his mistakes.

Commercial lending

What other sources of finance, perhaps less slow and encumbered with conditions, could the businesses turn to? Only two of the firms we visited had been entirely dependent on the ICDC, and seven others had grown from nothing by reinvesting their profits, without any external financing until they applied for a loan. But most had been established with the help of savings, and contributions from partners or shareholders, as Table 10 shows:

TABLE 10 *Sources of original capital excluding ICDC loans*

Businesses whose sources included:	Industry	Commerce	All	All%
Personal savings	16	27	43	49
Contributions from partners	21	6	27	31
Issue of shares	12	1	13	15
Assets of previous business	2	4	6	7
Sale of land or cattle	1	2	3	3
Bank loan	5	1	6	7
Government loan (not ICDC)	5	7	12	14
Credit finance	3	2	5	6
Other	3	6	9	10
No external finance apart from ICDC	4	5	9	10
Total of businesses*	47	40	87	100%

* The total of sources is of course larger, because a business could obtain capital from several sources.

Over half the industrial concerns were partnerships or small private companies, though they included two public companies and a co-operative. Shops can more easily grow from small beginnings under a single proprietor, who relies on his own savings, but two-fifths of the commercial concerns, too, were jointly owned. Even in the survey of market centres, where the businesses were generally much smaller, 31 per cent were owned in partnership. By far the commonest source of capital to start a business is private saving from employment or farm profits, and if the sum is too large for a man to find himself, he turns to friends and acquaintances—former schoolmates or fellow employees—or to members of his family.

But these informal sources cannot provide large amounts. Contributions can only be solicited amongst a man's acquaintance, who know his standing, and they seldom have much to give. Once a partnership or private company has been formed, it does not usually enlarge its membership unless it realizes early on that its present capital will be inadequate, or it plans a major expansion. Since the partners' or shareholders' return on their investment depends entirely on the profits to be distributed, and most businesses plough back the profit in the first few years, a late-comer gets less stake and less say in the firm for his money. The management is already in the hands of others whom the new shareholder has not chosen, and he does not feel so closely identified with it, or take such a pride in it. So it is as difficult to raise more working capital in this way as from Government.

Bank overdrafts or short-term credit from suppliers would be the most appropriate means of tiding a business over the interval between a contract and payment, or of providing a margin of ready money to meet temporary difficulties. But here the industrial businesses, especially, seemed unreasonably restricted, partly because they were not used to dealing with banks, and partly because some bank managers and suppliers evidently thought African businesses too risky to lend to, even when they had substantial and regular accounts.

Indians don't respect Africans. When I get supplies from an Indian, I'm sure that I'm paying five shillings where an Indian would get it for four shillings and fifty cents. And he'd give another Indian credit, but not me. The money I handle in my business—about 20,000 shillings—is not enough. I need bales of cloth for contracts. We have more orders than materials, and when the materials get finished, then we can't take any more work. I tried to get a bank overdraft, but the bank asked for security, or a guarantee from the ICDC. We really need credit. The clothes we make on contract are paid for when they are finished, and sometimes it takes two months to get paid. Meanwhile I want to get good cloth for suits, and I haven't the money.

We pay pay cash mostly for timber. The problem now is that we have big orders from schools, but we don't have the money to buy enough timber. I have applied to the bank for an overdraft, but they want marketable security. I showed them the furniture and machines, but they refused. We need 10,000 shillings. I thought the bank would help me, but now they refuse I don't know where to go. You can't get customers to pay in advance.

Both the businesses quoted were making steady progress, and maintained sizeable accounts.

The experience of the commercial firms had, on the whole, been better. Some had found their bank manager consistently helpful.

Each time I ask for an overdraft he comes and checks my books, and then he'll pay the supplier for me. I'll get two or three weeks to pay. I've had up to 20,000 shillings.

The bank manager always helps us out of trouble, so I can pay cash on time. This has helped us a lot—in fact, more than anything.[T]

The bank manager is a very good friend—the bank has been very helpful to me. I have a very good European here. Even if I send a cheque and I haven't got the money, he won't turn it back. . . . The difficulty is always ready money. Indian business is going on because they get recommendation from the bank, or from their friends. If Government would give recommendation to the bank, it would be alright, better than a loan. This ICDC loan costs me 702 shillings every month. The bank interest is the same—8 per cent—but a bank overdraft is better, because you can get it any time you need it.

The businessmen's comments on their relationship with their bank suggest that a few know their manager personally, and the manager in turn has taken an interest in their affairs. He looks at their books, knows their progress, and advises them how much credit they can have. Other bank managers will not use their personal judgment: they want security or government guarantee, or suggest that a businessman apply instead for a government loan. They do not trouble to inform themselves about the business, and even refuse invitations to visit it. And though more businesses had obtained a bank overdraft than had been refused, many had never asked, convinced that they would be unsuccessful.

Sometimes they believed that Asian managers, like Asian suppliers, were prejudiced against Africans—or even in collusion with their Asian competitors. 'I never asked, because there are only Asians in the bank, there are no Europeans or Africans, so I know they won't give me one.' More often, they seemed so used to looking towards Government for help that they had never thought of approaching the bank. In all, half the businesses had asked for an overdraft, and a third had been given one—but these were mostly commercial (Table 11).

TABLE 11   *Availability of bank overdrafts*

	Industrial	Commercial
Had obtained overdraft	10	19
Applied and refused	8	7
Never applied	29	14
Total no.	47	40

Frustrated or intimidated by their bank, they were scarcely more successful in obtaining credit from their suppliers. As we have already noticed in discussing the problem of credit to customers, African businesses are financially much more constricted than their Asian counterparts. Half bought entirely for cash—sometimes from choice, but often from necessity. Nearly half had been refused credit for at least some of their supplies, even for a few days. Since the Asian businesses with which they competed usually work on large credits for several months, they were at a serious disadvantage: if they could get credit at all, it was for a shorter period and at higher prices. They interpreted this discrimination as racial: Asian wholesalers protected their own community. But it could as well be simply commercial. A wholesaler will not give large credits to a firm he does not know, and therefore he charges more, because the order is smaller. As an Indian businessman put it: 'If an Indian shopkeeper buys 100 blocks of soap, and an African shopkeeper buys ten blocks, he can't compete. He can't buy at the same price. If you buy in quantity, it's natural to give a discount. It's not any kind of discrimination. What can you do about it? It's natural to lower your prices for a good customer. For instance, you may sell sugar at 143 shillings a bag to a man who buys many other things from you, just to please him. You take off that shilling. To someone else you are charging 144 shillings, and that causes trouble.' The discrimination is racial only in the sense that there are so few contacts between Asians and Africans that they have no basis for mutual confidence. 'There's one shop that will give me credit—an Asian who trusts me, he has been helping me for a long time. But the others, I can't convince them. They say an African won't pay, he hasn't got the money. Even cheques they won't accept.' Altogether, 36 per cent of the businesses could get credit for a month, 15 per cent for longer; but another 28 per cent were unable to buy any of their supplies on credit for however short a time, while the rest had never asked for credit. Suppliers who refused included government agencies which, troubled by bad debts, changed to strictly cash terms to all African businesses, irrespective of their record.

Financial trust

Amongst bankers and wholesalers, lack of confidence and personal acquaintance, not lack of resources, inhibited their lending to African businesses. Lack of confidence inhibited the ICDC too. For though it was short of funds, the conditions which encumbered its loans and constricted the working capital of the businesses it supported arose from mistrust of the borrowers' integrity or competence. At the same time, a corresponding mistrust discouraged businessmen from approaching banks and suppliers, or discussing their difficulties in time with the ICDC. This lack of mutual confidence seems a more immediate obstacle than any shortage of capital for investment.

The estrangement of races is partly an inheritance from the colonial past. An African bank official remarked, 'Africans don't feel easy with Europeans. You know, with Europeans we have that belief that if you lie, you'll get what you want, but if you tell the truth you won't get it. I've found that—it goes back to colonial days. On a settler's farm, if a man wanted a few hours off for a perfectly good reason, he knew he wouldn't get it if he told the truth, so he'd say "my wife is sick, I have to take her to hospital" and his boss would say O.K. So too, the European feels he can't trust Africans.' The history of insincerity in encounters between races makes African businessmen hesitate to use banking services, and banks cautious in answering their needs. Between African businessman and Indian wholesaler, the sense of alienation is as great and the tensions more explicit. African businesses begin to cut into the network of family and caste loyalties which sustained Indian commerce, threatening the livelihood of the immigrant community. But the African businessman still sees himself as the victim of racial collusion—offered worse terms, cheated in price and quality, subjected to unfair competition. Thus the range of familiar relationships in which he feels at ease are narrower than those he must handle in his financial affairs. He has to deal with suppliers and bank managers whose language, conventions and social ties are alien to him. The subtleties of expression, dress and manner which enable people of the same culture to gauge each other are all blunted. He lacks the personal contacts, the fluency of communication, the familiarity, assurance and conventional respectability to make his way easily in the commercial culture which surrounds him.

Just because of this isolation, Government is drawn in to open alternative channels of finance. But by this it runs the risk of consolidating the racial segregation it set out to redress.

If confidence is lacking simply in the economic viability of new enterprises, Government can set the example, so long as it is prepared to make mistakes. It shows by its support what can work, and more cautious investors profit by the demonstration. But scarcely any of the enterprises supported by the ICDC were new in this sense: similar businesses, in European or Asian hands, had long been established. The ICDC showed that Africans, too, could run them. The success, for instance, of the Mbuni company—the first African dry cleaner in Nairobi, and one of the earliest of businesses the ICDC financed—made a powerful impression. By such examples, the ICDC helped to prove that hardworking, efficient business management was to be found amongst African businessmen: and however obvious this should have been, the colonial tradition had clouded it with scepticism. But the ICDC could not show how these able entrepreneurs were to be identified, in a way that others might follow. Its procedures were slow and, naturally enough, at first sometimes muddled. It came increasingly to rely on self-protective measures—security, chattel mortgages on equipment, limited and circumscribed commitment of its own resources—which partly undermined the force of its example. The ICDC too, it seemed, was sceptical of African businesses, or at least of its ability to distinguish the competent. At the same time, its existence in itself suggested that African businesses were a special category, outside the concern of commercial lenders. So unwittingly it tended to perpetuate an informal racial segregation.

The crucial need is therefore to integrate African businessmen into the financial network of Kenya. In the long run, a special government loan fund cannot do this, because it stands itself apart from this network. Even if it tries to broaden its influence by working through commercial banks, or guaranteeing credit from suppliers, it only succeeds in relieving them of the risk, and so of the need to inform themselves about African businessmen. Yet without some kind of government intervention, commercial lenders may never bother to face the difficulties of incorporating African businessmen in their community of interest.

Could the ICDC have reconciled the conflicting pressures upon it less clumsily? It could fairly argue that some of the waste and confusion was caused by the businessmen themselves. If they had provided all the information and documents requested at the outset, there would have been fewer delays, and fewer expensive, abortive visits to the Corporation's office. Even so, the scheme had disadvantages from the ICDC's point of view, as well as the businessmen's. In the first place, a revolving loan fund took no account of the speculative nature of entrepreneurship. Whether the business succeeded or failed, whether the returns could be expected soon or late, the interest on the loan was still 8 per cent and still to be repaid over a few years. The ICDC was bound to meet disappointments where the loan would have to be written off. But it gained no compensating advantage from its outstanding successes. Nor could it adjust its return in the light of difficulties or development needs. In practice, it was occasionally forced by circumstances to behave as a partner in an enterprise it wanted to rescue—adding more money, forgoing repayments, taking part in management. But in these instances it seems to have written off its original loan without any compensating claim on future profits.

Secondly, the ICDC tended to be at odds with the businesses it helped to finance as soon as they ran into trouble. As a lender it became a threat, demanding repayments which the business could not sustain, and entitled to claim securities which were often the principal assets of the firm. In these circumstances, businessmen were likely to conceal their difficulties as long as they could, and the ICDC found it hard to offer any useful help.

Thirdly, it is politically difficult to concentrate preferential loans where they will be most useful. If there are many eligible applications—as there were for commercial, though not for industrial, loans—the fund tends to be rationed between the strongest contenders. Most of the ICDC's commercial loans were for 20,000 shillings or less, and they went to businesses which already had a substantial turnover. The amounts were generally much smaller than the borrowers asked—useful enough, but too small to initiate any radical development. Short-term credit from a bank or supplier would have been as cheap, as useful and much quicker to negotiate. It is hard to see how the loans to African retailers and wholesalers served any purpose which commercial credit could not have met. Since Government controlled the distribution of a growing range of goods through the Kenya National Trading Corporation, it could encourage a promising trader by appointing him distributor and allowing him limited credit. The commercial loans, therefore, seem redundant; and they relieved banks and suppliers of a service they ought to undertake.

From this we can begin to see the principles which should guide government intervention. Help will be most effective and most needed where new kinds of business, or new kinds of businessmen, are unable to raise money because private finance is badly informed about the risks. Government usually has more incentive, in the interests of national development or political equity, to discover what the risks are. But once it has proved the viability of new enterprises, it needs to conserve its scarce resources by moving on to pioneer further opportunities. Essentially, it has to mediate between the newcomers and the established commercial network, creating links, not separate channels of finance. It allies itself with new enterprises to introduce them into the economic system.

Loans may not always be the best way of doing this. If, instead of loans at fixed interest, the ICDC had invested equity in businesses it supported, some of its difficulties might have been resolved. It could have adjusted its financial help more flexibly, and compensated for losses by the profits on successful ventures. It could have claimed the right to be represented in the management of the business. It would then have been continuously informed of progress, able to give immediate advice, and less dependent on formal conditions to ensure that its help was properly used. It would no longer have needed to insist on security or designate so rigidly the use to which its funds were put, and would have been able to support the business with working capital with less fear of abuses. This kind of partnership represents the supportive relationship the ICDC hoped to establish more nearly than a contractual loan. Both sides would have had a shared interest in making the best of their position: the choice between reorganization, further investment or winding up their affairs would have had similar consequences for Government and private partners alike. Finally, the ICDC could have exploited its position to encourage the business to make use of commercial credit, and test the willingness of banks and suppliers to offer reasonable terms. It would no longer have been an alternative source of loans, but an applicant on behalf of the firm, and could have insisted more effectively than a private businessman alone that requests were not rejected out of indifference or prejudice.

In effect, something like this had come about informally with one or two companies which the ICDC had wished to rescue. The ICDC is also in partnership with several overseas firms, where it intends to sell out to private African shareholders eventually. If in the same way, it sold its equity in African businesses to its private partners or other investors when the enterprise was well established, it would come as close to a revolving fund as is likely to be practicable, when the purpose is to pioneer new kinds of activity. As it was, the ICDC had to report after its first four years that loans were at a standstill for lack of funds. Equity investment might well be more successful than loans, especially for industrial enterprises which cannot be developed effectively from small beginnings by the reinvestment of profits.

Our analysis suggests, too, that any loan scheme itself should be integrated from the outset with the commercial system. If the banks cannot incorporate lending to small African businesses and farmers within their present activities, Government might share with them the cost of developing better contacts. It takes time and trouble to find out the standing of an African business, the immediate profit to the bank is small, and most bank managers probably do not know where to begin. Political pressure by itself may only encourage a few defensive gestures—loans to politically prominent men, which can be written off for goodwill, or chairmen's statements which their branch managers ignore. If Government were prepared to meet part of the initial cost of staff and expert advice, it could press the rate at which banking services to African business expand.

All the problems we have considered arise from the nature of relationships and the form of institutions. Access to capital is inhibited by the risks which the lenders perceive, and the means they take to protect themselves: but these risks are seen in social rather than economic terms. They mistrust the competence or integrity of businessmen more than the viability of their businesses, and, sensing this mistrust, the businessmen themselves become defensive. Suspicions of racial prejudice, mutual ignorance and lack of confidence frustrate the growth of an inclusive network of commercial relationships. This is the heart of the problem for which policy must devise its remedies.

But in spite of the awkwardness of the ICDC's procedures, the caution of banks and discrimination of suppliers, the problems of access to external finance are not as fundamental as both businessmen and Government believe. When we look into the progress of the businesses the ICDC supported, the shortage of capital begins to seem an illusion, as the following three histories show.

The illusion of capital shortage

Thirty miles from district headquarters, where the main road crosses a stony river bed, a turning leads to Mikuni market. The lane, sandy and pot-holed, winds between sisal hedges and plots of parched maize. The rains here are uncertain. Families depend on the woodcarving industry, and their wage-earners in Nairobi or Mombasa to supplement the produce of their farms. The road runs out in a rough square of half a dozen country stores and one or two workshops, where lines of woodcarvers squat in the shade, chipping away at animal figures for the tourist trade. But the market is dominated by a large new concrete building, with two petrol pumps to one side of it, and a bar and hotel to the other— Mikuni Supply Stores. The shelves which cover the walls, the glass counters, the lines strung below the ceiling, are crammed with shirts, bolts of cloth, cutlery, crockery, hardware, groceries, cigarettes and medicines. The business seems too big for the neighbourhood. But with its two lorries and a van, it serves as wholesaler for the retail shops for twenty miles around.[1]

At the time of our visit the stock was worth 40,000 shillings to 60,000 shillings and the profits of the store, the bar and hotel together were 45,000 shillings in 1966, with all expenses—including the owner's salary—paid. Altogether, about 340,000 shillings has been invested in this business. But apart from a loan of 20,000 shillings from the Industrial and Commercial Development Corporation, the entire enterprise has been built up from its own profits.

The owner was born in 1931, five miles from the market, where his father kept a hotel—the first building in Mikuni. But until he was fifteen years old, the family could not afford to send him to school. Four years later, money for school fees ran out again, and at the age of nineteen, with 30 shillings from his mother, he began his business career—buying eggs in the neighbourhood, and selling them in Nairobi, 60 miles away. A year later, with a letter of recommendation from a schoolteacher to the District Commissioner, he won a place on a three months' traders' course—'and that's where I learned about business'. The fee was 75 shillings. By the end of the next year, egg sales had realized a profit of 500 shillings. and with this he bought a licence to trade in sisal. In the first year's sisal trading he made 2,500 shillings. Then the price slumped, and he prudently withdrew, putting 2,000 in the bank and 500 into his farm. But his ambition was still set on business. 'When I was in school, I had a friend whose father had a shop. I used to help him with his accounts at the weekends. I saw that this old man was making 500 shillings a month, far more than people earning salaries, who get only 90 shillings or 60 shillings. Since that time I determined to be a businessman. Since the very beginning, I had the urge to go into business. And I never wanted to go into partnerships—after six months partnerships collapse, there are quarrels and dishonesty. I wanted to build something up on my own, for my children to take over. And business has widened my mind, visiting different parts of the country, talking to salesmen, finding out what people need. This is what's made me determined to succeed. . . .ᵀ'

[1] In this and following illustrations, we have changed names and details so that the businesses cannot be identified. A reader who seems to recognize a business known to him is likely to be mistaken.

In 1956, sisal prices recovered, and he invested his savings once again in the trade. From then on, the business grew steadily. In 1957 he opened a small shop in the market. In 1958, with 7,000 shillings in hand, he bought a six-ton lorry worth 65,000 shillings at instalments of 4,000 shillings a month. Luckily, the rains were good next season, and the lorry was paid for. Since then he has bought another lorry, a pick-up, and built his present store at a cost of nearly £4,000. Only when all this was established did he apply to the ICDC for a loan, to supplement his working capital. Since then, the business had gone on growing.

In a side street of a town of small workshops and thriving markets stands the Sunshine Garage, hidden behind the carcasses of stranded buses. It takes its name from its origins. 'I started this business myself under a tree by the petrol station—out in the open, that's where I got the name. I had no licence, and the municipality worried me too much. I started with a spanner—five shillings, that's all the capital I had. But I'd been friendly with a Minister for a long time. I was a politician, and he'd been a Member for my constituency. I used to see him at every rally, every meeting—I was secretary of the Party at that time. He asked me why I didn't start my own business. So I tried, working in the open under that tree there, until the municipality told me to close down. So I went to a European farm as a mechanic, and worked there for a year. Then an Asian bought the farm, so I left. I don't like working with Asians. I started again, just in the open. I was alone for a month, and then I asked three others to join me. But the municipality was still worrying us because we didn't have a proper plot or a licence. Then my friend the Minister intervened with the Ministry of Local Government, who wrote to the Council asking them not to force us to close down until we could find a suitable plot. I got to hear of two plots, so I asked the Minister to come out and look at them. He talked to the owners, and advised us to buy this one. It was 20,000 shillings, but we only had 11,000 in the bank, so he guaranteed us another 9,000 on his own security. Then he gave me an application form to apply to the ICDC, and we got a loan of 20,000 shillings a few months later.' From this they repaid the 9,000 shillings.

Apart from the ICDC loan, and the 11,000 shillings the four partners had raised from their own savings, the business had no other capital. But after two years of reinvesting their profits, they had installed a lathe, grinder, drill, vices, gas and electric welding equipment, bought a lorry and built a concrete store for a stock of spare parts. The business was now worth about double its original capital, and there was as much again in a savings account. 'But we haven't made any progress at all yet', remarked the founder of the business. 'We want to take on another experienced mechanic. And I'd like to become a machine-tools agent upcountry and import spare parts. Though really I'm quite pleased. I would never have done it without my friend's advice. I thought, God knows how I can start a business without capital. But since he promised to help me . . . I think God sent him to help me. He said he too came from a poor family, and knew the problems.'

In the same town, there is an African dry-cleaning firm—the only plant of its kind in the district. The company has sixteen shareholders, five of them brothers. It owns a second dry-cleaning plant in another town, and runs a taxi service with two Peugeot station wagons. The equipment is the most up to date available, and has been ingeniously installed to achieve the greatest economy of water and fuel—'the Italian *fundi*[1] who put it in for me said he'd never seen anything like it, but it seems to work alright.' The dry-cleaning machine itself has been labelled by the managing director with arrows and a legend, so that every worker on the staff can see for himself how it operates. This is the style of the management: accounts, records, equipment are kept in scrupulously methodical order, born of a fascinated love for the details of commercial technology.

The two dry-cleaning plants were financed at a cost of 130,000 shillings. The shareholders originally contributed just under 18,000 shillings, with which they bought their first dry-cleaning equipment. When this had been running successfully for a few months, they applied to the ICDC for a loan of 80,000 shillings. 'The purpose of the loan', they wrote, 'is to expand the present business. Initially we started on a pilot basis with the minimum of equipment. Although we have only been in business three months, sales have far exceeded expectations. We are operating twelve hours a day, and we are not able to cope with the business.' After a year's negotiations, the ICDC approved a loan of 50,000 shillings, at 8 per cent interest, on the security of their equipment. But meanwhile they had already bought and installed the

[1] Craftsman (a Swahili word often used in Kenya in place of its English equivalent).

machinery with their own money, by paying an initial instalment of 18,000 shillings. The machinery for their second plant was paid for half out of profits and half by hire-purchase through a credit finance company. Later they bought another 30,000 shillings worth of equipment with a bank overdraft. The net profit for the first year was 60,000 shillings, which had all been ploughed back into the business.

Each of these three enterprises—wholesaler, blacksmith, dry cleaner—were, when we visited them, profitable and growing. They were managed by men of three different tribes, but with much else in common. None had more than five years primary education, but all three knew their trade from years of practical experience—and they seemed all three alert, enthusiastic and ambitious, unassuming but resourceful. None began with any substantial capital of his own, and they came from families, like most families in Kenya, with little land, and barely the income even to pay for a few years' schooling for their children. Yet none of these businesses depended, in the last resort, on government help for its creation. They came into being because, at a crucial point of decision, their founders risked all they had—one on a lorry he could not afford, others on a plot they lacked the money to buy, others on equipment for a service that might have found no market. The ICDC helped them to consolidate their success and to grow more quickly. It did not create them.

In general the most important single source of finance for the businesses the ICDC supported was not its own loans, nor the shares contributed, nor any overdraft or credit, but the reinvested profits of the enterprise. For though the ICDC usually provided the greater part of the external capital, its loan amounted to less than half the present value of the concerns. Most of the businesses had ploughed back all their profit, and had net assets worth considerably more than had ever been invested from outside. If we exclude the seven which had failed, and two which could not estimate their present value, the commercial businesses had invested on average 56,000 shillings (including the ICDC loan, their original capital, and any other shares, loans or contributions from outside) and were worth 156,000 shillings when we visited them.[1]

[1] The figures for commerce exclude also one very large concern, whose value had increased from about 1,900,000 shillings to 2,300,000 shillings. The estimates of present value were sometimes taken from audited accounts, but were generally only

The industrial businesses had invested 76,000 shillings and were worth 113,000 shillings. Half the commercial businesses had better than trebled their value, while 45 per cent of the industrial businesses had increased by at least 25 per cent. The difference can be explained by the higher investment in industry, the higher rate of failure, and their shorter life: only 30 per cent of the industrial concerns had been running more than five years, but 67 per cent of the commercial. Even so, nearly half the industrial businesses had substantial profits to reinvest within the first year or two of operation.

To an African entrepreneur with only a few years education, and a few hundred shillings in post office savings, with no security to to offer, no friends amongst the Asian wholesalers in his nearest town, nothing achieved to convince his acquaintances to trust him with their money, capital must seem the crucial obstacle. Yet most of the businesses made a start with very few initial resources, and grew as much from their own momentum as from outside help. And those which depended most on Government were the least successful. Altogether, we came across only 14 businesses where negotiations with the ICDC began before they were already operating. All of these were industrial concerns, including several dry cleaners and sawmills, and the loans made up the greater part of their initial capital. In this sense, the ICDC helped to start them. They would have been hard put to find enough money to begin without its support—though other similar businesses had been able to buy a minimum of equipment before they applied for a loan. But only four of these 14 were initiated by Government, in the sense of suggesting the activity and promoting its organization. All four had been unsuccessful. One—an ambitious manufacturing concern—had at last found a profitable basis in association with an overseas firm after losing a lot of money; one seemed about to collapse through quarrels in the partnership, and the doubtful competence of its manager; one had struggled ably for several years to overcome a fundamental miscalculation of the economic possibilities, before it reluctantly gave in before the cost of pursuing ever-dwindling supplies of raw material; and one was defeated by technical difficulties it could not solve. In the last of these instances, the owners had proposed an altogether different

---

rough calculations based on the assets of the business. Though they are not accurate, they are reasonably realistic, and should be within a 10 per cent margin of error.

activity, and been over-persuaded by the ICDC. Because of this, they lacked confidence: when troubles started, they looked to the ICDC, while the ICDC expected them to assume responsibility for the concern. 'We couldn't get the machines to produce. If at all we'd thought of the idea ourselves, we'd have gone as far as we could, or we'd have trained someone. But we were blind in all this. We'd definitely have been better off if we'd stuck to our first idea.' Experience suggests that the ICDC was wiser to act as facilitator than as promoter, using its funds to encourage enterprise rather than to implement ideas of its own.

From every point of view, the role of government finance seems, therefore, to be narrowly circumscribed. Unless it pioneers loans to new kinds of enterprise, it tends to be redundant, but if it takes too strong an initiative, it overwhelms the entrepreneurial drive of its clients. It can help businesses forward at crucial stages in their growth, but if it encourages them to expand too soon it may destroy them; and if it goes on helping them when they are well established it only institutionalizes their segregation from the network of private finance. It is a subtle role, and so tends to be encumbered with precautions which take too long: the delays and restrictions may then outweigh its benefits. But it is just as damaging to lend improvidently, and confirm the prejudice against African business by losing a lot of money.

These constraints derive from the nature of the need for government intervention. It is not that capital as such is unavailable. Business ventures can attract rural savings on easy terms and commercial credit is not over-extended. Even the ICDC's shortage of funds was in a sense artificial. If there were many promising African enterprises stagnating for lack of investment, Government could allocate more of its resources to the small business scheme or raise overseas backing to enlarge it. The need is to improve access to capital where social barriers inhibit economic relationships—in the Kenya government's terms, to overcome the racial discrimination inherited from the colonial past—rather than create capital. But the circumstances where a public loan scheme can provide capital no private lender will venture, and yet not incur much greater risks, are likely to be transitional and particular. Government finance has therefore to steer a very finely drawn line.

This argument leaves out of account, however, the second

major form of intervention open to Government: training in skills. The reluctance of private finance to support African businessmen arises not only from lack of information, but from plausible doubts about their competence. If they cannot organize their labour, keep accounts or manage technical processes, money will not help them, and the social structure which isolates them from the financial network is likely to deny them experience of these skills too. If a loan scheme can be supported with training and advice, the margin of potentially competent businesses too risky for private investors but not for Government might be broader. In time, such training might establish a businessman's credentials for support from private investors too. But this presupposes that African businessmen are handicapped by inexperience of skills which are readily teachable, and to this question we now turn.

9

EDUCATION AND TRAINING

An entrepreneur needs three kinds of skill: a practical imagination, which enables him to recognize opportunities new at least in his own world of experience; an ability to order the day-to-day routine of his business so that money is accounted for, employees know their work, orders are recorded and fulfilled, the plant repaired and serviced; and enough general knowledge to support these first two skills, since even the most imaginative organizer is helpless without information.

But the relevance of general education or specific vocational skills must vary with the stage of development a business has reached. A crucial obstacle at one point scarcely matters at another. Without some competence at reading, writing and simple arithmetic, it is hard to practise business at all; beyond this, education may become important again only at a much higher level of sophistication, when a businessman needs to command a wide range of general knowledge and handle professionally trained subordinates. Similarly, he may not need much managerial expertise while he pioneers small enterprises under his personal supervision; but as his activities outgrow these bounds, he can be faced with problems of organization he is helpless to control. So, too, a craftsman repairing bicycles in the market place, or making chairs and cupboards for his neighbours, does not need great skill. His customers do not expect and cannot afford well finished work, and his competitors are equally unsophisticated. Even if he could do better, his skill is unusable at this level because it has no market. Only as he begins to buy expensive equipment, and so has to sell a much greater volume of production, do quality and control of costs become crucial. For at this stage he begins to compete with European or Asian firms, and it is no longer enough to turn out on demand a usable article whose cheapness excuses its clumsy workmanship. If we think of the relationship between skills and business activities in this way, as a series of thresholds, then at different stages of development different kinds of ignorance will become an obstacle. And once that obstacle is overcome, more training or experience in that skill will be redundant, at least for the time being.

For this reason alone, success in business is not likely to be closely and continuously associated with education or vocational training. Any attempt to teach entrepreneurial skills would have to determine very exactly what handicaps a businessman at a particular point in his growth. But it is uncertain, besides, whether an entrepreneur ever really acquires the skills he uses through formal education. The great innovators of the industrial revolution were characteristically self-taught. Thomas Telford, for instance, whose roads, bridges and canals transformed the transport links of Britain, was the son of a shepherd, apprenticed at the age of fourteen to a stonemason. Richard Arkwright, mill owner and inventor of the spinning jenny, was a barber's apprentice at sixteen. Andrew Carnegie, who developed the Pittsburgh iron and steel workshops into a great industrial empire, was fourteen when he took his first job—at a dollar a week, as a weaver's assistant in a cotton factory. Henry Ford was working in a machine shop at seventeen, William Morris repairing bicycles at sixteen. None of them had much more schooling than most African businessmen. Their fathers—farmers, shepherds, craftsmen—followed the occupations common to rural Africa. And they began their working lives with as few advantages.[1]

Even so, Kenya is not, as America 100 years ago, an underpopulated land of vast unexploited resources, nor like nineteenth century Britain the pioneer of a revolution in applied science. The machines and techniques of African enterprise come from more advanced societies, and it competes in the same markets.

[1] 'Possibly it may already have struck the reader with surprise, that not only were all the engineers described in the preceding pages self-taught in their professions, but they were brought up mostly in remote country places, far from the active life of great towns and cities. . . . Strange indeed it is that the men who have built our bridges, docks, lighthouses, canals, and railways should nearly all have been country-bred boys. Edwards and Brindley, the sons of small farmers; Smeaton brought up in his father's country house at Austhorpe; Rennie, the son of a farmer and freeholder; and Stephenson, brought up in a hamlet, an engine-tenter's son. But Telford, even more than any of these, was a purely country-bred boy, and was born and brought up in a valley so secluded that it could not even boast of a cluster of houses of the dimensions of a village' (Smiles, Vol. 2, p. 292).

It has to assimilate the achievements of the industrial revolution, not re-enact it in on another stage. In a technologically sophisticated world, the range of opportunities open to a self-taught entrepreneur may be much more constricted. The expectations of his customers do not grow with his ability to satisfy them, as in an earlier age, but are already formed by the products of the most advanced industrial nations. The businessman himself is inhibited by his unfamiliarity with the techniques of modern industry, which set the ultimate standard for his own ambitions. The promotion of African enterprise, as an attempt to transfer economic power from rich nations to poor, from white races to black, may be teachable by means which were not open to the pioneers of the industrial revolution.

Certainly the industrial businessmen whom the ICDC supported were much aware of the gap between their knowledge and their aspirations, and looked to Government for advice and training even more insistently than they looked for loans. They saw themselves as novices in business, whose mistakes came from ignorance rather than lack of invention, and envied the experience of their European and Asian rivals. But the problems of providing useful training are as complex as those which beset financial aid. A creative imagination itself perhaps cannot be taught at all, and the value of improving specific skills depends on whether a business has reached a threshold of competence in that skill. As a business develops, too, advice is harder to give, because the problems are as unfamiliar to Government and its consultants as to businessmen themselves. Techniques, methods, organization, all have to be thought out afresh in the setting of Kenya's economy, and the experience of other countries is only speculatively useful.

At the same time, education or training may actually discourage entrepreneurship by opening less risky opportunities of earning a living, with perhaps higher prestige. To understand how education relates to business, we have to look on education not only as a source of knowledge, but as the principal system of allocating status and chances in life. In this sense, as we discussed in chapter 3, denial of education may be the spur to original enterprise. Hence the correspondence between education, training, practical experience and the achievements of the businessmen we interviewed was not consistent. The potential value of training

will perhaps become clearer when the complexity of these relationships have been unravelled.

The influence of education

At every level of business activity, we interviewed men who had
completed a primary education and others who had never been to
school, craftsmen with trade-school grades and self-taught
improvisors. Experience and education were no guarantee of
success: the son of a poor family who could never afford school
fees nor find skilled employment might prove to be an outstanding
entrepreneur. Two of the largest enterprises—one with over 100
employees—were run by men with no formal education at all;
while one of the few graduates, from an Indian business school,
was managing a concern with only three workers and two
apprentices.

The uneducated, untrained entrepreneurs had often taught
themselves, grasping at every opportunity that came their way.
Several of the Kikuyu businessmen, for instance, had spent years
in detention during the Emergency, and these 'hard core Mau
Mau' (as the colonial administration classified them) occupied the
tedious hours of prison life by teaching each other. 'I was a leader
of Mau Mau in Nairobi, secretary of a Mau Mau society', explained
the manager of two businesses, and partner in a cattle ranch,
whose father had been a labourer at six shillings a month on a
European farm. 'I never went to school, and in 1953 I was detained for six years. But when I was in detention camp, there were
people who were very eager to teach us. And after I had learned
some English, I did a correspondence course. I was paying thirty
shillings a month from the money they paid us in the camp. And
again, when I was in detention I read a lot of books, especially
books by Dale Carnegie—"How to win Friends". They are very
nice.' The detainees were determined patriots, who even before
Independence saw their struggle in economic as well as political
terms, and planned how they, as Africans, could prove themselves
in business. They discussed their future careers, exchanged experiences of sawmilling, bus companies, shops they had run, and even
formed provisional partnerships.

Some businessmen, too, had taught themselves a trade by
curiosity and intelligence alone. A carpenter told us how as a

child he had found a six-inch nail, and hammered it into a crude chisel on a railway line. With the chisel he made carts for other children to carry water. Then he watched someone making a bed, and made a bed himself with his chisel and a panga. He sold it for two shillings, and bought fifty-cents worth of nails and a saw for a shilling. The son of a widow, he had no money for schooling, or even for clothes: he dressed in skins. But bit by bit he bought more tools, and his furniture became less clumsy. He was always studying furniture to see how it was made, and then drawing out plans at home—'I was very curious'. As he grew up, he took a labourer's job in a sawmill, still making furniture in his spare time. Eventually the firm discovered his talent and employed him as a carpenter. But they never trained him. When we met him, he was running a busy furniture workshop with contracts from schools and a hospital and planned to start a small sawmill of his own.

Children often take up trading to help pay their school fees, and probably learn more about the principles of business in competition with their schoolmates than they will ever hear in the classroom. Many of the successful businessmen from the area of Nyeri district which we studied particularly, for instance, had engaged as schoolboys in the egg trade. Every Saturday morning, the boys walked ten miles into the township to sell the eggs they had bought from the farmers around their homes. The ablest trader began buying his eggs early in the week, to ensure his stock, and arrived in town before his mates, to catch the best of the market. But to calculate how soon to buy without the eggs going stale, and how many to carry without breaking them, or coming too late, took shrewd commercial judgment. The most successful of this generation of schoolboy egg traders is now the most outstanding of its businessmen: he beat his competitors by cutting school on Friday afternoons—confident that he could catch up on his school work—and put himself a day ahead of the race. Some of the older businessmen we interviewed had made long journeys to settlers' farms and Masai country, earning a few shillings and trading their wages for livestock, before they were fifteen.

Yet despite the success of some uneducated men and the variety of experience, the businessmen were as a whole more educated than most of the population. According to the 1962 census, two-thirds of the men in Kenya had never been to school—over half even in Central Province, the most educationally advanced region. But only 23 per cent of the businessmen we interviewed in the market centres were completely uneducated, and 7 per cent of the businessmen supported by the ICDC. The disparity is still marked when the growth in educational opportunities over the years is taken into account: the businessmen included a higher proportion with primary or secondary education than the age group most comparable with their own[1] (Table 12).

TABLE 12 *Education of businessmen and the general population*

| | Per cent with years of formal education | | |
	None	1–8 (*Primary*)	9 or more (*Secondary*)
Males over 15 (Kenya)*	68%	31%	1%
Males 25–29 (Kenya)*	51%	46%	3%
Market businessmen	23%	73%	4%
ICDC-supported businessmen	7%	68%	25%

* The census figures exclude the Northern Province—the most arid and sparsely settled area.

These figures also suggest that the level of education rises with the scale of business, since the two groups of businessmen are as different from each other as they are from the general population. The businesses supported by the ICDC were on the whole much larger than the others: 70 per cent had more than five workers—mostly between six and twenty, but including nine businesses with over forty—while nearly half the businesses in the market centres had no employees at all, and only 4 per cent more than five. When the businesses are sorted by size, a consistent association appears between number of workers and years of schooling. Though the proportion of wholly uneducated businessmen remains about the same irrespective of the number of workers, there are more men with secondary education in the larger concerns, and fewer with less than four years schooling. As Table 13 shows, the more workers a business employs, the more likely that it will be run by a

[1] Three-quarters of the ICDC-supported businessmen and two-thirds of those in the market centres were between 30 and 50 years old when we interviewed them. Few, therefore, would have been less than 25 at the time of the census, four or five years before. Many would already have been over 29. The comparison therefore under-estimates the educational difference between businessmen and others of their generation, since the proportion of educated men declines consistently with age. In 1962, 40 per cent aged 15–19 had no education, 44 per cent at 20–24, 56 per cent at 30–34, 70 per cent at 40–44, 80 per cent at 50–54, up to 90 per cent amongst men in their seventies.

relatively educated man—though at every level, most businessmen have still never gone beyond the senior years of primary school.

TABLE 13 *Education and size of business*

| | Per cent with years of formal education | | | |
	Less than 4	*4–8*	*9 or more*	*Total no.*
Market businessmen:*				
no employees	40%	56%	4%	379
1–5 employees	35%	60%	5%	421
6 or more employees	25%	62%	13%	32
All	36%	60%	4%	832
ICDC-supported businessmen:				
1–5 employees	27%	58%	15%	26
6–10 employees	17%	58%	25%	24
11 or more employees	8%	62%	30%	37
All	20%	55%	25%	87

* Excluding 16 where adequate information was not gathered.

Amongst the businesses supported by the ICDC, however, the nature of the enterprise influenced the level of education it attracted as much as its size. The industrial concerns were generally larger—half of them had over ten workers compared with a third in commerce—but even size for size they were more often run by relatively educated men. Only 17 per cent of the industrial businessmen with fewer than six employees had less than four years education, as against 36 per cent of commercial men. With more employees, the proportion with little education was much the same in both groups, but many more of the industrialists had some years of secondary schooling—46 per cent to 8 per cent, for those with six to ten workers; 33 per cent to 23 per cent for those with more than ten. Since these percentages are based on very small numbers, too much cannot be made of them. But businesses which use more sophisticated methods might be expected to attract more educated men. Though they were not on the whole technically complex, the industrial enterprises supported by the ICDC still required an understanding of modern machines, and more facility in reading catalogues, estimating installation and running costs, testing the skill of prospective employees than rural shopkeeping or small craft workshops.

If the size and technical requirements of a business are taken as rough indications of its sophistication, then our findings suggest that the kind of business a man undertakes is partly influenced by his education. But it does not follow that more education would raise the number of *successful* enterprises: it may influence a man's confidence or ambition rather than his competence in business. In practice, we found a direct relationship between the success of an enterprise and the education of its owner only amongst the businesses in the market centres: that is, although more sophisticated businesses attract more educated men, paradoxically education is not associated with successful management as it is in simpler businesses.

We divided the businesses in the market centres according to whether they made as much as 300 shillings profit a month—a figure which seemed to distinguish the more successful businesses better than any other classification.[1] It represents a substantially higher income than unskilled workers could earn at the time, even in Nairobi. A businessman's chance of making as much as 300 shillings improved consistently, the longer he had been to school (Table 14):

TABLE 14   *Education and size of profit*

| *Market businessmen making profits** | *Percentage with years of formal education* | | | |
	Less than 4	*4–8*	*9 or more*	*All*
Under 300/– p.m.	79%	68%	57%	72%
300/– p.m. or more	21%	32%	43%	28%
Total %	100%	100%	100%	100%
Total no.	215	374	28	617

* Excluding businessmen who could not estimate their profit.

[1] The estimates of profit were only rough. A quarter of the businessmen could, or would, not give us any figure, and they have been excluded from the analysis. Others may have been mistaken or purposely misleading. But the interviewers were asked to make their own assessment of each business—from the quantity and range of stock, the number of customers they saw, the neatness and sense of activity they noticed—and their impressions on the whole confirm the businessmen's own claims. The interviewers judged 69 per cent of the businesses claiming to make a profit of 300 shillings or more to be above average in quality, and 3 per cent below average. Of the businesses claiming to make less, they thought only 28 per cent above average and 22 per cent below. The correspondence between higher stated profits and the interviewers' assessment does not become much closer if the line is drawn at 400 shillings or 500 shillings rather than 300 shillings, but becomes markedly less close when a lower figure is taken.

This is still so when the size of business is held constant. For though, as we have seen, more educated men tended to employ more workers, and these larger businesses were on the whole more profitable, even the smallest businesses were more likely to realize 300 shillings a month as the education of their owners increased. Similarly with age: businessmen in their thirties and forties tended to make higher profits than either younger or older men, but in every age group the more educated were more successful. Amongst men under 30, only 8 per cent with less than four years schooling made as much as 300 shillings a month, but 20 per cent of the rest; in the 30–39 age group, 29 per cent of the less educated and 34 per cent of the more educated made 300 shillings; in the 40–44 age group, 24 per cent and and 46 per cent; and for older men, 14 per cent and 34 per cent. Thus except in their thirties, education improved the businessmen's chances of realizing a higher level of profit by 15 per cent or 20 per cent.

All the analysis so far suggests that the longer children go to school, the more they will learn there that can be useful to them later in business. The larger the business, or the more profitable, the more likely it is that the man running it will have been to school for several years at least, and perhaps even taken a teacher-training course after primary school, or spent a few years at secondary school. If this is so, then the development of African businesses would be quicker if more educated men were encouraged to turn to a business career. Yet the evidence of the ICDC-supported businesses suggests that the advantage of more education disappears just at the point where the scale of activity begins to be large enough to attract educated recruits. The achievement of these larger businesses seemed to bear no relationship at all to the education of the men who ran them.

The ICDC-supported businesses cannot be very meaningfully distinguished by their level of profit. They were much more various in size and activity than the market businesses, many were only in their second or third year of operation, and the amount of their profits could often only be calculated after the year's end, so that any accurate figures available were already out of date. Instead, we have divided them into five groups, on the basis of all the information we could gather: those which were profitable and expanding; profitable but not growing; doubtful (not yet profitable, or undergoing reorganization, the future unpredictable); apparently failing;

and already failed. By these criteria, twenty of the industrial and fourteen of the commercial enterprises fall into the first category—both profitable and expanding. But there is hardly any tendency for the more educated owners to be concentrated in this group of businesses[1] (Table 15):

TABLE 15   *Education and progress of ICDC-supported businessmen*

| | Years of formal education | | | |
	Less than 4	4–8	9 or more	All
Owners of profitable and expanding businesses	35%	39%	43%	39%
Others	65%	61%	57%	61%
Total %	100%	100%	100%	100%
Total no.	17	48	21	86*

* Excluding one business too new to assess its prospects.

Nor does an analysis by age groups suggest that education would be any more clearly associated with the progress of the business if age were held constant, though our sample is too small to show this with adequate numbers.

At first sight, it seems puzzling that an otherwise consistent association between education and achievement should break down just as businesses begin to become more sophisticated. But more sophisticated businesses tend also to be more specialized, both in the markets they serve and the products they sell. So it is not after all unlikely that general education should become less relevant as business activities progress. Conversely, specialized training should become more important. And this seems to be so: the relationship between practical experience and achievement develops in the opposite way to education. Apprenticeship, training or employment in a relevant trade seems to have no influence on the success of simpler businesses, but is associated with the progress of the industrial enterprises supported by the ICDC—the category of business where success seems to have least to do with education. The rural shopkeepers or craftsmen who had been to a training school, or been apprenticed or employed in the trade they followed, were not as a whole making any more substantial

[1] If commercial and industrial businessmen are looked at separately, the most progressive commercial men do tend to have rather more education than the others, but not the progressive industrialists. But the numbers in each category become too small to put much confidence in the differences.

profits than the rest. But amongst the industrial businessmen supported by the ICDC, 60 per cent running profitable and expanding firms had some related practical experience, as against only 36 per cent of the rest. Experience only in other trades than their present business did not help, suggesting that training or employment in a skilled trade are only useful when they are specifically relevant to the jobs in hand.

Education, then, is associated with the size and nature of the business a man attempts, but it does not improve his chances of doing well beyond a simple level of activity: and conversely, only as businesses become more sophisticated does practical experience in that work begin to affect his prospects. This suggests two critical thresholds in the development of business skills. The first is elementary literacy. A businessman needs to be able to read and write enough to understand a catalogue, or a bank statement, send an order, prepare an invoice; he needs to know enough arithmetic to add up his accounts; he needs enough Swahili or English to talk to an Asian wholesaler. These are all skills which a primary school teaches. A boy who has never been to school must start in business at a disadvantage: he has to teach himself these skills. So amongst the uneducated, only the most determined and intelligent are likely to survive in business, even on a small scale. But once a schoolboy has mastered reading, writing, arithmetic and simple English, he does not learn much more that would help him in a business career. He does not need algebra to keep his books, nor to have stumbled through *Macbeth* or *The Merchant of Venice* to write a commercial letter. 'What use has algebra been to me?' as one prominent shopkeeper exclaimed. ' "Every debit has a credit, and every credit has a debit", has been much more help.'

Why then should secondary education have any influence on business at all? In practice, as we have seen, the more ambitious the enterprise, the more likely that it will be run by a man with some secondary schooling. But as well as a threshold of basic skills, there is also a threshold of ambition which the prospective businessman must cross. It is easier to teach yourself literacy than a sense of assurance that you too can run a garage, a bus company, a bakery, a wholesale store like the Asian whose prosperity you envy. To be more educated than most of your generation gives a sense of superiority which raises your expectations: even without any experience of business, a schoolteacher would hardly be content to be a petty shopkeeper. The retailers or craftsmen in the market centres and the industrial businessmen supported by the ICDC related their ambitions to different scales of achievement. The country shopkeepers were trying to make a little more than they could hope to earn from unskilled employment or farming their small-holdings. But the industrialists were trying to compensate for their exclusion from the well paid and prestigious occupations open to the graduates of higher education. As we saw in the analysis of the social origins of entrepreneurs, they turned to business when their vocational aspirations had been frustrated. Able men, who find that schooling well beyond the average still does not qualify them for satisfying jobs, will set their business aims in terms of the opportunities they might have had, if they had pursued their education even further. Thus the more educated businessmen tended to undertake bigger and more sophisticated enterprises, not because their education had qualified them, but because their reference group was of an altogether higher status.

This pattern of ambition, however, could lead them into the trap of running their businesses as if they were civil servants, like the men by whom they set their standards—going too much by the book, too impressed with prestigious customers, too well dressed and too bound to their neat office desks. At the same time, their education had not taught them much that was directly useful to the specialized business which attracted them. So education influenced the size and nature of their undertaking, not their chances of success. Unless they had experience of working in an established firm, it was hard to find out what kind of equipment they needed, the realities of costing and pricing, where they could recruit skilled employees. If they had to work all this out for themselves, they depended all the more on their own craftsmanship to cut, trim, fashion their material into something people would buy at a price that paid their workmen, machinery and rent. Without either experience or training, or skilled assistants to guide them, their mistakes were likely to run them out of business before they could learn from them.

Here lies a second threshold of skills which businessmen must cross as they develop. A man can teach himself a craft, as many did, by trial and error. But once he installs equipment on any scale, he defines his product and his market within much narrower limits, where the margins of price and quality have little tolerance for miscalculation. Even in retailing, the development from general store to specialized outlet, from country to town, involves a change in the range and quantity of stock that calls for much more informed judgment. The stages of growth are not a continuous progress by gradual increments of capital and experience: there are decisive steps when only a different order of investment and skill, a shift to a different kind of market, can push the scale of business much further. The businesses supported by the ICDC—and especially the industrial businesses—represent such a stage in development.

The men who ran them were therefore greatly preoccupied by the need for training and advice in the management of modern businesses. They envied European businessmen their knowledge and long commercial history, and rated their experience a greater asset than any other advantage—capital, connections, privileged status—that Europeans might possess. Unlike the businessmen in the market centres, who seldom mentioned any possible government aid apart from loans, nearly two-thirds of the ICDC-supported businessmen asked for advisory services and practical training. They wanted loans too, almost as often: but they recognized the futility of capital without the expertise to use it. Can practical advice, relevant to the needs of a particular business, be effectively organized as a public service?

The problems of training entrepreneurs

The ICDC itself, with a total staff of about 30, could not provide either the time or the range of expertise to advise businesses generally. It had helped some to choose equipment,[1] but for the most part it had to assume that the businessmen it supported knew what they were about. The only other source of advice specifically for business were the trade development officers, who are posted in each province under the Ministry of Commerce and Industry. But none of the businessmen contacted them, except to inquire about loans, or forward their applications. The trade development officers are responsible for licences and loan applications, and the organization of short courses in book-keeping, rather than advice on technical problems of managing a business, for which they are

[1] Three-fifths of the industrial businesses had been advised by the ICDC on choosing equipment, or by the suppliers of machinery in installing it.

not equipped. So there was a need for technical advice and training which, when these businesses were starting, had not been met.

Assistance of this kind is intrinsically difficult to organize, because the needs of each business are different. As we have seen, the businessmen were handicapped not by lack of general knowledge but by ignorance of specific techniques and methods. An advisory service would therefore have to call upon a wide range of experience and skills, and apply them to the particular problems which each business presented. Even if it could recruit a staff versatile enough to give useful advice to many of its clients, such a service would be expensive. It is much more economical to identify needs which businesses share, and organize courses to meet them. So, in practice, help tends to concentrate on methods of book-keeping, as the one skill which all businesses use, and few African businessmen have learned. Is poor accounting as serious a handicap as this would imply?

Amongst both the market businesses, and the businesses supported by the ICDC, achievement does seem to be related to the quality of accounting, judged by the crude measure of the number of books kept. Since each book is a different kind of financial record, the number of books should represent the thoroughness of accounting—assuming that the entries are well maintained, and the information used. Three-quarters of the most progressive of the ICDC-supported industrial firms, for instance, keep at least three books, but less than half the others: half the most progressive commercial enterprises keep three or more books, less than a quarter of the others. And in the market centres, the businesses making 300 shillings profit each month or more were twice as likely to keep three books, half as likely to keep none.[1] The profitable and growing ICDC-supported businesses were also rather more likely to have their accounts audited—though this might have been as much a consequence as a cause of their success, since the fee is substantial.

As a less crude measure, in the interviews with the ICDC-supported businessmen we tried to explore their methods of

[1] Thirteen per cent of the more profitable businesses kept no books, 42 per cent one book, 27 per cent two books and 18 per cent three or more. For the businesses making less than 300 shillings the proportions are 32 per cent none, 42 per cent one, 18 per cent two and 8 per cent three books or more. Only 3 per cent of the ICDC businesses kept no books at all, 18 per cent only one—nearly all of them amongst the less progressive—32 per cent kept two and 47 per cent three or more.

costing, pricing and estimating profit. Here, it must be admitted, the interviewers floundered in as much confusion as their informants, as we struggled to sort out the complexity of pragmatic adjustments. Depreciation, for instance, is commonly ignored, or left to the accountants: but sometimes included in a rough and ready way in the cost of running a machine, or recognized as a charge on the profits reinvested. Some businesses, such as butcheries, need only the simplest of procedures. An animal is bought one day: two days later it has either been sold or gone bad. The butcher knows what he has made immediately. But a mining company may be investing for years in experiment and development before it begins to see much profit. A furniture maker or a tailor can adjust his prices to his costs, since each piece is custom made. A dry cleaner or baker must charge the going rate. So the ease and immediate relevance of costing varies greatly from one kind of business to another, according to how it fixes its prices, and the proportion of its costs to be distributed on overheads. But we understood enough to classify the businesses into those which did not seem to estimate their costs at all (of which there were only six); those which used rule-of-thumb calculations, based on experience or the conventional wisdom of the trade (54 businesses); and those which worked out their costs systematically (27 businesses). A higher proportion of the profitable and growing businesses worked out costs systematically—44 per cent, compared with 23 per cent of the rest.

Yet, though the performance of the business was related to the quality of the book-keeping, it did not relate to the qualifications of the book-keeper. As it happens, the only two ICDC-supported businesses whose books were kept by qualified accountants were among the relatively less successful; while the books of nine highly successful enterprises were kept by men with no previous training or experience at all. As a whole, 69 per cent of the most progressive businesses had a book-keeper with training or experience, and 56 per cent of the others—a difference which could easily be fortuitous. Clearly, many of the successful businessmen were keeping reasonably complete accounts without the help of previous training or experience, or a qualified assistant. Men who had taken a full-time course in book-keeping were no more likely to do well than the rest.[1] We doubt whether courses in book-keeping provide

[1] Forty-five per cent who had taken a full-time course, and 40 per cent who had not,

the kind of experience these businessmen most needed, because
a man who recognizes the importance of accounting will already
have worked out a system adequate for his purpose.

So long as the purpose of accounts is taken to be the determination of profit or loss, and an overall record of how the money has
been spent, rough methods may serve well enough. There are
profitable businesses whose only records are a jumble of invoices,
shoved in a drawer with old pencil stubs and dog-eared catalogues;
and businesses with neatly ruled ledgers, whose methodical
columns of figures glumly document accumulating losses. Both
know where they stand. If they want to know why they stand so,
and what can be done about it, then they do begin to need a more
sophisticated analysis of where the money goes. These questions,
however, can only be answered in the particular circumstances of
each company. Accounting and costing become an aspect of the
problems of management which beset the enterprise as a whole.
So, when inadequate accounting does begin to be a serious handicap, the missing skill is not competence in routine book-keeping,
but a weakness of organization.

In any scheme to train or advise businessmen, the same fundamental difficulties reappear. The essential quality, an entrepreneurial creativeness, probably cannot be taught, at least to adults whose
habits of mind are formed. So training falls back upon skills which
can be systematized into routines generally relevant to business—
book-keeping, management techniques, trades. But once they
have been abstracted from the specific problems of an enterprise,
such courses scarcely compensate for lack of practical experience.
They are probably more useful to the craftsmen or clerks an
entrepreneur employs than to the entrepreneur himself. The
Japanese-sponsored Industrial Training Centre in Nakuru came to
recognize that most of its trainees were better fitted for employment than for running their own concerns. Only the Management
Training Centre in Nairobi, which opened in 1966 with the help
of the International Labour Office, experimented with more
imaginative courses for African businessmen. Apart from two

---

were running profitable and expanding businesses. There were also 40 businessmen
in the market centres who had studied book-keeping full time: 60 per cent were
making 300 shillings a month or more, while only a quarter of other businesses made
as much. But the businessmen who are selected for these courses tend already to be
the most outstanding, so the training is as likely to be a result of their success as a
cause of it.

courses in accounting, it also planned for 1968 two on starting and managing a small retail business, and two on manufacturing.

These courses took the participants, step by step, through the stages of establishing a business. 'With a background of general guidance from the course leader, participants conduct negotiations with the actual types of people with whom they come into contact in their business life. These include solicitors, bank managers, estate agents, finance company managers, wholesalers' representatives, accountants and auditors, credit managers, insurance agents, shop fitters, display experts, personnel experts, etc. Additionally they come face to face with retail customer reactions and learn both from guidance and experience how best to sell and handle complaints.' The members of the manufacturers' course also were to 'come into actual contact—and conduct negotiations—with such people as plant and machinery suppliers, raw-materials suppliers, industrial engineers, marketing experts, etc. The proposed factory is planned in some detail, and an actual model is produced.' After two weeks of this exercise—which was to take place in the evenings, so as not to interfere with the participants' supervision of their businesses—the course leader was to spend two weeks visiting each participant, to offer individual guidance. The Centre also established a 'business doctor' service, to which those who had taken the course could turn at any time for further advice.

These courses were designed and led by a New Zealander, and the similarities between the New Zealand and Kenya economies— their agricultural base and the pattern of small-scale commercial enterprise—may have helped him to sense the needs of African businessmen. Unluckily for Africa, management training—like most of the techniques of modern industrial society—has evolved in America and Western Europe to meet the needs of much more advanced economies. To adapt it to serve Africans struggling beyond petty shopkeeping demands itself an entrepreneurial imagination. The courses for African businessmen occupied only a small part of the Management Training Centre's programme. It announced about three dozen courses in over two dozen subjects for 1968—including critical path techniques and effective public speaking—mostly designed to meet the needs of Government and big businesses. Educational institutions seem drawn, inexorably, towards the clients with the highest status. Management experts, like other professionals, tend to invest the most sophisticated of their techniques with the most prestige, and training African businessmen is probably less rewarding professionally, and less within their scope, than training managers for large organizations. Any attempt to institutionalize training runs the risk that it will lose sight of the unique needs of the society it serves, and elaborate a routine of expertise, professionally impressive but not much to the purpose.

Even if these courses for African businessmen can be sustained against institutional pressures, they will be less effective, the wider the range of businesses they try to cover. Sawmiller and baker, tinsmith and printer do not face the same problems. And they are more useful to a newcomer than an established businessman, who must already have mastered the essentials of the subject matter to survive. In the end, the means by which the ICDC-supported businessmen gathered the skills they needed were probably more practical than any formal training. Some had worked in responsible jobs, where they saw how a business was run; or they hired experienced employees from established Asian or European firms; or brought in a trained book-keeper. They checked the methods and prices of competitors, consulted the representatives of companies from whom they bought equipment and supplies, and some had contacts amongst the managerial staff of large European firms, who befriended them with advice. They needed help in extending this network of acquaintance rather than a formal substitute for it.

If the first threshold of skill is literacy, and the second practical knowledge of specialized activities, the ICDC-supported businessmen were approaching a third. The successful amongst them had more or less mastered the technical and book-keeping problems they were likely to encounter. But their success was driving them towards a scale of operation and range of interests where the very qualities which had brought them so far—their individualism and restless ambition—were threatening to over-reach themselves and topple the whole structure. They began to face problems of management which did not arise simply from inexperience, but from more profound causes bound up in the pattern of relationships within the enterprise. Whom were they to trust, as partner, assistant, employee? How were they to establish the basis of a working agreement, and ensure that it was honoured? They had reached a threshold of organization, where their further progress depended on finding answers to these questions which fitted a larger scale of activity than any they had yet attempted. But here there was little experience to guide them, or skill to teach, for the problems could only be solved in terms of their own society, and their place as innovators in it.

10

CONCLUSIONS

We have looked at the situation of African businessmen from different points of view—as a problem of resources, of management and establishing markets; in the perspective of a man's career, his values, and the history of his society. In conclusion, we will try to integrate these different aspects in a rounded description.

An African entrepreneur in Kenya is typically intelligent, experienced and ambitious. These qualities are the principal assets he brings to his endeavour, and they reinforce each other. Because he is intelligent he has found more responsible and skilled employment than most men of his education. He has travelled widely, understood how businesses are run, learned crafts, and this experience has given him confidence in his ability. It has also made him restlessly dissatisfied. His frustration is partly a sense of the backwardness of his people, an awareness of opportunities exploited by foreigners in his country which ought to be within his grasp. But it is also a more personal frustration at the chances he has missed through lack of schooling. He cannot hope to earn the money, the prestige or responsibility in employment for which he believes his abilities fit him, and which from experience he knows he could handle. He is held down to subordinate, uncreative positions by the examinations he has never taken. Hence his driving ambition to realize through his own enterprise an achievement that will command the same respect as occupations of the highest status. His aims in business are defined by the causes of his frustration: the colonial civilization which dominated his childhood, and still informs society with its conception of success; and the administrative and political élite from whom he is excluded. He therefore emphasizes those purposes which business shares with Government—reducing unemployment, raising the standard of living, modernizing the economy until it stands comparison with an advanced industrial state—and takes the European example as his model. Money is secondary to the establishing of business as an occupation of recognized social importance; until he has achieved enough to fulfil these ambitions, he lives modestly and continually reinvests his income. All this conforms to the teaching of the Church in which he was brought up, which to him is another expression of the economic maturity of the civilization he is seeking to emulate.

Thus the pressures of circumstance which determine who becomes an entrepreneur, and what drives him on, form him into a man who will work very hard to create a modern, progressive business, and take very little out of it for his own pleasure. He invests his self-respect in the achievements of the business itself, caring little for the show of prosperity, since to be rich is not alone a mark of the status he is seeking. He needs to prove that business can make a contribution equivalent to education, and this concern for social usefulness, for business as another kind of productive knowledge, makes him identify his enterprise with the welfare of his workers and his community. He sees trade unions as irrelevant, because there is no conflict of interest, and pays, in his own eyes, as fairly as he can. For him entrepreneurship expresses the spirit of African socialism.

All these qualities promote his success. But the circumstances which create them also create their counterpart in the constraints which inhibit his achievement. The lack of higher education, which provides his incentive, also isolates him. He does not have the sophistication or social contacts to handle confidently his relationships within the economic system of which he is part. He is suspicious and hostile towards the Asian suppliers on whom he depends, and shy of banks. They, for their part, are doubtful of his competence, because he is an African newcomer to the business, and they have few means of assessing his worth. He cannot talk to them within the conventions of a common culture, and never meets them socially. Even with the African élite, educational snobbery, or the fear of it, is likely to constrain relationships. Yet this social world to which he cannot belong defines his ambitions, and imposes principles of economic exchange which his business has to meet. Hence he models his business organization on European practice, as he understands it—impersonal, contractual, and governed by principles of rational efficiency. He therefore repudiates the traditions of his society as irrelevant to a modern, progressive enterprise. Finding that kinship tends to intrude disruptive claims upon business, he turns away from it without further experiment, uninfluenced by the success of Asian family businesses, with which he cannot identify. Both his desire to emulate European achievements, and his hostility to the alternative commercial culture of his Asian competitors, reinforces his indifference to the family, and his insistent segregation of business relationships from customary loyalties.

He is therefore doubly isolated, within both his community and the wider society, withdrawing from the one to meet the demands of the other, and belonging to neither. This insecurity drives him back upon a mistrustful, self-reliant style of management, where he attempts to keep all aspects of the business under the control of himself and his working partners—whom he may not trust either. The growth of his business is constrained by the limits of what he can personally supervise, and thus he is unable to master the organizational problems of the substantial business of his dreams, while he dissipates his attention on a string of petty investments. Ironically, the self-conscious modernity of his ideals leads him towards a dead end where he stultifies his chances of achieving them. In these circumstances he appeals for further training, more capital, more restriction on Asian competition, without seeing the underlying sources of frustration in his own style of management. By themselves, the help he seeks may only institutionalize his isolation under government protection, leaving him still with a restricted market to exploit.

This seemed the characteristic situation of the businessmen whom the ICDC supported. Though a few had begun to concentrate their energies in a single firm, rejecting even the appeal of farming, and a few others had drawn from family or friends a team of management which might have adapted to an integrated structure of responsibilities, we did not find one enterprise where these qualities had come together to exploit a potentially large market. Yet the chances that African entrepreneurship can help to develop middle-sized industrial enterprises seem to depend on men like these. The shopkeepers and craftsmen in rural markets are less ambitious, experienced and self-confident. Their purposes are set, not by exclusion from the élite, but by the difficulty of finding even unskilled employment, and they lack the resources or the aspirations to struggle with the risks of innovation. The élite themselves, though they invest in business, do not have the incentive to commit themselves to it, while the earnings and prestige of Government are both higher and more secure. Thus the circumstances from which the most determined entrepreneurs have so far arisen are likely to set the problems of promoting African businesses for some time to come.

These circumstances are intricately related, entangling businessmen in a web of influences which cannot be unravelled by any simple plan. Wherever we pick up the thread, it leads back to its starting point, compounding cause and effect. The isolation of African businessmen makes it difficult for them to raise capital, which leads to government intervention and the consolidation of their isolation. Their insistence on the segregation of business from other social relationships leads to a mistrustful search for autonomy which cramps their management: yet management training could easily reinforce the attachment to principles of rational efficiency which made them repudiate kinship and community loyalties in the first place. Thus it becomes impossible to isolate any single policy as crucial, or even by itself helpful.

Although we have emphasized the importance of integrating economic relationships, of creating trust and widening contacts, this too is only one aspect of a complex interaction. Though it is a more fundamental problem than the provision of capital or training of skills, its solution might still be derived from them. Whatever their reservations, banks would no doubt think African business a good investment if its chances were sufficiently weighted by protection and subsidy, and a network of mutually supportive relationships could grow from this. The history of entrepreneurship in Mahiga suggests that African businessmen were ready from the first to explore the commercial opportunities created by European settlement. They had so little success because they lacked the capital and skills to match Asian competition, while the colonial administration was indifferent or restrictive, directing openings for trade towards the immigrant communities. The isolation of African businessmen can be seen as a consequence of policies which ignored the opportunity to train and finance them, in the crucial early years before European and Asian dominance of the economy was established. Whatever factor we single out as a constraint upon entrepreneurship is inextricably bound up with others.

Conclusions

The relationship between these factors, therefore, matters more than the weight of any one of them. The way in which ideals, the colonial experience, vocational chances, education or the lack of it, loan schemes, the size of markets, competition, dispositions of character all react upon each other cannot be resolved into a compound of measurable influences, where from discrete increments we can predict proportionate outcomes. Once a threshold of skill is passed, for instance, education or experience may have no influence on success until an altogether higher level of sophistication is reached, and then the formal education which promoted entrepreneurial confidence becomes a disincentive. Or again, the detachment of business from claims of kinship has enabled it to recruit workers and reinvest profits in economically more rational ways, but if it were possible now to reconstruct family businesses on these principles, their management would be more secure. The relationships are not linear: a handicap at one stage of development later becomes a potential asset, assets become liabilities or dwindle into insignificance, effects become causes. The situation can only be understood as a whole, as it evolves over time.

We have brought out the interdependence and mutability of the influences determining entrepreneurial behaviour, because the search for practical proposals tends to overlook them. Policy decisions cannot escape some attempt to measure the costs and benefits of a particular intervention, however hard it may be to determine the value of any single course of action in a tangle of circumstance. The need to choose pulls towards a simplified, selective analysis, asserting the primary importance of one factor or another. The conflict is characteristic of all development planning. To understand the problems of a society struggling to evolve a radically different structure, its history, social, political and economic circumstances are all relevant, and all connected. But the analysis drawn from this point of view does not readily answer the questions facing Government, which cannot control most of these circumstances, nor look much further than the few alternatives immediately open to it. Government can direct the allocation of public resources, but much less easily integrate its various policies, or ensure the quality of their implementation. An analysis which explains situations in terms of subtle and intricate relationships between factors largely beyond government control is therefore awkwardly intractable. It is tempting instead to argue for one policy of measurable cost, where a given expenditure would promise a predictable return.

Our study suggests that any such single-minded prescription would be misleading. The encouragement of entrepreneurship can only be a sensitive and complex undertaking where the quality of assistance matters more than the amount, and the success of any policy depends on other actions which support it. Neither loans, for instance, nor training or protection are likely to do much good unless they are co-ordinated and their relationship worked out in detail. The weaknesses of Kenya's policies for promoting African business have not been in the purposes themselves, so much as the way they have been carried out, and the lack of integration between them. Loans have been given to enterprises which were then denied government-controlled supplies; technical training has not been related to market opportunities or the provision of loans; industrial estates have been built for firms which could not hope to succeed without tariff protection which Government would not consider; a state wholesaling agency was moving into competition with private African wholesalers, who received loans from the ICDC which they did not need, or needed only in much larger amounts; public agencies ignored African business in procuring their supplies, or paid them so late that they could not fulfil further orders. Thus the Kenya government—like most governments—vitiated its intentions by its inability or indifference in co-ordinating its actions. At the same time, it overlooked aspects of the businessmen's needs where it might also have intervened. As we review the kinds of help which seem to follow from our analysis, it has always to be kept in mind that they will only reinforce each other if they are designed to do so, not just notionally, but in practical detail.

Policies implied by the situation of African business

Entrepreneurship is concerned with the allocation of resources, not their creation. Unless money, skills, and materials could be more productively reorganized, an entrepreneur has no opening. But an absolute want of resources must be very rare. The most efficient economies are probably the poorest and most primitive, for only in a totally isolated subsistence economy is the present use likely to represent the best possible arrangement of all that is known to be usable. Once a society is opened to the outside world, money to lend and skills to hire will surely be available somewhere. If, for instance, a farming community rejects an improved seed because it lacks the labour for its more intensive cultivation, and the labour is simply not to be found, no opportunity for entrepreneurship exists. But if there are unemployed in search of work within reach of the community, and financiers who might loan the cost of their wages, then an entrepreneur has a chance. If he fails, it is either because he cannot pay as much for these assets as some other users, is less efficient than his rivals, or because he cannot gain access to them.

These are the three potential obstacles an entrepreneur confronts: he may be unable to buy assets at a price which attracts them from other uses; he may be unable to use them as economically as his competitors; or, though he can pay for them and exploit them profitably, their redistribution may be inhibited by ignorance, mistrust, prejudice—the awkwardness of the relationships which mediate exchange. If we can determine which kind of obstacle is causing the most serious obstruction, we can see more clearly what kind of help is most needed.

The first obstacle was not a characteristic difficulty of the African businessmen we met. So long as their plans worked out, they could afford the cost of both labour and capital. Unemployment was so widespread, trade unionism so undeveloped, that they needed to pay very little for unskilled hands. A firm in difficulties could still find workers, even when its wages were below the minimum rates laid down by Government, and irregularly paid. In practice, when they could, the businesses paid fairly, and they were ready to offer more than their competitors for scarce skills. Equally, they could raise capital through partnerships and shares for no more than the promise of eventual profits. People seemed willing to risk their savings in speculative ventures on very informal terms. Nor did the rate of interest on loans trouble the businessmen. They complained of the slowness of the ICDC, the cost of negotiating with it, of the amounts lent and the security required, but not of the 8 per cent it charged. If banks would co-operate, some preferred to borrow commercially, because the procedures were simpler, though the rates might be higher. And several gambled successfully on the hire purchase of lorries, paying them off within a year, despite the charges. The businesses never defaulted on loans because the cost in itself was more than they could sustain, but because machines did not work, supplies ran out, they failed to reach their market or were overtaken by competitors, or because they preferred to risk arrears for the sake of faster growth. So African businesses were not inhibited by inability to buy the resources they need at the going rate.

The second obstacle—comparative inefficiency—does undermine the chances of some kinds of business. A small enterprise cannot usually compete with large, because it cannot take advantage of economics of scale. If a single firm can reach a wide market, a business which only attempts to serve a part of the market is likely, sooner or later, to be driven out. So long as African businesses are small, their opportunities lie only where the cost of transport, the convenience of customers, the perishability of goods, or the nature of demand restricts the extent of the market. Wholesaling, retailing, transport companies and service industries, which become less attractive, the further they are from their customers; furniture making, tinsmithing, tailoring, where goods are made to the customer's specification; and curios for the tourist trade all seem viable. The chances for small sawmills, bakeries, or any kind of standard manufacture are correspondingly unpromising. If bread became a staple, rather than a luxury, some of the African bakers might grow with the demand to a competitive size: meanwhile, they depend precariously on bad roads and local contacts to outwit more powerful competitors. The small sawmills may have to amalgamate, or turn to retailing timber and carpentry.

Inefficiency arising from incompetence in specific skills is a less serious handicap. An entrepreneur can teach himself the basic skills he needs, and hire more specialized knowledge. We found no evidence that training in book-keeping—the most widely useful technique of business—was related to achievement. It seems that in a small enterprise, an able man soon sees where accounting matters, and devises a system adequate for his purpose; while a bigger firm can recruit a trained book-keeper. Experience is more relevant, and the industrial businessmen often took up activities they had learned in employment. But if they had experienced workers, technical ignorance did not necessarily handicap them. Lack of skills is therefore more a problem of recruitment than of training entrepreneurs. Though some skilled workers, such as qualified mechanics, were becoming hard to find, the successful businessmen had paid high wages to secure the men they needed.

On the whole, then, the businesses supported by the ICDC could afford to pay for the resources of capital and skills they needed, and could use them competently, within the limits set by the scale of their organization. The most serious obstacles to their progress were embedded in the structure of relationships. These handicaps lead to a style of management which becomes inefficient as a businessman outgrows his small beginnings, but they originate in the third kind of obstacle—constraints upon an entrepreneur's access to resources.

Until recently, these constraints were enforced by the political system. Land was not freely exchangeable, since the right of purchase was restricted by race. African land could not be used as security for borrowing, not only because there were no unambiguous individual titles, but because the European or Asian lender was not free to take possession. And so long as farming was largely for subsistence, most land and labour were not integrated with the monetary economy. Thus resources were allocated within distinct social and economic systems, but not easily between them. Independence abolished the formal constraints upon African entrepreneurs, but it could not create the relationships of a new inclusive system. African businessmen still had to succeed within a commercial network dominated by alien cultures, where their range of acquaintance and shared conventions were slight. The intervention of Government to compensate for their financial isolation tended to perpetuate this segregation, by providing an alternative system of credit. African businessmen had few contacts outside their own community, by which to develop a wider market. The network of economic relationships they needed to exploit had no social counterpart, through which to negotiate opportunities.

At the same time, the need to integrate their enterprises with this wider system drove them to repudiate the conventional expectations of African society. They adopted the principles of businesslike efficiency which seemed to inform European concerns, taking competence as the only valid criterion of employment, reliability the only criterion of credit, and differentiating business relationships rigorously from social obligations. But this left them with no basis of trust, since the values which sustained such a conception of commercial contract were foreign to African traditions. So management depended on a close personal supervision, which made trust unnecessary. And this greatly restricted the size of businesses which they could handle. The origins of African entrepreneurs did not give them any claim upon relationships that might have helped to overcome this isolation. They arose characteristically from an occupational class whose lack of educational qualifications denied them promotion above relatively well paid but still subordinate positions. They were not a self-conscious group, defined by a distinguishing religion or culture, and so could not appeal to the mutually protective solidarity of a minority to support their economic relationships. Since, too, their ideal of business derived from the European example, they regard African traditions as out-dated, and did not think of intermediate forms of organization easier for African society to assimilate.

Thus whether we look at finance or management, at the size of businesses in relation to the market opportunities, at the creed or origins of businessmen, the same obstacle reappears—the lack of a social network with conventions, values and points of contact to facilitate both the internal and external relationships of business. The problem is hard to tackle directly. But we outline below five proposals to illustrate how we think our analysis might be interpreted in practice. Each aims to integrate an entrepreneur and the people he deals with less awkwardly, or to create more trust between them.

A marketing advisory service A marketing service would help to introduce African businessmen to potential customers both in Kenya and abroad, advise them on the markets they might enter, whom to contact, how to organize distribution, where to advertise. It would give some helpful advice, but its essential function would be to put people in touch with each other, so that they could do business. It should not itself market goods, for then it would only encourage the isolation of the businessmen it tried to help: once it had established contacts for them, its work would be done. Such a service is needed, because African businessmen have little acquaintance with larger-scale industry and commerce, do not know their way about the national or international market, and are too socially unsophisticated, and unsure of their English, to reach the right people in the management hierarchies of big companies, or even their own government. The service could also co-ordinate the policy of Government as a customer of African business, guiding departments and public authorities to likely African suppliers, and encouraging competitive tenders. But it must identify with the interests of African business, rather than of government departments, so that its loyalty to its clients is unequivocal.

Training of relationships Training in management needs to emphasize relationships rather than techniques. Courses for African businessmen could invite bankers, accountants, import agents, staff of international companies, commercial attaches, civil servants, to join discussions and explain their interests. If the courses were informal enough, people of different races and different communities would come to understand and respect each other, and the personal contacts might afterwards be useful. At the same time, African businessmen will have to delegate more responsibility, if their enterprises are to grow, and they need assistants whom they are prepared to trust. If courses in management for the potential staff of African businessmen were run side by side with courses for entrepreneurs, the courses themselves might help to establish confidence between them. Both these suggestions derive from the same principles: that if you want to develop a working relationship, you cannot train one party to the relationship without the other; and that the training will be more useful, if it leads spontaneously from learning to practice. A management training centre can also help to work out a sense of common purpose, to which everyone who takes part in its courses is more or less committed. No policy can ensure the spread of a generally respected commercial ethic. But an institution can stand by a code of behaviour, defend it, teach it, and give it the prestige of its own authority, so that the code becomes formally assimilated within the structure of society.

Government equity Government equity in African businesses would often fit the purpose better than loans. Loan schemes on special terms are inherently cumbersome: since they are designed to provide capital where the risks seem high by commercial standards, their procedures involve more elaborate and less routine scrutiny of applications. In the end, the advantage to the borrower may be outweighed by the cost and delays. At the same time, he may be less able to obtain commercial credit, or less ready to ask for it, because he is regarded as a risky client for whom Government should take responsibility. Banks are then slow to take a serious interest in African business, even when the risks are no higher than elsewhere. They are used to leaving the task to Government, and see no need to invest their own time and trouble in learning how to do it. So Government should withdraw from lending to African businesses like wholesaling, whose viability has been established. But the first African enterprises in a new field will still be hard to finance commercially, since there are no precedents to assess their competence. Goverment will need to go on backing pioneers. But equity participation would be more adaptive than a loan scheme, create fewer conflicts of interest between Government and business, and enable Government to compensate for its support of relatively unsuccessful ventures by its share in the profits of others. It would entitle Government to advise the management through its representative, and to act with its private partners in negotiations with banks and suppliers. If the private owners held a right to buy out Government, once the business was established, fears of covert nationalization should be allayed.

Banking staff Some commercial banks have appointed officers in their Nairobi headquarters with a special responsibility for working with African business. They will need similar officers in most of their main branches, while they build up a network of knowledge and acquaintanceship amongst the businessmen in each community—and without such a network, they will probably only lose money if they try to increase their financial help. The difficulty is that these officers will be most needed where the immediate opportunities for lending are few, since it must take time to assess what is possible, and the cost of training and employing them cannot be recovered quickly. If this is a serious drawback, we think it would be better for Government to subsidize these costs than to attempt to meet the same needs through a loan scheme of its own.

Legal aid Conflicts in business partnerships often arise because titles are unclear, and the structure is unwieldy. The number of partners who can be registered is limited to 20, and in older established businesses especially, there may be many supernumerary shareholders who are not formally represented: they are merely consulted by the partner to whose share they have contributed. Businessmen are often confused by the difference between registered partnerships, companies and co-operatives, and unclear about their legal responsibilities.[1] Some businessmen, too, did not understand the implications of the conditions attached to the ICDC's loans, while they were unable to enforce the collection of debts from their own customers for lack of adequate records. There would be less mistrust and misunderstanding if the law were made clearer, either by legislating simpler articles of association, by advice or by publicizing standard forms of agreement. ICDC officials gave such help where they could, but they were not trained in law, and it was not their primary responsibility.

These proposals would be relatively inexpensive. Two of them need only the redirection of present resources—from loans to shares, from conventional management courses to more original experiments designed especially for African business. All are intended to integrate relationships and create more confidence in them. The same principles of action can be worked out in other institutions—grants for higher education, for instance, might include practical experience abroad for businessmen. These five proposals are certainly not exhaustive, but examples of how we think our analysis might be applied.

Entrepreneurship in general

The situation of African businessmen in Kenya has been profoundly influenced by the colonial experience, but even in countries with a different history a similar pattern of circumstance can be traced. Immigrants often, like the Kenya Asians, consolidate a racially distinct commercial network, since entrepreneurship is a characteristic response to minority status. Throughout the world, the offshoots of international companies graft themselves onto

[1] Of 37 African trading or farming ventures registered as public companies between 1964 and 1967, 'Only three appeared to have complied with all the registration requirements of the Act. . . .' '. . . either in the Registrar's Department or in some other Ministry a team of export company advisers and an inspectorate should be made available to assist and guide newly formed companies in complying with the technicalities of our company legislation' (Coward, pp. 36, 37). See also Marris.

backward economies without taking root there. The racial and cultural divisions which inhibit entrepreneurship in Kenya have their counterparts in nations whose political history has been less obviously dominated by racial segregation. Internal barriers to exchange—of tribe, class or religion—are common everywhere. Most poor countries are also poorly integrated, and use what resources they have less efficiently than rich. The disparity between the scale of the economy, and the range and integration of systems of human relationship, is probably a universal handicap to entrepreneurship.

The form entrepreneurship takes will still vary greatly from place to place, and from one time to another, according to the particular constellation of circumstances. But we have tried below to formulate a set of propositions, defining our interpretation of the Kenya experience in terms which we think would apply everywhere.

1 The opportunity for entrepreneurship arises whenever resources could be reallocated more productively. Only the poorest and most isolated economies are likely to offer no such opportunities at all. Societies recently opened to the outside world, or where internal barriers are breaking down, are likely to provide the most widespread opportunities. But rapid changes also disrupt society in ways which make the opportunities hard to realize.

2 Entrepreneurs will come forward to take advantage of these opportunities only if they cannot find the money, power or prestige they expect for themselves in established occupations. The rewards of entrepreneurship are speculative, and therefore only attractive to those who are already frustrated in their ambitions and, at the same time, confident that they can handle the risk. A downwardly mobile social class, a disenfranchised religious or cultural minority, or a competitive, open educational structure are each likely to produce entrepreneurs. They will not appear readily in stable, homogeneous societies; nor in stable homogeneous communities which isolate themselves from the wider system, or control the distribution of resources within it.

3 Entrepreneurs are held back when they cannot outbid other users of the resources they need; cannot use them efficiently; or

cannot gain access to them. The first two are not strictly obstacles to entrepreneurship. For if a man cannot afford to pay as much for capital and labour as other users, his project is not likely to be any more productive: and similarly, if his inefficiency prevents him from realizing the profit he should make. But these handicaps become relevant under a policy which seeks to manipulate opportunities for entrepreneurship in favour of otherwise uncompetitive sorts of people. Such a policy has to accept an economic sacrifice for its social or political ends.

4 The essential obstacles to entrepreneurship arise from constraints on the exchange and reorganization of resources. Firstly, assets may not be freely tradable between sectors of economic activity—as when land, labour, produce and services are exchanged within a system of subsistence farming, but their value is not translatable into money;[1] or when segregation prevents one race from owning the same resources as another; or religion, the self-protection of a professional guild, or class snobbery bars entry to certain undertakings. Secondly, the relationships between people may be so tenuous that there are few points of contact where exchanges can be negotiated, opportunities and available resources discovered—as when communications are poorly developed, or cultural differences discourage meeting. Finally, the sanctions and values which protect commercial transactions may be so equivocally shared or poorly assimilated that exchanges are impeded by mutual mistrust.

5 Where the relationships through which an enterprise is organized are reinforced by narrow loyalties—of kinship, sect, or cultural minority—the informal sanctions against default will be stronger, the shared values more binding. But the range of such a pattern of organization will be more constricted. A business where all responsibility is held by one person is the narrowest of all, then family or sectarian businesses. But a pattern of individual responsibility is likely to arise where there is no basis for group loyalties in business, and may more easily evolve into a wider system, informed by principles common to society as a whole.

6 The encouragement of entrepreneurship therefore depends upon broadening the range of social interaction; strengthening

[1] See, for example, Barth.

239

the sanctions against abuse of commercial obligations; diffusing a creed which justifies the principles of business to customers, workers and Government as well as entrepreneurs themselves; and bringing all relevant assets within a single system of exchange.

Entrepreneurship in a socialist society

This formulation treats entrepreneurship as a private economic endeavour, but it can be conceived, in its widest sense, as an aspect of a more fundamental task—to integrate a viable nation out of many disparate, mutually suspicious and unready parts. In Kenya, the opportunities for entrepreneurship arise from two processes which have been at work since the beginning of the century: a continual enlargement of the scale of economic and social interaction, and a breaking down of internal barriers. Imperial rule brought the produce of the country into an international market of exchange, built roads and railways to carry it, and overcame tribal resistance to movement. Independence finally abolished racial discrimination against African participation. These changes have invalidated all conservative preconceptions of economic value. The most productive distribution of skills, savings and land has now to be revised in the light of a market where both people and goods can move more readily, over greater distances, than ever in the past.

At the same time, these processes of change are profoundly disruptive. They evolve disjointedly, undermining institutions and beliefs before their successors have taken shape; piecemeal innovations are abortive, for lack of complementary adjustments; the uncertainties and frustrations generate defensive reactions— rigidity in government, intolerance, tribalism, mistrust. So the opportunities are not easily realized. The disintegration of the old order, which gives rise to them, also provokes daunting obstacles to their fulfilment. Overwhelmed by these difficulties, a society may drift into anxious authoritarianism, reimposing an awkward control which sacrifices the chances of growth to an illusion of coherence. Or it may remain segmented, with enclaves of prosperity unrelated to the rural poverty lying beyond the suburbs of a modern city.

The problems do not arise only in nations which encourage

private enterprise, nor will they yield to ideological rebuke. A socialist society faces the same need to reallocate its resources more productively: indeed, historically, socialism has gained most ground in states where the task of economic and social reintegration appeared most daunting. But a radical reconstruction of the ideological basis of society does not resolve the problems. It can only shift the balance of constraints and opportunities in ways which promise a more dynamic evolution. The risk is that entrepreneurial vitality will exhaust itself in the triumph of the revolution: as the moment of liberation recedes, the need to reimpose social control will create new rigidities which inhibit further exchange. Ideals turn into inflexible doctrine, asserting the primary importance of orthodoxy. The disparity between economic and social systems becomes politicized, as the party predominates in every aspect of life. Political assets—one's connections, ideological conformity, position in the government hierarchy—tend to determine control over economic assets, but not the other way about. So economic exchange has to be mediated by a political system where the values are different, and only very imperfectly related to economic performance. A state entrepreneur cannot automatically increase his resources, as he proves how productively he can use them: nor does he necessarily forgo them, if his enterprise is inefficient. A competent manager may be driven to create his own informal, illegitimate systems of exchange to outflank the awkwardness of political control—bargaining materials with his counterparts in other industries, falsifying accounts to provide a margin of unrecorded assets under his own direction. Thus a centralized socialist system tends to erect its own barriers to entrepreneurship. Within the network of relationships which govern economic activity, some are regulated by straightforward criteria of economic performance, others by criteria of political performance, and the two are only roughly equivalent. Thus a rather similar incompatibility of systems of exchange arises, as when subsistence and monetary economies exist side by side. This is still likely, even if the system attaches great importance to productivity, since the kind of performance which earns political rewards demands different skills. The difficulties may be no more insuperable than those of capitalist systems, and the authority of a national ideology may be more successful in overcoming racial or tribal divisions, or establishing a universally respected system of beliefs to sustain trust in economic relation-ships. But the need for entrepreneurship, and the disparities in the social structure which obstruct it, seem bound to arise irrespective of the political system, in ways which are fundamentally com-parable.

A note of advice to African businessmen

Finally, what advice does our inquiry suggest for African business-men themselves, whose insight into their problems has informed this analysis? They had much practical wisdom to offer a new-comer, speaking from experience of their own mistakes as well as their achievements, which we have already quoted: on the importance of studying the market; on relating capital require-ments, skills and potential markets before starting; on finding trustworthy partners and technically qualified employees; on keeping accounts and closely supervising workers and costs; on concentrating capital and energy in a single enterprise; on personal integrity, thrift and working hard; on the dangers of drinking, sociable friends, and the claims of family; on searching for the best wholesale prices, avoiding credit to customers, cultivating one's bank manager.

Ideally, the progress of a successful businessman might run something like this, after he has first gained experience in employ-ment. He would start by considering critically his own abilities and means. Then he would survey the market, and select a likely site. Next he would recruit capital, choosing as his partners men he trusts, and treating them with scrupulous honesty: he should never, for instance, attempt to pay himself more at the outset, nor act without consulting them. He will then need some experienced employees, and must be prepared to pay them well. Here, too, he needs men he can trust, and as the business expands, he should give them increasing responsibility. His investigation into whole-sale prices for his own supplies must be as thorough as his market survey, taking into account, too, the cost of transport. He will need to keep good books, watch his costs, and work out conditions of credit which save him from the worst risks. But he had best, from the first, allow something for bad debts in his expenses. He should live cheaply, plough back his profits, and pay himself a small salary, to separate his personal income from the resources of the business. In this way, he can hope to keep his obligations to family and kin to what he can afford. If his books are clear, and the business profitable, he can press his bank to trust him: and if the manager is unhelpful he should find another bank. Above all, he should concentrate on making a single enterprise grow, and develop its organization, learning and adapting continually.

Lastly he will still need the courage to face many disappointments. In the words of the manager of a prosperous dairy, 'I would encourage him that business is a good thing, but warn him that it's like a gamble, like the three card trick. To play this you have to be brave, because if you take your money out of your pocket and start a business and you find it's going down and you're a coward, your spirits go down and automatically you go out of business. Whereas you should know what the reason is, like credit or going out too much with friends, or family expenses, and then you can do something about the cause instead of closing. You should have this ability to know where you are losing, and be enterprising enough to get out of the situation. . . . Avoid credit. Scale down expenses. Be patient and don't expect too much too soon. Be brave or you'll lose the trick.ᵀ'

SUPPLEMENTARY TABLES

1 *Sorts of business*

Nature of business*	Market businesses	ICDC-supported businesses	Businesses owned by Mahiga men	Asian businesses
Retailing	43%	16%	26%	36%
Wholesaling	2%	28%	5%	31%
Restaurant or bar keeping	15%		20%	4%
Butchery	6%	2%	12%	
Service industry ⎫	21%†	21%	7%	9%
Manufacturing ⎭		31%	5%	13%
Building contracting		1%		5%
Transporting		1%	13%	1%
Other	13%		12%	1%
Total %	100%	100%	100%	100%
Total no.	848	87	104‡	281

* Many businesses combine retailing, for instance, with tailoring, restaurant keeping or wholesaling, or a taxi service with other activities. The classification follows the principal interest of a business. Slightly different classifications have been used in the text: we have generally included butchers with other retailers, for instance, when discussing the ICDC-supported businesses, but distinguished different kinds of manufacture.

† Most of these are craftsmen both making and repairing things.

‡ This is the total of businesses of which the 55 men from Mahiga were owners or principal partners. They had interests in 130 businesses altogether.

2 *Businessmen from Mahiga: centre of business activity by age*

Centre	Under 40	40 and over	All
Nyeri, Karatina or Kiganjo	9%	31%	18%
Thompson's Falls, Nanyuki, Naivasha	15%	40%	26%
Embu, Meru	9%	5%	7%
Nakuru, Eldoret, Subukia	31%	5%	20%
Western and Nyanza Province	18%	9%	15%
Nairobi	9%	5%	7%
Coast or Uganda	9%	5%	7%
Total %	100%	100%	100%
Total no.	33	22	55

Supplementary Tables

3 *Previous occupation of market businessmen*

Occupation before taking up business	Profit under 300/- p.m.	Profit 300/- p.m.+	All
Farming	17%	15%	17%
Employed: unskilled	18%	10%	16%
skilled manual	23%	27%	25%
clerical, teaching	15%	21%	17%
army, police	4%	6%	4%
At school	6%	5%	5%
In detention	1%	1%	1%
Hawker or petty trader	8%	9%	8%
No occupation	8%	6%	7%
Total%	100%	100%	100%
Total no.	445	178	786*

* Including businesses where profit could not be estimated, but excluding one market where the question on previous occupation was not asked.

4 *Attitude to employment of ICDC-supported businessmen*

Would prefer employment	5%
Would prefer employment if income higher	12%
Would not prefer employment even for higher income	83%
Total %	100%
Total no.	87

5 *Satisfactions of business: ICDC-supported businessmen*

None	1%
Can make more money	20%
Independence	51%
Learn more, wider experience	21%
Contributing to national development	32%
Total no. of businessmen	87

6 *Job description medians: Mahiga High School Forms I–III 1968 (92 boys)*

Job category	Job description	Would like job v. much (5) vs. Would dislike job v. much (1) / Job preference	Job has v. high prestige (honour, respect) (5) vs. Job has low prestige (honour, respect) (1) / Prestige	Man with job is v. educated (1) vs. Is v. uneducated (5) / Education	Is a v. clever man (1) vs. Is not a clever man (5) / Cleverness	Is a v. rich man (5) vs. Is a v. poor man (1) / Wealth	Is a v. happy man (1) vs. Is not a happy man (5) / Happiness	Has a v. easy life (5) vs. Has a v. difficult life (1) / Easy life	Works v. hard (5) vs. Does not work hard (1) / Hard-working
Government jobs/ professional	District officer	4·81	4·84	1·10	1·38	4·65	1·35	4·79	3·87
	Health inspector	4·78	4·83	1·11	1·37	4·46	1·42	4·73	4·25
	Agricultural officer	4·73	4·71	1·18	1·46	4·37	1·42	4·71	3·83
Non-government professional	Doctor	4·77	4·77	1·11	1·17	4·43	2·05	3·56	4·79
	Priest/clergyman	2·61	3·91	1·74	1·85	3·46	1·40	4·09	4·18
Teachers	Govt. secondary teacher	4·50	4·50	1·10	1·37	4·12	1·48	4·69	3·58
	Harambee sec. teacher	3·50	3·42	1·39	1·73	3·90	2·17	3·50	4·36
	Primary headmaster (P.1.)	4·06	4·08	1·40	1·82	4·04	1·76	4·52	3·91
	Primary teacher (P.2.)	3·26	3·33	1·75	1·97	3·73	2·21	3·76	4·12
Sub-professional/ clerical	Veterinary assistant	4·17	4·01	1·40	1·58	3·86	1·71	4·26	4·05
	Community dev. asst.	3·90	3·86	1·42	1·79	4·11	1·60	4·56	3·79
	Clerk in office	4·10	4·10	1·27	1·62	4·04	1·46	4·72	4·18
	Dairy co-operative clerk	3·03	3·02	1·90	2·19	3·64	2·25	3·79	3·89
	Radio announcer	4·03	4·09	1·22	1·66	3·95	1·42	4·65	4·09
	Politician	3·77	3·95	1·34	1·39	4·13	1·92	3·70	4·30
	Headmas...		3·02	2·70	2·31	3·69	2·26	2·82	2·77

246

Skilled/semi-skilled Builder (stone houses)	2·31	2·63	3·09	1·93	3·81	2·94	1·85	4·69
Motor mechanic	3·35	3·45	2·17	1·99	3·86	2·27	1·96	4·85
Soldier	3·40	4·06	2·64	2·25	3·61	3·12	1·76	4·71
Policeman	3·24	3·54	2·29	2·20	3·59	2·60	2·37	4·56
Lorry driver	1·93	2·22	3·15	2·88	3·35	2·73	2·23	4·12
Self employed, business Shopkeeper: Nyeri	3·53	3·59	2·85	2·13	4·34	1·75	4·15	4·22
Othaya	2·87	2·98	2·83	2·41	4·10	2·09	3·98	3·92
Mahiga	2·57	2·92	3·05	2·35	4·04	2·14	3·72	4·23
Taxi driver (own car)	3·31	3·25	2·88	2·50	4·16	1·94	4·20	4·09
Bar owner Mahiga	2·34	2·44	3·13	2·59	4·09	1·97	3·23	4·00
Butcher Mahiga	2·40	2·47	3·16	2·61	3·79	2·26	3·64	4·18
Teashop keeper Mahiga	1·70	1·97	3·32	2·81	3·27	2·60	2·26	4·14
Tailor Mahiga	1·78	1·84	3·63	3·12	3·01	2·92	2·22	4·37
Hawker	1·11	1·15	4·52	3·44	2·00	3·98	1·13	4·60
Farmers Farmer with 15 acres Mahiga	3·05	3·17	3·14	2·75	4·14	2·16	3·68	4·73
Farmer with 15 acres settlement	3·12	3·31	3·24	2·85	3·88	2·24	3·09	4·77
Farmer with 2 acres Mahiga	1·22	1·27	4·00	3·35	1·77	4·17	1·18	4·75
Farm labourer European farm	1·23	1·39	4·61	3·75	2·00	3·88	1·27	4·78
Unskilled Coffee-factory worker	1·35	1·50	3·55	3·12	2·24	3·43	1·34	4·72
Road worker	1·15	1·21	4·58	3·30	1·85	4·01	1·11	4·85
Turn-boy	1·10	1·15	4·54	3·02	1·67	3·94	1·11	4·76
Traditional Traditional doctor	1·20	1·59	4·56	1·77	2·96	2·54	1·34	4·31

7 *Active membership in social or political organizations: ICDC-supported businessmen*

None	36%
Chamber of Commerce	25%
County or town councillor	10%
School committee	29%
Local committee of political party	9%
Social or sports clubs	8%
Total no. of businessmen	87

CHAPTER 4

8 *Religion and business: ICDC-supported businessmen*

Influence of religion on business:

No religion	7%
Religious beliefs have been of material help in business	11%
Religious beliefs have been of spiritual help only	47%
Neither	35%
Total %	100%
Total no.	87

9 *Qualities of a successful businessman as seen by businessmen supported by the ICDC*

Qualities mentioned:

Hardworking	32%
Honest	36%
Avoids drink, women	30%
Experienced, has practical knowledge	20%
Understands book-keeping	21%
Friendly	38%
Ruthless, competitive	1%
Single-minded	15%
Imaginative	13%
Other	17%
Total no. of businessmen	87

10 *Commonest reasons for failure in business*

Reasons mentioned	ICDC-supported businessmen	Market businessmen
Giving credit, bad debts	18%	47%
Lack of capital	30%	20%
Extravagance, women	43%	53%
Lack of customers	8%	9%
Lack of knowledge of book-keeping, poor management	50%	31%
Too many dependants	8%	11%
Dishonest partners	13%	6%
Bad employees	16%	8%
Lack of integrity	10%	
Too many different interests	19%	
Asian, European competition	5%	
Laziness		9%
Other answers		15%
No answer		2%
Total no. of businessmen	87	848

11 *Reasons for the success or failure of businesses known to the businessmen supported by the ICDC*

Reasons suggested by ICDC-supported businessmen for the failure of African businesses they knew:

Extravagance or laziness	42%
Poor management or accounting	36%
Lack of capital	18%
Dishonest or quarrelsome partners	13%
Too many business interests	10%
Too many dependants	10%
Giving credit	9%
Bad employees, poor supervision	9%
Dishonesty	4%
European or Asian competition	3%
Other	10%
Total no. of businessmen	67*

* The other 20 did not know any business failures well enough to comment.

Supplementary Tables

Reasons suggested by ICDC-supported businessmen for the outstanding success of African businesses they knew:

Hard work, concentration	33%
Good management, accounting	30%
Good at attracting customers	17%
Enough capital	12%
Government loan	12%
Experience	10%
Trust between partners	8%
Integrity	8%
Other	22%
Total no. of businessmen	60*

* Eighteen others could not suggest reasons for success, 9 could not think of any business they judged outstandingly successful.

12 *Reasons why businessmen had taken up business*

	ICDC-supported businessmen	Market businessmen
Lack of education	5%	5%
Poor prospects in farming	2% }	
Unable to find employment	6% }	15%
Dissatisfied with employment	28%	
Training or experience in business activities	23%	11%
To contribute to development, provide jobs	16%	1%
Enjoys business	26%	14%
Saw an opportunity	43%	2%
Influenced by advice	13%	4%
To make money		33%
To occupy retirement		3%
Inherited business		2%
Other reasons	3%	11%
Total no. of businessmen	87	848

13 *Qualities of European businessmen as ICDC-supported and Asian businessmen perceived them*

Qualities of Europeans	ICDC-supported businessmen	Asian businessmen
Experience, knowledge	60%	3%
Access to capital, credit	38%	26%
Integrity	21%	1%
Good business connections	12%	52%
Helpful to Africans	12%	
Unhelpful to Africans	1%	
Tricky, dishonest		
Thrifty, hardworking	5%	1%
Privileged position		6%
Intelligent, adaptable		2%
Education		3%
Good business management		10%
Fixed prices		2%
Other answer	25%	4%
No distinctive qualities, no answer		25%
Total no. of businesses	87	281

14 *Qualities of Asian businessmen as perceived by themselves and ICDC-supported businessmen*

Qualities of Asians	ICDC-supported businessmen	Asian businessmen
Experience, knowledge	38%	41%
Access to capital, credit	47%	19%
Integrity, honesty		4%
Good business connections	45%	
Helpful to Africans		
Unhelpful to Africans	26%	
Tricky, dishonest	25%	
Thrifty, hardworking	18%	16%
Intelligent, shrewd		9%
Ownership of property		1%
Mutual help among Asians		9%
Monopoly, lack of competition		1%
Education		1%
Other	7%	7%
No distinctive qualities, no answer		25%
Total no. of businessmen	87	281

15 *Advantages of African businessmen as perceived by ICDC-supported businessmen*

Advantages of Africans	ICDC-supported businessmen
Preferred by African customers	28%
Political advantages	5%
Other	4%
None	64%
Total no. of businessmen	87

16 *Reasons given by Asian businessmen for success of Asian business*

Reasons for Asian success	Asian businessmen
Hard work	85%
Thrift, soberness	33%
Intelligence, native ability	13%
Honesty, trustworthiness	18%
Ability to calculate risks	5%
Ambition, drive	6%
Experienced, long established	19%
Good business management	12%
Communal co-operation	11%
Good at attracting customers	2%
Capital	3%
Other answer	5%
Don't know, just luck	1%
Total no. of businessmen	281

17 *Training given to African employees by Asian businesses*

Training of Africans	Asian businesses
No training given, trained when hired	11%
Guidance, supervision on job	38%
Training or advice apart from job	1%
No African employees	23%
Unskilled African employees only	27%
Total %	100%
Total no.	281

18 *Work of African employees in Asian businesses*

Work of African employees	Asian businesses
Unskilled only	27%
Some skilled, no clerical or managerial	42%
Skilled and clerical, no managerial	7%
Skilled, clerical and managerial	1%
No African employees	23%
Total %	100%
Total no.	281

19 *Is it fair to discriminate in favour of Africans? Views of Asian businessmen*

	Asian businessmen
Is fair:	
because it is their country	12%
because they are backward	14%
other or no special reason	2%
Is not fair:	
because everyone has equal rights	61%
because Africans have abused preferential treatment	2%
other or no special reason	1%
Fair for some reasons, unfair for others	2%
Don't know, no opinion	6%
Total %	100%
Total no.	281

20 *Asian businessmen's experience of partnerships with Africans*

No experience, never considered African partner	79%
No experience, has considered African partner	17%
Partnership successful	1%
Partnership unsuccessful	3%
Total %	100%
Total no.	281

21 *Asian businessmen's views on partnership with Africans*

Partnership is practicable and would have advantages		44%
	practicable but offers no advantages	6%
	not practicable	33%
	doubtfully practicable	17%
Total %		100%
Total no.		281

CHAPTER 5

22 *Division of ownership of businesses*

No. of owners	ICDC-supported businesses	Market businesses
1	46%	68%
2	13%	15%
3	7%	6%
4	6%	3%
5	7%	2%
6–10	18%	4%
11–20	3%	1%
Over 20		1%
Total %	100%	100%
Total no.	87	848

23 *Number of employees*

No. of employees	ICDC-supported businesses	Market businesses
None		45%
1		22%
2– 5	30%	29%
6–10	28%	4%
11–20	24%	
21–30	8%	
31–40		
41–50	2%	
51–100	5%	
Over 100	3%	
Total %	100%	100%
Total no.	87	848

24 Businessmen's perception of their wage rates

	ICDC-supported businesses
Wage rates are considered to be:	
Average	54%
Above average	24%
Below average	14%
No answer	8%
Total %	100%
Total no.	87

25 Trouble with employees

	ICDC-supported businesses	Market businesses
Labour disputes	8%	
Stealing	35%	26%
Incompetence	9%	5%
Slacking, drunkenness, lateness	19% ⎫	19%
Absenteeism	8% ⎭	
Disobedience, rudeness, personal		
disagreements	5%	2%
No difficulties	38%	61%
Total no. of businesses	87	479*

* Excluding businesses with no employees in preceding year.

26 Ownership of land by commercial and industrial businessmen supported by the ICDC

	Industrial	Commercial	All
None	18%	10%	14%
Less than 3 acres	16%	5%	11%
3– 5 acres	18%	13%	15%
6– 10 ,,	18%	18%	18%
11– 15 ,,	2%	5%	4%
16– 20 ,,	6%	2%	5%
21– 50 ,,	13%	21%	16%
51–100 ,,	4%	16%	9%
Over 100 ,,	4%	10%	7%
No estimate	1%		1%
Total %	100%	100%	100%
Owns more than 1 farm	4%	35%	18%
Total no.	47	40	87

27 *Ownership of other businesses*

| | ICDC-supported businesses | | |
Ownership of other businesses	Industrial	Commercial	All
Owner or substantial partner in 1 other	26%	23%	24%
Owner or substantial partner in 2 other	6%	13%	9%
Owner or substantial partner in 3 or more	2%	5%	4%
Owner or substantial partner in no other	66%	59%	63%
Total %	100%	100%	100%
Total no.	47	40	87

Ownership of other businesses	Market businesses
Owns other business in same market only:	
of same kind only	1%
including other kinds	11%
Owns other business in same market *and* elsewhere:	
of same kind only	1%
including other kinds	2%
Owns other business elsewhere only:	
of same kind only	4%
including other kinds	3%
No other business owned but owns plot in same market	1%
No other businesses owned	76%
No answer	1%
Total %	100%
Total no.	848

28 *Origins of employees in ICDC-supported businesses*

	Industrial	Commercial	All
Employees all from same location	15%	30%	22%
all from same district	15%	30%	22%
all same tribe	20%	18%	19%
all African	33%	15%	24%
include different races	17%	7%	13%
Total%	100%	100%	100%
Businessmen denying any tribal preference	91%	80%	86%
Total no.	47	40	87

CHAPTER 6

29 *Employment of relatives by market businessmen of different tribes*

Tribal origin of employer	None related	Employees Some related	All related	Total %	Total no. of business-men
Kamba	46%	19%	35%	100%	52
Kikuyu	67%	16%	17%	100%	141
Luhya	57%	13%	29%	100%	54
Luo	68%	9%	23%	100%	56
Gusii	87%	11%	2%	100%	46
Kalenjin	33%	46%	22%	100%	46
Swahili and Mijikenda	29%	14%	57%	100%	14
Taita	26%	38%	36%	100%	47
Other	80%		20%	100%	10
All	57%	19%	24%	100%	466

CHAPTER 7

30 *Classes of customers to which businessmen said they usually extended credit*

Credit to customers	ICDC-supported businesses	Market businesses	Asian businesses
No credit given	38%	25%	23%
Credit given to:			
government institutions, schools	18%	1%	2%
other businesses	16%		10%
known and trusted customers	29%	62%	46%
friends		11%	
relatives		3%†	1%
most or all customers	10%	2%	23%
Total no. of businesses*	87	848	238‡

* Percentage totals more than 100 per cent since businessmen might give more than one answer.
† But see also the answers in the next table, when they were specifically asked about relatives.
‡ The 43 Asian businesses outside Nairobi are excluded from tables where their characteristics differed from the Nairobi sample.

Supplementary Tables

Is credit given to relatives?

	Market businesses
Not at all	60%
Only on the same conditions as anyone else	20%
Sometimes	10%
Usually	8%
Other answer	2%
Total %	100%
Total no.	734*

* This question was added after some of the interviews had been completed.

31 *Is it necessary to give credit?*

	Market businesses
Yes and does	29%
Yes but does not	3%
No but does	48%
No and does not	20%
Total %	100%
Total no.	828*

* Excluding inadequate answers.

32 *Credit to customers and progress of business*

	% of businesses refusing all credit	(100 =)
Market businesses with profit under 300/- p. m.	21%	(445)
Market businesses with profit of 300/- p. m. or more	35%	(178)
ICDC-supported businesses, not expanding profitably	45%	(53)
ICDC-supported businesses, expanding profitably	26%	(34)

33 *Action on bad debts*

Action on bad debts	ICDC-supported businesses	Market businesses	Asian businesses, Nairobi
No substantial bad debts	39%	40%	32%
Substantial bad debts:			
court action taken	24%	12%	35%
,, ,, threatened	16%	6%	5%
other action	9%		3%
no action	12%	42%	25%
Total %	100%	100%	100%
Total no.	87	848	238

Supplementary Tables

34 Credit from suppliers

Length of credit obtained from suppliers	ICDC-supported businesses	Asian businesses, Nairobi
None	49%	27%
Up to one month	36%	12%
Over one month	15%	61%
Total %	100%	100%
Total no.	87	238

35 Race of suppliers

	ICDC-supported businesses	Market businesses
All Asian	32%	23%
All African	8%	18%
All European	14%	3%
Asian and European	25%	6%
Asian and African	8%	32%
African and European		4%
All three	8%	14%
Government agency only	5%*	
Total %	100%	100%
Total no.	87	834†

* A quarter of the other businesses also got some supplies from government agencies.
† Excluding 14 which did not depend on any supplies.

36 Attracting customers

How market businessmen said they tried to attract customers away from their competitors:

Good service, quality	26%
Good manner, friendliness	52%
Better range of stock	9%
Offering credit or discounts	14%
Integrity	2%
Appealing to friends	1%
Cleanliness, neatness	4%
Fair prices	4%
Other answer	2%
Does not try to attract customers	15%
Total no. of businesses	848

How ICDC-supported businessmen tried to meet competition:

	Profitable & expanding businesses	Others	All
Higher quality	41%	26%	32%
Lower prices	32%	19%	24%
Better access to market	3%	6%	5%
Personal contacts	12%	9%	10%
Racial or political pressure	24%	11%	16%
Other	12%		5%
No competition	21%	13%	16%
No way of meeting competition		26%	16%
Total no. of businesses	34	53	87

37 *Competition faced by different sorts of ICDC-supported businesses*

Extent of competition	Retail	Whole-sale	Service industry	Manu-factur-ing standard articles	Manu-factur-ing to order	All
No serious competition	31%	8%	26%	12%		16%
Competition from within same district only	69%	88%	64%	38%	80%	69%
Competition from outside district		4%	10%	50%	20%	15%
Total %	100%	100%	100%	100%	100%	100%
Total no.	16	24	19	18	10	87

CHAPTER 8

38 *Government help requested by African businessmen*

Percentage of businessmen mentioning various kinds of help	ICDC business-men	Percentage of business mentioning various kinds of help	Market business-men
Loans	59%	Loans	85%
Training and advice	64%	Training and advice	14%
Government regulation of prices	1%	Credit facilities for supplies	2%
Government help in access to supplies	25%	Changes in licensing restrictions	4%
Government help in organizing African businesses	13%	Regulation of wholesale prices	10%
Closer supervision of loans	30%	Improve market facilities	5%
Control of competition	14%	Organization of wholesale co-ops	13%
Nationalization	10%	Reduce or change taxation	2%
Help in finding markets	15%	Other	18%
Control rents, build new premises	5%	No help government can give	2%
Fairer taxation	1%		
Other	20%		
None	1%		
Total no. of businessmen	87	Total no. of businessmen	848

39 *Length of time between application and issue of ICDC loans*

Up to 6 months	22%
6 months to 1 year	41%
Over 1 year	23%
Over 2 years	14%
Total %	100%
Total no.*	81

* Excluding those where the loan had not been finally issued or our information is inexact.

Supplementary Tables

CHAPTER 9

40 *Age and standing of business*

	Age of market businessmen			
Profit of business	20–29	30–39	40–49	50+
Under 300/- p. m.	83%	67%	65%	79%
300/- p. m. or more	17%	33%	35%	21%
Total %	100%	100%	100%	100%
Total no.*	138	236	158	81

* Excluding businesses where profit could not be estimated, and 10 where age was not known.

	Age of ICDC-supported businessmen			
Progress of business	20–29	30–39	40–49	50+
Static, doubtful or failing, etc.	33%	56%	61%	80%
Profitable and expanding	67%	44%	39%	20%
Total %	100%	100%	100%	100%
Total no.*	6	34	31	15

* Excluding one where age was not given.

41 *Age, education and profit: market businesses*

	% of businesses earning 300/- profit p.m. or more by age and education			
Education	20–29	30–39	40–49	50+
Less than 4 years	8% (27*)	29% (55)	24% (78)	14% (51)
4 years or more	20% (111)	34% (179)	46% (79)	34% (29)

* Figures in brackets are the total of businessmen in each age and educational category equivalent to 100 per cent.

42 *Technical training and progress of businesses*

| | Training or previous experience of market businessmen | | |
| | | Trained in | Trained in |
Profit of business	None	present trade	other trades
Less than 300/– p.m.	74%	74%	64%
300/– p.m. or more	26%	26%	36%
Total %	100%	100%	100%
Total no.	318	147	148

| | Training or previous experience of ICDC-supported businessmen | | |
| | | Trained in | Trained in |
Progress of business	None	present business	other business
Static, doubtful or failing, etc.	62%	52%	68%
Profitable and expanding	38%	48%	32%
Total %	100%	100%	100%
Total no.	37	25	25

43 *Influence of experience on progress of industrial and commercial businesses supported by ICDC*

| | Industry | | Commerce | |
| | Profitable and | | Profitable and | |
	expanding	Other	expanding	Other
No training or experience	30%	36%	57%	52%
Training or experience in skills related in business	60%	36%		12%
Training or experience in other skills	10%	28%	43%	36%
Total %	100%	100%	100%	100%
Total no.	20	27	14	26

44 *Book-keeping and progress of business*

| No. of books kept | ICDC-supported businesses | | | Market businesses | | |
	Profitable and expanding	Others	All	Profit 300/- p.m. +	Profit under 300/- p.m.	All
None	3%	4%	3%	13%	32%	32%
1	6%	26%	18%	42%	42%	38%
2	26%	36%	32%	27%	18%	20%
3 or more	65%	34%	47%	18%	8%	10%
Total %	100%	100%	100%	100%	100%	100%
Total no.	34	53	87	178	445	844*

* Including businesses for which profit was not estimated, but excluding 4 where book-keeping was not known.

| Books kept by | ICDC-supported businesses | | |
	Profitable and expanding	Others	All
Qualified accountant		4%	2%
Trained staff	47%	38%	42%
Experienced but untrained staff	22%	14%	17%
Staff without training or experience	28%	40%	35%
No books kept	3%	4%	4%
Total %	100%	100%	100%
Total no.	34	53	87

45 *Methods of costing and progress of business*

| | ICDC-supported businesses | | |
	Profitable and expanding	Others	All
Costs not estimated	3%	9%	7%
Costs roughly estimated	53%	68%	62%
Costs systematically estimated	44%	23%	31%
Total %	100%	100%	100%
Total no.	34	53	87

CHAPTER 10

46 *Advice to African businessmen starting a business*

Advice offered	ICDC- supported businessmen	Market businessmen
Avoid or be careful of giving credit	21%	50%
Start with enough capital	31%	22%
Keep good accounts	46%	23%
Cultivate good relationships with customers		26%
Be honest		7%
Avoid extravagance		21%
Beware of friendships		4%
Be determined, get ahead		11%
Know your trade		13%
Plan carefully	32%	
Choose good site		8%
Other answer	24%	25%
No advice	2%	5%
Total no. of businessmen	87	848

INTERVIEW SCHEDULES

Interview No.

UNIVERSITY COLLEGE, NAIROBI,
INSTITUTE FOR DEVELOPMENT STUDIES

BUSINESS SURVEY

Introduction We are helping with a study of African businessmen which is being carried out at University College, Nairobi. The research is to find out more about African businesses—what progress they are making, what their difficulties are, how Government might be able to help them. The information is important for planning the development of Kenya. We hope you will agree to help us by answering a few questions about your business. We are not government officials. Nothing you tell us about your business will be passed on to Government or made public without your permission, so we hope you will talk to us quite freely. We shall be making a report on our research to Government, but we will not mention the names and details of particular businesses.

1. May I ask your name? (There is no need to ask for the name immediately, if you think it would be better to ask later.)

2. (i) Are you an owner or part-owner of this business?
   (Note: the question refers to the business, not the building.)
   (ii) If not, do you manage it for someone else?
   (iii) If you are the manager, who owns it?

3. (i) Is the business owned in partnership?

(ii) If so, how many partners are there?
(iii) Are they related to each other?
   (*a*) none related
   (*b*) some related
   (*c*) all related
   If related, what are the relationships (e.g. brother, cousin, father, son, etc.—note whether the relationship is on the mother's or father's side— e.g. put mother's brother, or father's brother, not just uncle).

266

4. Kind of business:

Supplies

5. Where do you obtain your supplies: (put yes or no against each)
   (*a*) Wholesaler not in same market?
   Asian:
   African:
   European:
   (*b*) From vans which come to the market?
   Asian:
   African:
   European:
   (*c*) Locally? (i.e. farmers or co-ops, wholesalers in same market)
   African:
   Asian:
   (*d*) Elsewhere? (e.g. meat from cattle auctions) (describe where)

Pricing

6. (i) Is the selling price fixed on all items, or does it sometimes vary
   (*a*) with customer's ability to pay?
   (*b*) according to cost of repair, suit, furniture, etc.?
   (*c*) according to bargaining between buyer and seller?
   (*d*) in any other way?
   (ii) Do you reduce the price of goods which are difficult to sell? even below what they cost you?

Credit

7. (i) Do you give credit to any customers?
   (ii) If you do, to which customers? (e.g. friends, or relatives, or people with good salaries, etc.)
   Do you always give credit to your own relatives? (why? or why not?) And if you take anything from the business for your own use, do you pay for it?

(iii) and what are your conditions?
maximum amount of credit to each customer:
maximum length of time in which to pay (e.g. 1 week, 1 month, 3 months):
other conditions (e.g. deposit, paying previous deb:, etc.):
(iv) How many customers do you give credit to? And what is the total amount of credit each month?
About how many customers do you have in a month?
(or give percentage of customers to whom he gives credit)

8. (i) Have you had any trouble with bad debts?
   (ii) If yes, how much? (give total amount overdue in past twelve months):
   (iii) What do you do about people who don't pay: (e.g. take them to court)?
   (iv) How many have you taken to court in the past twelve months?
   (v) If none taken to court, why not?

9. (i) Do you think it is necessary to give credit in order to get customers?
   (ii) Why do you think that?
   (iii) Did you give more credit in the past than you do now, or less? Why have you changed?

Competition

10. (i) Are there other African-owned businesses in the market like yours?
    (ii) Do you think in this market there are: too many businesses like yours?
    or too few?
    or just about the right number?
    Why do you think that?

11. If this is not the only African business of its kind in the market:
    (i) Do you try to get customers to come to you and not to others? If so, how?
    (ii) (*a*) Are prices fixed by law or by the suppliers (e.g. bottled beer)?
    (b) If some are not, do you have an agreement with other businesses like yours in this market to charge the same prices?
    (*c*) or do you try to give lower prices than others?
    (iii) Do you sell anything or give any service which other businesses like yours here do not provide?
    If so, what made you decide to do it?

12. Is there any competition between this business and
    (*a*) Asian business? or
    (*b*) Other businesses outside this market?
    If so, has it hurt your business? how have you been able to deal with it?

Employees

13. (i) How many people are employed in this shop? (include apprentices—and the manager, if not owner or part-owner of the business)
    (ii) How many of them are related to the shopkeeper (belong to the same family)?
    (iii) What is the relationship? (be as exact as possible—e.g. full brother, half brother, etc.)

14. (i) Have you had any trouble with employees?
    —stealing?
    —staying away from work?
    —other?

(ii) If so, how did you deal with it?
(iii) How many employees have you had to dismiss in the past 12 months?

15. How much are the employees paid?

16. (i) On the whole, do you think it is better to employ relatives or non-relatives?
    Why, do you think?
    (ii) Which are more reliable, relatives or others? (why?)

17. (i) Suppose two men came to you for a job. One is recommended by a friend of yours, as a hard-working man who could do the job. The other is a stranger, but he has more education and experience. Which would you choose, the first or the second? (Why?)
    (ii) Which of these businessmen do you think is running his business in the better way?
    The first takes anyone he thinks can do the work, but sacks them immediately if he's not satisfied with them. The other employs people he knows, talks things over with them when they do not work well, and tries to help them.

Loans

18. (i) Has the business ever had a loan?
    If so, from whom:

	Amount:
Government?	
County Council?	
Bank?	
Friend?	
Other?	

    (ii) If not, has the owner ever applied for a loan?
    If so, to whom did he apply?

19. (i) Do you keep any accounts for the business?
If so, what?
(ii) Have you ever studied book-keeping?
If so, where?   for how long?

(Ask Questions 20–32 of the Owner)

20. (i) Where do you live now:
In the market?
Within 5 miles of the market?
Elsewhere in the same district?
Same Province?
Other (write in):
(ii) Where were you born:
Within 5 miles of the market?
Elsewhere in the same district?
Same Province?
Other (write in):
(iii) What year were you born?
(If not known) Roughly how old are you?

21. (If the business owner is a woman, do not ask this question and put n/a)
We would like to ask a little about your family.
(i) How many sons did your father have, who are older than you, not counting those who died in childhood?
(ii) How many sons did your father have who are younger than you?
(iii) How many children (boys and girls) did he have altogether?
If your father had more than one wife:
(iv) How many sons did your mother have, who are older than you?
(v) How many sons did she have who are younger?
(vi) How many children altogether?
(exclude those who died in childhood in every case)

22. (i) How much education have you had? (include teacher training and higher education, but not technical training)
(ii) Have you had any technical training? (e.g. carpentry, black-smithing) (note whether in training school or apprenticeship)

23. Do you own any land?
If yes,
(*a*) how many acres?
(*b*) what cash crops and grade cattle do you have?
(c) which is more important to you, your farm or your business? which is more profitable?

24. Do you own any other business? If yes, what? (note kind of business, and where)

25. (i) How long have you been running this shop?
(ii) How long have you been a shopkeeper?
(iii) What were your main reasons for taking up business?
(iv) What was your occupation at the time when you first started running your own business? (or just before you started?)

26. If you had any savings to invest at present, what is the first thing you would do with them?
Why?

27. (i) On the whole does this business make a profit?
(ii) How much would you estimate your profit is each month, when all your business expenses have been paid? (that is, what is the profit after labour, transport, stock, materials, and rent have all been paid for—excluding family expenses):
(iii) Have you put any of your profit back into the business?
(iv) What else do you spend the profit on?

28. What are your greatest difficulties?

29. Do you think there is any way Government could help the progress of African businesses? How?

30. What advice would you give to a friend just starting up in business?

31. What do you think are the commonest reasons why businesses fail?

32. Here is the description of two shopkeepers:

One is very friendly and patient, he gives credit to people who are poor, and is well liked by his customers. He keeps the same stock as other shops, and charges the same prices. The other never gives credit, and does not spend so much time being friendly to his customers. But he keeps more kinds of stock than other shops, and he knows where to buy his goods cheaply, so his prices are lower.
Which of them is the most like the kind of businessman you would like to be?

Interviewer's Comments:

Note especially: does the shop look well stocked?
is there much variety of stock?
did you see many customers?
did the business look busy?

From your own observation, would you say this business was:

Doing better than most?

About average?

Doing less well than most?

(write in yes or no)

Date: Interviewer:

Interview No. ☐☐☐

UNIVERSITY COLLEGE, NAIROBI, INSTITUTE FOR DEVELOPMENT STUDIES

SURVEY OF ASIAN BUSINESSES

Introduction   We are helping with a study of Asian businesses which is being carried out at University College, Nairobi. We hope you will agree to help us by answering a few questions about your business. We are not government officials: no particulars of your business will be made public without permission, or passed on to Government. No names or details of individual businesses will be published in any report of the study. Its purpose is just to gather some general information about Asian businesses to compare with another study of African businesses, and to gather the views of businessmen like yourself about the possibilities and difficulties of helping African businesses to develop, and the problems you face yourself. Studies like these should help to bring about a better understanding between communities in Kenya, so we very much hope you will agree to spare a little time to answering our questions.

1. *Kind of business*
   Wholesale   1
   Retail (inc. tailoring)   2
   Service industry   3
   Manufacture   4
   Building and construction   5
   Transport   6
   Agency (e.g. travel, credit)   7
   Hotel, bar, lodging house   8
   Other (write in)

Kind of goods sold or service given:

2. *Ownership*
   (*a*) Are you the owner or the manager of this business?
   owner   1
   manager   2
   (b) Is this business a partnership or a company, or just owned by one person or his family?
   sole ownership   1
   joint family ownership
   (not formally partner-
   ship or co.)   2
   partnership   3
   private Co. Ltd.   4

271

2. *Ownership—cont.*

    private Co. not Ltd.   5
    public Co.   6
    co-operative   7

If so, are all, some or none of the other owners

    Relatives?
    Other members of your community?
    Other Asians?
    African?
    European?

3. *Employees*

(i) How many people work in the business?

(ii) How many of them are:
    relatives? (excluding informant)
    other members of your community?
    other Asian?
    African?
    European?

(iii) (If employees include relatives) What is their relationship to you?

(iv) On the whole, do you think it is better to have members of your own family or outsiders
    as business associates?
    as employees?

Why do you think that?

Which are likely to be more reliable, relatives or others?

(v) (If employees include Africans) What kinds of jobs do the African employees do?

(vi) (If any Africans in skilled jobs) What training have you given them? Or were they all already trained?

(vii) (a) Do you think it is possible for Asian businessmen to do more to help train Africans for skilled jobs and business management?
    In what way?

What are the difficulties?

(b) Have you ever tried to do this yourself?

If so, was it successful:
    from your point of view?
    from the trainees' point of view?

4. (a) When this business first started under present ownership, could you tell me how the capital was raised? (We are not asking you to tell us the amount or details)

    from the owners' own savings?   1
    from selling property or investments?   2
    from members of the family?   3
    from friends?   4
    from offering shares?   5
    bank loan?   6
    loans from community associations?   7
    credit from suppliers?   8
    inherited business?   9
    bought by instalment from previous owner?   x
    other? (write in)

(b) Has more external capital been put into the business since? (If yes) What has been the principal source of further financing?

(c) Have you invested any profits from your business in Kenya, apart from this business?
If so, what kinds of investment have you made?

(d) Do you have any members of your family outside Kenya to whom you have given financial help? If so, what kind of help?

5. (a) Where do you get most of your supplies?
Kenya:
    from European firms?   1
    from Asian firms?   2

from African firms or
farmers? 3
Govt. Agencies? 4
Outside Kenya (i.e. direct import):
from India or Pakistan? 5
other countries? 6
Other? (write in)

(*b*) Do you regularly get credit from your suppliers? for how long?

(*c*) Are any of your major suppliers related to you?

6. (*a*) Do you give credit to your customers?

(*b*) If so, to which customers do you give credit, and on what conditions?
Do you feel there is more risk in giving credit to African customers than others? Why?

(*c*) Have you had trouble with bad debts? (give approximate amount of debt over time)

(*d*) (If so) What action have you taken?

7. *Helping African businesses*
(i) The government is trying to develop African businesses. What do you think is the best way of doing that?

(ii) Do you think there are ways the Asian business community could help?

(iii) Do you think it is sometimes fair for government to give special preference to Africans over other citizens, or not? why do you think that?

(iv) (*a*) There's a suggestion that there should be more Asian-African partnerships in business. What do you feel about that—is it practicable? Would there be a mutual advantage in it?

(*b*) Have you ever gone into partnership with an African businessman yourself?
If so, how did it go?
If not, have you ever seriously considered it?

8. *The future for Asian businesses*
(i) The Asian community has been outstandingly successful in Kenya in trade and commerce. What do you think are the most important reasons for their success?

(ii) (*a*) What advantages do you think Asians have compared with Africans as businessmen in Kenya?

(*b*) What advantages, on the other side, do you think Africans have compared with Asians?

(*c*) And what do you think are the advantages of European businessmen compared with either Asians or Africans?

(iii) Looking into the future, do you think the Asian community is likely to grow larger or smaller relative to other races? In business, and in general? why do you think that?

(iv) If you were asked to advise a boy—of ten say—from your own community about his future, what would you recommend? (prompt—kind of job? should he settle in Kenya?)

(v) When you retire, where do you plan to settle down?

(vi) Do you think Asian businesses are bound to suffer if African businesses expand?

(vii) What do you think are the outstanding problems facing Asian business in Kenya at present?

9. (*a*) From the point of view of your own community, do you think anything could be done to bring the different communities in East Africa closer together?

(*b*) Do you think it is possible for the different groups amongst the Asian people in East Africa to act together?
If so, what do you think should be the main purposes of such united community action?

(*c*) Do you think that inter-marriage is a good way of trying to bring the different communities together?

(*d*) What do you think are the advantages of citizenship for non-Africans in Kenya?
and the disadvantages?

10. *Personal*
Lastly, may I ask you a few questions about yourself:
(i) How old are you?
(ii) Where were you born?
(iii) How long have you been living in Kenya?
(iv) Where did you go to school? for how many years?
(v) How long have you been running this business?
(vi) How long have you been in business?
(vii) What was your occupation before you first went into business?
(viii) What language do you speak at home?
(ix) What is your religion?
(x) Of what country are you a citizen?

Interviewer's comments:

Interviewer:

Date:

SCHEDULE FOR STUDY OF ENTERPRISES
SUPPORTED BY ICDC LOANS

I. *Nature of the enterprise*

1. Name and address of Enterprise:
   Branches:
   Name(s) of principal owners:

2. Formal structure:
   (Private Co., Co-operative, Public Co., etc.)

3. Activities:

II. *Origins of the enterprise*

1. Who started it?
   Name
   Occupation
   Relationship to others involved.
   (e.g. same family or clan, same
   school, how were they known to
   each other?)

2. What were the aims and opportunities foreseen in starting it?
   (Note social or political as well as
   economic aims)

3. When did it start?
   Date first conceived:
   Date it began to operate:

4. How was it originally financed?
   (Individuals, Banks, ICDC,
   credit from suppliers, etc.)
   Source
   Amount
   Date

5. (i) How was the ICDC loan
   negotiated?
   (Note: who first approached,

how first heard of ICDC, time
taken to negotiate loan, amount
asked, reasons for any reduction,
security offered, cost of negotiations, whether loan paid in cash
or through invoices, terms of
loan.)
(ii) Who sponsored the application?

6. Was any technical advice or
   assistance received at the outset?
   From whom? What kind?

7. Summary of capital investment
   Original capital
   (excluding ICDC
   loan):   Source:
   ICDC loan:
   Other loans: Source:
   Subsequent capital
   investment: Source:

   _____

   Total:
   Present capital
   value: _____
   Difference: _____represented
                          by:
                     fixed
                       assets:
                     other
                       assets:

8. Have any profits of the enterprise been invested in other
   activities?
   If so:
   Nature of investment
   Amount
   Terms of investmen‐

III. *The running of the enterprise* (Note: if business has failed, ask these questions retrospectively)

A. *Personnel*

1. The directors:
   (Who are they? what is the relationship between them? How were they recruited? and when?)

2. The management:
   (i) Functions
   Salary
   owner/shareholder?
   (ii) How recruited (e.g. qualifications, recommendation, personal relationship)
   (iii) What are the qualifications and experience of the member of staff who looks after the books and accounts?

3. Other employees:
   (i) Kind of occupation
   Number
   Wage rate
   (ii) How were they recruited? (e.g. qualifications required, recommendations, personal relationship)
   (iii) (*a*) Are wages above or below average?
   (*b*) Any bonuses, overtime, payments in kind, discount privileges?

4. In general, is preference given to relatives of management, members of the same clan, tribe or religion in choosing staff?
   What is the tribal distribution of employees?

5. From the experience of this enterprise, are relatives usually more reliable or less reliable than others as business associates or employees? Why?

6. Have there been any disputes or other difficulties within the staff?

If so, what happened, and how were they resolved?

7. What precautions are taken against theft, bad work, poor time-keeping, malingering by employees? How far are they trusted?

8. (i) Are advances of salary given? (When and on what terms?)
   (ii) Are regular discussions held with employees?
   (iii) Any other comments on how relationship with employees is handled:

B. *Customers*

1. (*a*) Who are the customers? (e.g. by race, locality, occupation, etc.)
   How were they found?
   (*b*) Do you advertise? How?

2. (i) (*a*) Is credit given to any customers? (If so, on what terms and to whom? How is it decided whether a customer is credit-worthy?)
   (*b*) Besides credit—any other privileges to good customers (e.g. discounts)?
   (*c*) Are any free services given to customers as goodwill (advice, use of telephone, etc.)?
   (ii) If no credit given now, was it formerly?
   (iii) (*a*) Has the enterprise had any experience of bad debts?
   (*b*) If so, how are they pursued?

C. *Suppliers*

1. (i) Does the enterprise
   lease—
   rent—
   own—
   its premises?

(ii) If lease or rent:
    (*a*) amount?
    (*b*) from whom does it rent?
    (*c*) has rent gone up?

2. From whom does the enterprise obtain supplies (e.g. European, Asian, African)?

3. On what terms (if any) is the enterprise able to get credit, defer payments, overdraw?

4. Are there difficulties in getting supplies? (Slow delivery, poor quality)

D. *Competitors*

1. Does the enterprise have competitors in its market? (esp. Asian or European competitors)

2. If so, what have been the competitors' tactics? (e.g. price cutting, boycotts, discrimination by suppliers, etc.)

3. And what have been the tactics of the enterprise?

E. *Costing*

1 How is the selling price determined? (E.g. from costs +, or prevailing market price)

2. How are costs, overheads worked out? (Especially, note allowances for depreciation. What costs are taken into account?)

3. How is the profit margin calculated? (Is it known whether the enterprise is making a profit?)

4. (i) What records are kept. (E.g. cash book, journal, ledger. Any others?)
(ii) Are accounts audited? (If so, note fee)

F. *The experience so far:*

1. Problems encountered, profit or losses, expansion, changes of plan, staff:

2. How much of any profit has been distributed, how much reinvested? Are loan instalments up to date? Amount of profit?

3. Future plans: (or if business has failed, reasons for failure)

IV. *The originator(s) of the enterprise*

(These questions to be asked of whoever took the principal part in originating the enterprise. If there was more than once such originator, the information should be gathered for each of them, as far as possible).

1. Why did you decide to start this enterprise? (esp. why this kind of business, rather than another? why go into business, rather than any other way of earning a living?)

2. Personal history:
(i) Birthplace:
(ii) Approximate date of birth:
(iii) Father's occupation and status in his community: (e.g. if a subsistence farmer, was he relatively well off or poor, chief or elder, etc.)
(iv) Is your father still living? If not, how old were you when he died?
And your mother?
(v) (If Father died in Ego's childhood): who brought you up?
(otherwise)
were you brought up in your father's homeland? If not, where?
(vi) How long have you been living here?

(vii) Education:
Kind of school:
To what level?
(viii) What did you do after you left school?
(ix) Record of jobs, activities, and previous business ventures (Note especially how he came to start his first business venture)
(x) Have you had any business training? (from e.g. commercial course, working for a firm)

3. (i) Religion:
(ii) How active a part do you play in your church?
(churchgoing, church elder, officer of church organizations, etc.)
(iii) Have you always belonged to this religion?
  (a) If not: how did you come to join it?
  (b) If so: were your parents also members of this church?
    were there many members of this church in the community where you grew up?
(iv) How many others involved in this enterprise are of the same religion?
(directors, management, employees)
(v) Has your religion helped you in any way in this enterprise?
(either practically—personal contacts, help from religious institutions, or in terms of its teaching)
(vi) Do you have any strong convictions about drinking? smoking?

4. (a) Apart from this business, are you owner or part owner of any other? (specify)

(If so) who manages it on your behalf?
(b) Do you own any farm or homestead? (Roughly how many acres: and how much under cash crops. Any grade cattle?)
(If so) who looks after it?
Do you have any plans to buy more land?
Have you invested any business profits in your farm? Why (rather than in the business itself)?

5. Do you hold any paid job (apart from this enterprise)?

6. Apart from those we have discussed—church, business, farm —are you involved in any other activities, such as chamber of commerce, social or political organizations, cultural societies, tribal associations?
(If so) Do you hold any office in them?
Did you help to start any of them?

7. (i) Are you married?
No. of wives:
Occupation:
Children: No. under 16:
          No. over 16:
Occupation of children over 16:
(ii) How many members of your own family are involved in any way with this enterprise?
Or with any of your other enterprises?
(iii) Have you been approached by members of your family for jobs? Have you had to refuse any requests?
(iv) In general, in your experience, is it an advantage or a disadvantage to involve your family in business?

(v) (*a*) Apart from your wife (wives) and children, what family responsibilities do you bear?

(*b*) What requests for help do you get from your family, and how do you handle them?

(*c*) Do they expect to get things out of your business for free? such as?

(*d*) Do you receive help from any members of your family? (in cash or kind, or unpaid services)

8. (*a*) What do you think are the most important qualities of a successful businessman?

(*b*) Do you know of any businesses which have been outstandingly successful? Why, do you think?

9. (*a*) What do you think are the commonest reasons why people fail in business?

(*b*) Do you know of any businesses which have failed? Why, do you think?

10. What advice would you give to a friend just starting up in business?

11. (*a*) What advantages do you think Europeans have over Africans as businessmen?

(*b*) What advantages do you think Asians have over Africans as businessmen?

(*c*) Do you think that Africans have any compensating advantages?

12. What do you think are the outstanding problems of African businesses?

13. What should Government do to help African businesses most effectively?

14. Would you prefer to be employed if you could earn as much? Or if you could earn more? Why not?

15. Do you worry about the business —lose sleep, appetite? What do you worry most about?

Descriptive note of the enterprise: its premises, location, and the community in which it is situated.

Date of interview:

Interviewer:

REFERENCES

BARTH, FREDRIK, 'Economic Spheres in Dafur', *Themes in Economic Anthropology*, ed. Raymond Firth, (Tavistock, 1967).

COWARD, D. J., 'Administration of the Companies Act in Kenya', *Private Enterprise and the East African Company*, ed. P. A. Thomas, (Tanzania Publishing House, 1969).

DAVENPORT, ROBERT W., *Financing the Small Manufacturer in Developing Countries*, (McGraw-Hill, 1967).

GEERTZ, CLIFFORD, *Princes and Pedlars*, (Chicago University Press, 1963).

HARRIS, ALFRED and GRACE, 'Taita Domestic Groups', *The Family Estate in Africa*, ed. Robert F. Gray and P. H. Gulliver, (Routledge & Kegan Paul, 1964).

Industrial and Commercial Development Corporation of Kenya, *Annual Reports*, (1963–66).

International Labour Office, *Services for Small-Scale Industry*, (I.L.O.: Geneva, 1961).

JACOBS, ALAN, *The Traditional Organization of the Pastoral Masai*, (D.Phil. thesis, Oxford University, 1965).

Kenya Archives, Annual Reports of Rumuruti and Nyeri Districts, (1909 to 1926).

Kenya Development Plan, 1966–1970.

Kenya Population Census, 1962: Vol. III, *African Population*, (Ministry of Economic Planning and Development, 1966).

KENYATTA, JOMO, *Facing Mount Kenya*, (Secker and Warburg, 1953).

LEVINE, ROBERT A., 'The Gusii Family', *The Family Estate in Africa*, ed. Robert F. Gray and P. H. Gulliver, (Routledge & Kegan Paul, 1964).

LEVINE, ROBERT A., *Dreams and Deeds: Achievement Motivation in Nigeria*, (University of Chicago Press, 1966).

LONG, NORMAN, *Social Change and the Individual:* A study of the social and religious responses to innovation in a Zambian rural community, (Manchester University Press, 1968).

LUGARD, FREDERICK, *The Rise of our East African Empire*, Vol. I, (Blackwood, 1893).

MARRIS, PETER, 'The Law and African Business', *Private Enterprise and the East African Company*, ed. P. A. Thomas, (Tanzania Publishing House, 1969).

MATSON, A. T., 'Buganda Merchant Venturers', *Uganda Journal*, Vol. 32, Part 1, (1968).

MCCLELLAND, DAVID C., *The Achieving Society*, (Van Nostrand, 1961); 'The Achievement Motive in Economic Growth', *Industrialization and Society*, ed. Bert F. Hoselitz and Wilbert E. Moore, (UNESCO: Mouton, 1963).

References

National Christian Council of Kenya Working Party, *Who Controls Industry in Kenya?*, (East African Publishing House, 1968).

RAY, ROBERT S., 'The Structure of Employment in Kenya', *Education, Employment and Rural Development*, ed. James R. Sheffield, (East African Publishing House, 1967).

ROUTLEDGE, W. S. and K., *With a Prehistoric People*, (Edwin Arnold, 1910).

SCHATZ, SAYRE P., 'Economic Environment and Private Enterprise in West Africa', *The Economic Bulletin of Ghana*, Vol. VII, No. 4, (1963). 'Aiding Nigerian Business: the Yaba Industrial Estate', *The Nigerian Journal of Economic and Social Studies*, (July, 1964).

SCHUMPETER, JOSEPH A., 'The Creative Response in Economic History', *Journal of Economic History*, Vol. VII, No. 2, (1947).

SMILES, SAMUEL, *Lives of the Engineers*, (John Murray, 1862)

STALEY, EUGENE, 'Development of Small Industry Programmes', *A Contribution in Methods of Industrial Development*, (OECD; Paris, 1962).

SUTTON, FRANCIS X., HARRIS, SEYMOUR E., KAYSEN, CARL and TOBIN, JAMES, *The American Business Creed*, (Harvard University Press, 1956).

WEBER, MAX, *The Protestant Ethic and the Spirit of Capitalism*, trans. Talcott Parsons, (Allen and Unwin, 1930).

INDEX

Aberdare mountains 25, 32
African businessmen
  advantages 252
  isolation 226–7, 233–4
  see also ICDC-supported business-
    men; Mahiga businessmen;
    Market businessmen
Age of businessmen
  and attitude to relatives 143
  and profit 262
Alliance High School, interviewers
  from 16
Asian businesses
  historical origins 7
  interview schedule for 271–4
  position in Kenya economy 5–6
  sample 18–19
  sorts 244
  see also Asian businessmen
Asian businessmen
  African hostility to 94–8
  attitude to Africans in business
    96n, 253–4
  attitude to European businessmen
    96n
  attitude to relatives in business
    143–4
  credit to customers 155
  exclusiveness and minority status
    75–6
  help to Africans by 95–6
  perceived advantages 93
  reasons for success 252
  training of Africans 252
  see also Asian businesses
Athamaki. See Muthamaki

Bad debts 154–6, 258

Baganda traders 75n
Bakeries 164–6
Banking staff 236
Baringo, Lake 49
Barth, Fredrik 239n
Book-keeping 219–21, 264
Brothers
  in business 127, 138, 149
  and land tenure 146

Calvinism 78–9
Capital
  invested in ICDC-supported busi-
    nesses 187–8, 202–3
  shortage of working 183–4
  sources 189
Carnegie, Dale 87, 209
Chinga 34
Colonial policy towards agricultural
  development 6–8
Competition in different sorts of
  business 164–8, 260
Coward, D. J. 237n
Credit
  to customers 153–61, 257–8
  from suppliers 155, 259
Customers
  attraction 157, 259–60
  credit to 153–61, 257–8
  race 152
  racial prejudices 98

Davenport, Robert 170n
Development Finance Co. 11
Development Plan 1966/70 11, 169,
  171
Directors of Kenya companies, by
  race 12

Diversity of business interests 122–126, 256

Education
and age 211n
and ambitions 216–17
of businessmen 210–11
discourages entrepreneurship 101
in Mahiga 53
and profit 213–14
and progress of business 215–16
and size of business 211–12
and success in business 65–6
Embu 34, 45
Employees
advances of pay to 114–15, 161n
attitudes towards relatives as 135–9, 143
numbers 254
origins 256
racial and tribal diversity 141–2, 145
recruitment 108–9
relatives amongst 139–41, 143, 144–5, 149
theft by 110–11
trouble with 115–16, 255
wages 114
Employment of men in Kenya 60–61
Entrepreneurship
defined 1–3
influenced by values 81–3, 101–2
in Java and Bali 56–7
in Masai trade 37–42
problems of analysing 19–20
in socialist societies 240–2
as transfer of power 6
and vocational frustration 62–7, 73–4
Equity participation by Government 235–6
European businessmen, perceived characteristics 91–3, 251
European settlement
in colonial period 6–8
influence on Kikuyu 90–1
and trade with Mahiga 47–8

Failure of businesses
and bad debts 156
reasons for 86, 88, 249
Family relationships. *See* Relatives
Farming, development of African 8–9. *See also* Land consolidation; Land-holding
Father–son relationships
in business 37–8, 149–50
in land-holding 146
Ford Motor Co. 4n
Fort Hall 46. *See also* Muranga

Geertz, Clifford 56
Goods of Masai trade 33–4, 45–6
Government policy towards business 170–2, 196–8, 229–30, 235–6
Gusii 17, 71, 146n, 148

Harris, Alfred and Grace 146n
Harris, Seymour 82n
Hindu joint family 145–6

ICDC-supported businesses
accounting by 219–21
capital invested in 187–8
Government help wanted 261
initiated by ICDC 203–4
interview schedule for 15, 255–279
relatives involved in 149
sample 14–15
sorts 14, 244
trouble with employees in 115
see also ICDC-supported business-men
ICDC-supported businessmen
advice from 242–3, 265
attitude to Asians 93–8
attitude to employment 62–4, 245
attitude to Europeans 91–3, 251
attitude to farming 120–2
attitude to relatives in business 135–9
attitude to smoking and drinking 86–7

attitude to tribe and race of employees 141–2
attitude to wages 114
birthplace 58
church-going 84
credit to customers 154
detained as 'Mau-Mau' 209
diversity of business interests 123
education 64–5, 211–12
Government aid wanted 179, 218
moral values 83–8
political activities 67–9, 248
previous occupation 60–2
reasons for taking up business 89, 250
religion 57–8, 248
satisfactions 245
symptoms of strain 101
technical advice to 218n
see also ICDC-supported businesses
Independent schools in Mahiga 53
Indonesia, entrepreneurship in 56–57
Industrial and Commercial Development Corporation (ICDC)
attitude to defaulters 185
businesses initiated by 203–4
capital contributed by 202–3
foundation 10–11
lending by 181–3, 188
policy 169–70, 195–8
technical advice from 218
Industrial estates 11, 169–70
Industrial Training Centre, Nakuru 11, 221
International Labour Office 5n
Interview schedules 15, 17, 266–79
Interviews
language used 15
number 15–19

Jacobs, Alan 30n
Jehovah's Witnesses in Zambia 77, 80, 81, 88

Kalenjin 17, 147–8
Kamba 17, 71, 148

Kaysen, Carl 82n
Kenya currency 10n
Kenya National Trading Corporation 10, 171
Kenyatta, Jomo 146n
Kiambu 26n, 72
Kiburu Kinja 25n
Kiiru Ngecu 25n
Kijabe station 45–6
Kikuyu
entrepreneurial values 41–2
importance of livestock 29
influence of European settlement 90–1
influence of Masai culture 30–2
marriage with Masai 37–8n
perception of early European settlers 47
predominance as entrepreneurs 70–2
traditional land rights 146n
see also Kikuyu–Masai trade
Kikuyu–Masai trade
Asian competition with 44, 46
decline 43–6
disrupted by fighting 32n, 35
goods exchanged 33–4
leaders 37–41
levels of participation 39–40
organization 32–7, 44, 45–6
profits 36–7
turns into shopkeeping 46
Kirere Kihara 25n
Kirianjau Munya 25n
Kisii. *See* Gusii

Laikipiak Masai 30, 43
Laikipia Plateau 30, 43, 44
Land consolidation 117–18, 147
Land-holding
of businessmen 118–20, 255
in Mahiga 26–8
and population density 147–8
restrictions on 233
traditional 146
Legal aid 236–7
LeVine, Robert 80n, 146n
Livestock, importance to Kikuyu 29

Loans
  defaulting on 185
  delay in approval 182, 261
  dilemmas of policy for 179–80
  equity as alternative 196–7, 235–236
  expense of obtaining 182–3
  interest rates 231–2
  political influence on 69, 72n
  size 186–8, 196
  tribal distribution 70–1
Long, Norman 78n
Lugard, Frederick 31n
Luhya 17, 71, 148
Luo 17, 71, 72n, 148
Luo Thrift Society 68n

McClelland, David 77n, 79–80, 99
McNamara, Robert 1
Magana 26
Mahiga
  boys' egg-trading 210
  drive for education 53
  entrepreneurship 228
  evolution of business 49
  informants on history 25n
  land-holding 26–8
  sample of businessmen 17–18
  settlement 25–6
  trade with European settlers 47–48
  trade with Tugen 49
  see also Mahiga businessmen
Mahiga businessmen
  age and spread 50, 244
  early enterprises 49
  management problems 50–2
  sample 17–18
  size of partnerships 51
  sorts of business owned 50, 244
Management
  and employment of Europeans 126
  of ICDC-supported industries 107–16, 124–5
  and industrial revolution 105–6
Management training 235

Management Training and Advisory
  Centre, Nairobi 12, 221–3
Mangore Waithaka 25n
Market businesses
  books kept 219
  interview schedule for 17, 266–270
  relatives involved in 149
  sample 16–18
  sorts 244
  trouble with employees in 115–116
  see also Market businessmen
Market businessmen
  advice from 265
  attitude to farming 120
  attitude to relatives in business 139
  attitude to tribalism in business 141
  book-keeping training 221n
  credit to customers 154–7
  education 211–14
  Government aid wanted 179, 261
  methods of attracting customers 162
  previous occupation 61–2, 245
  reasons for taking up business 250
  see also Market businesses
Marketing service 173–4, 234–5
Markets
  description 16–17
  for small-scale industry 172–3
Marris, Peter 237n
Masai
  contempt for Kikuyu 30, 32
  economy 25, 30
  Kikuyu perception of 30–2
  warfare between 30
  see also Kikuyu–Masai trade; Laikipiak Masai; Purko Masai
Matson, A. T. 75n
Mau Mau 67, 102, 209
Mexican villages, entrepreneurship in 77, 80
'Mikuni Supply Stores' 198–200

Minorities, entrepreneurship among
    56–7, 75–6
Muranga   34
Muthamaki   29, 41

Nairobi   11, 12, 18
National Christian Council of Kenya
    12n
Ndia   34
Ndorobo   26n
Njama ya Ihii   41
Nyeri   44, 45, 48, 50, 210

Odinga, Oginga   68n
Overdrafts   190–2
Owen, Robert   106
Ownership of businesses
    form   140
    numbers involved   254

Partners
    Asian view of African   254
    mistrust   125–6
    problems with   50–2
    racial and tribal mixture   141
    relationships   107, 139–40, 143,
        149
Profit
    influenced by education and age
        213–14, 262
    reinvestment   202–3
    and technical training   263
Progress of business
    by age   262
    defined   214–15
    and education   213–16
    see also Success of businesses
Protection of African business
    170–2
Protestant ethic   78–80
Purko Masai   30, 43, 44. *See also*
    Masai

Racial segregation in Kenya eco-
    nomy   6–13
Ray, Robert   61n
Relatives
    credit to   157–9, 258

employment   137–41, 143–5, 149,
    257
partnerships with   140, 143, 149
Religion of businessmen   57–8, 84
Retailing, constraints on African
    161–3
Rift Valley   17, 25, 30, 43, 45, 47, 50
Rothchild, Donald   18
Routledge, W. S. and K.   29n
Rumuruti Market   43n, 44
Russian Ambassador sought   74

Sampling methods   13–19
Schatz, Sayre   126n, 170n
Schumpeter, Joseph   2n, 5n, 19n
Shopkeeping, growth of African
    9–11
Small Industries Revolving Loan
    Fund   180, 181, 195
Small Industry Research and Train-
    ing Centre   11
Small-scale businesses, importance
    in industrial economies   4–5
Smiles, Samuel   87, 207n
Socialism and entrepreneurship
    240–2
Sons. *See* Father–son relationships in
    business
Staley, Eugene   5n
Success of businesses
    and accounting   219–21
    and concentration of interests
        123–6
    and credit to customers   160–1
    and education   213–16
    and personal qualities   84–6, 248
    reasons   86, 250
    by type   169, 232
'Sunshine Garage'   200–1
Suppliers
    credit from   155, 192–3
    race   152–3, 259
Sutton, Francis   82n

Taita   17, 71, 146n, 148
Tanzania   91n
Technical training   215–16, 220–1,
    263

Telford, Thomas   207
Tobin, James   82n
Trade between Kikuyu and Masai.
   See Kikuyu–Masai trade
Trade development officers   218
Trade unions   113–14

University College Nairobi, inter-
   viewers from   18
U.S.A.I.D.   11
U.S. Rubber   5n
U.S. Steel   5n

Vocational frustration   225–6
Vocational preferences of schoolboys
   66, 101, 246–7

Wage rates   114, 231, 255
Weber, Max   78–9, 81
Wives
   as employees   110, 149
   as farmers   119, 123

Zambia   77, 80